LYLE
1,001 ANTIQUES WORTH A
FORTUNE
(WHICH NOT A LOT OF PEOPLE KNOW ABOUT)

LYLE

1,001 Antiques Worth a Fortune
(Which not a lot of people know about!)

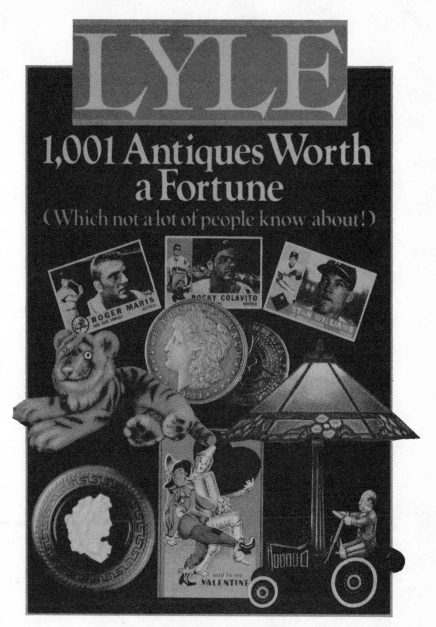

Anthony Curtis

A PERIGEE BOOK

Perigee Books
are published by
The Putnam Publishing Group
200 Madison Avenue
New York, NY 10016

Library of Congress Cataloging-in-Publication Data

Curtis, Tony, date.
    Lyle : 1,001 antiques worth a fortune (which not a lot of people know about) / Anthony Curtis.
        p.   cm.
"A Perigee book."
Includes index.
ISBN 0-399-51757-X
1. Antiques—Catalogs.   I. Title
NK1125.C885   1992   91-43431   CIP
745.1′075—dc20

Cover design by Jack Ribik

Front cover: Baseball cards courtesy Alan Kirchoff; photos of Steiff tiger, "scarecrow/tin woodman" valentine, Marx coo-coo car, and *Gone With the Wind* premium cameo brooch courtesy Hake's Americana and Collectibles, York, PA; coins courtesy Jack Ribik.

Printed in the United States of America
     3   4   5   6   7   8   9   10

This book is printed on acid-free paper.

Acknowledgments

AB Stockholms Auktionsverk, Box 16256, 103 25 Stockholm, Sweden
Abbots Auction Rooms, The Auction Rooms, Campsea Ash, Woodbridge, Suffolk
Abridge Auction Rooms, Market Place, Abridge, Essex RM4 1UA
Allen & Harris, St Johns Place, Whiteladies Road, Clifton, Bristol BS8 2ST
Jean Claude Anaf, Lyon Brotteaux, 13 bis place Jules Ferry, 69456 Lyon, France
Anderson & Garland, Marlborough House, Marlborough Crescent, Newcastle upon Tyne NE1 4EE
Antique Collectors Club & Co. Ltd, 5 Church Street, Woodbridge, Suffolk IP 12 1DS
Auction Team Köln, Postfach 50 11 68, D-5000 Köln 50 Germany
Auktionshause Arnold, Bleichstr. 42, 6000 Frankfurt a/M, Germany
Barber's Auctions, Woking, Surrey
Bearnes, Rainbow, Avenue Road, Torquay TQ2 5TG
Biddle & Webb, Ladywood Middleway, Birmingham B16 0PP
Bigwood, The Old School, Tiddington, Stratford upon Avon
Black Horse Agencies, Locke & England, 18 Guy Street, Leamington Spa
Boardman Fine Art Auctioneers, Station Road Corner, Haverhill, Suffolk CB9 0EY
Bonhams, Montpelier Street, Knightsbridge, London SW7 1HH
Bonhams Chelsea, 65–69 Lots Road, London SW10 0RN
Bonhams West Country, Dowell Street, Honiton, Devon
British Antique Exporters, School Close, Queen Elizabeth Avenue, Burgess Hill, Sussex
William H Brown, The Warner Auction Rooms, 16–18, Halford Street, Leicester LE1 1JB
Butterfield & Butterfield, 220 San Bruno Avenue, San Francisco CA 94103, USA
Butterfield & Butterfield, 7601 Sunset Boulevard, Los Angeles CA 90046, USA
Central Motor Auctions, Barfield House, Britannia Road, Morley, Leeds, LS27 0HN
H.C. Chapman & Son, The Auction Mart, North Street, Scarborough.
Christie's (International) SA, 8 place de la Taconnerie, 1204 Genève, Switzerland
Christie's Monaco, S.A.M, Park Palace 98000 Monte Carlo, Monaco
Christie's Scotland, 164–166 Bath Street Glasgow G2 4TG
Christie's South Kensington Ltd., 85 Old Brompton Road, London SW7 3LD
Christie's, 8 King Street, London SW1Y 6QT
Christie's East, 219 East 67th Street, New York, NY 10021, USA
Christie's, 502 Park Avenue, New York, NY 10022, USA
Christie's, Cornelis Schuytstraat 57, 1071 JG Amsterdam, Netherlands
Christie's SA Roma, 114 Piazza Navona, 00186 Rome, Italy
Christie's Swire, 1202 Alexandra House, 16–20 Chater Road, Hong Kong
Christie's Australia Pty Ltd., 1 Darling Street, South Yarra, Melbourne, Victoria 3141, Australia
A J Cobern, The Grosvenor Sales Rooms, 93b Eastbank Street, Southport PR8 1DG
Cooper Hirst Auctions, The Granary Saleroom, Victoria Road, Chelmsford, Essex CM2 6LH
Nic Costa/Brian Bates, 10 Madely Street, Tunstall
The Crested China Co., Station House, Driffield, E. Yorks YO25 7PY
Clifford Dann, 20/21 High Street, Lewes, Sussex
Julian Dawson, Lewes Auction Rooms, 56 High Street, Lewes BN7 1XE
Dee & Atkinson, The Exchange Saleroom, Driffield, Nth Humberside YO25 7LJ
Diamond Mills & Co., 117 Hamilton Road, Felixstowe, Suffolk
Dowell Lloyd & Co. Ltd, 118 Putney Bridge Road, London SW15 2NQ
Downer Ross, Charter House, 42 Avebury Boulevard, Central Milton Keynes MK9 2HS
Hy. Duke & Son, 40 South Street, Dorchester, Dorset
Du Mouchelles Art Galleries Co., 409 E. Jefferson Avenue, Detroit, Michigan 48226, USA
Duncan Vincent, 105 London Street, Reading RG1 4LF
Sala de Artes y Subastas Durán, Serrano 12, 28001 Madrid, Spain
Eldred's, Box 796, E. Dennis, MA 02641, USA
Ewbanks, Welbeck House, High Street, Guildford, Surrey, GU1 3JF
Fellows & Son, Augusta House, 19 Augusta Street, Hockley, Birmingham
Finarte, 20121 Milano, Piazzetta Bossi 4, Italy
John D Fleming & Co., 8 Fore Street, Dulverton, Somerset
G A Property Services, Canterbury Auction Galleries, Canterbury, Kent
Galerie Koller, Rämistr. 8, CH 8024 Zürich, Switzerland
Galerie Moderne, 3 rue du Parnasse, 1040 Bruxelles, Belgium
Geering & Colyer (Black Horse Agencies) Highgate, Hawkhurst, Kent
Glerum Auctioneers, Westeinde 12, 2512 IID's Gravenhage, Netherlands
The Goss and Crested China Co., 62 Murray Road, Horndean, Hants PO8 9JL
Graves Son & Pilcher, 71 Church Road, Hove, East Sussex, BN3 2GL
W R J Greenslade & Co., 13 Hammet Street, Taunton, Somerset, TA1 1RN
Peter Günnemann, Ehrenberg Str. 57, 2000 Hamburg 50, Germany
Halifax Property Services, 53 High Street, Tenterden, Kent
Halifax Property Services, 15 Cattle Market, Sandwich, Kent CT13 9AW
Hampton's Fine Art, 93 High Street, Godalming, Surrey
Hanseatisches Auktionshaus für Historica, Neuer Wall 57, 2000 Hamburg 36, Germany
Andrew Hartley Fine Arts, Victoria Hall, Little Lane, Ilkely

Hauswedell & Nolte, D-2000 Hamburg 13, Pöseldorfer Weg 1, Germany
Giles Haywood, The Auction House, St John's Road, Stourbridge, West Midlands, DY8 1EW
Heatheringtons Nationwide Anglia, The Amersham Auction Rooms, 125 Station Road, Amersham, Bucks
Muir Hewitt, Halifax Antiques Centre, Queens Road/Gibbet Street, Halifax HX1 4LR
Hobbs & Chambers, 'At the Sign of the Bell', Market Place, Cirencester, Glos
Hobbs Parker, Romney House, Ashford, Ashford, Kent
Hotel de Ventes Horta, 390 Chaussée de Waterloo (Ma Campagne), 1060 Bruxelles, Belgium
Jacobs & Hunt, Lavant Street, Petersfield, Hants. GU33 3EF
James of Norwich, 33 Timberhill, Norwich NR1 3LA
P Herholdt Jensens Auktioner, Rundforbivej 188, 2850 Nerum, Denmark
G A Key, Aylsham Saleroom, Palmers Lane, Aylsham, Norfolk, NR11 6EH
Kunsthaus am Museum, Drususgasse 1–5, 5000 Köln 1, Germany
Kunsthaus Lempertz, Neumarkt 3, 5000 Köln 1, Germany
Lambert & Foster (County Group), The Auction Sales Room, 102 High Street, Tenterden, Kent
W.H. Lane & Son, 64 Morrab Road, Penzance, Cornwall, TR18 2QT
Langlois Ltd., Westway Rooms, Don Street, St Helier, Channel Islands
Lawrence Butler Fine Art Salerooms, Marine Walk, Hythe, Kent, CT21 5AJ
Lawrence Fine Art, South Street, Crewkerne, Somerset TA18 8AB
Lawrence's Fine Art Auctioneers, Norfolk House, 80 High Street, Bletchingley, Surrey
David Lay, The Penzance Auction House, Alverton, Penzance, Cornwall TA18 4KE
Brian Loomes, Calf Haugh Farm, Pateley Bridge, North Yorks
Lots Road Chelsea Auction Galleries, 71 Lots Road, Chelsea, London SW10 0RN
R K Lucas & Son, Tithe Exchange, 9 Victoria Place, Haverfordwest, SA61 2JX
Duncan McAlpine, Stateside Comics plc, 125 East Barnet Road, London EN4 8RF
John Maxwell, 75 Hawthorn Street, Wilmslow, Cheshire
May & Son, 18 Bridge Street, Andover, Hants
Morphets, 4–6 Albert Street, Harrogate, North Yorks HG1 1JL
D M Nesbit & Co, 7 Clarendon Road, Southsea, Hants PO5 2ED
Onslow's, Metrostore, Townmead Road, London SW6 2RZ
Outhwaite & Litherland, Kingsley Galleries, Fontenoy Street, Liverpool, Merseyside L3 2BE
J R Parkinson Son & Hamer Auctions, The Auction Rooms, Rochdale, Bury, Lancs
Phillips Manchester, Trinity House, 114 Northenden Road, Sale, Manchester M33 3HD
Phillips Son & Neale SA, 10 rue des Chaudronniers, 1204 Genève, Switzerland
Phillips West Two, 10 Salem Road, London W2 4BL
Phillips, 11 Bayle Parade, Folkestone, Kent CT20 1SQ
Phillips, 49 London Road, Sevenoaks, Kent TN13 1UU
Phillips, 65 George Street, Edinburgh EH2 2JL
Phillips, Blenstock House, 7 Blenheim Street, New Bond Street, London W1Y 0AS
Phillips Marylebone, Hayes Place, Lisson Grove, London NW1 6UA
Phillips, New House, 150 Christleton Road, Chester CH3 5TD
Pinney's, 5627 Ferrier, Montreal, Quebec, Canada H4P 2M4
Pooley & Rogers, Regent Auction Rooms, Abbey Street, Penzance
Rennie's, 1 Agincourt Street, Monmouth
Riddetts, Richmond Hill, Bournemouth
Ritchie's, 429 Richmond Street East, Toronto, Canada M5A 1R1
Derek Roberts Antiques, 24–25 Shipbourne Road, Tonbridge, Kent TN10 3DN
Rogers de Rin, 79 Royal Hospital Road, London SW3 4HN
Russell, Baldwin & Bright, The Fine Art Saleroom, Ryelands Road, Leominster HR6 8JG
Sandoes Nationwide Anglia, Tabernacle Road, Wotton under Edge, Glos GL12 7EB
Schrager Auction Galleries, 2915 North Sherman Boulevard, Milwaukee, WI 53210, USA.
Selkirk's, 4166 Olive Street, St Louis, Missouri 63108, USA
Skinner Inc., Bolton Gallery, Route 117, Bolton MA, USA
Southgate Auction Rooms, Munro House, Cline Road, New Southgate, London N11.
Henry Spencer, 40 The Square, Retford, Notts. DN22 6DJ
G E Sworder & Son, Northgate End Salerooms, 15 Northgate End, Bishop Stortford, Herts
Taviner's of Bristol, Prewett Street, Redcliffe, Bristol BS1 6PB
Tennants, 27 Market Place, Leyburn, Yorkshire
Thomson Roddick & Laurie, 24 Lowther Street, Carlisle
Thomson Roddick & Laurie, 60 Whitesands, Dumfries
Venator & Hanstein, Cäcilienstr. 48, 5000 Köln 1, Germany
T Vennett Smith, 11 Nottingham Road, Gotham, Nottingham NG11 0HE
Duncan Vincent, 105 London Road, Reading RG1 4LF
Wallis & Wallis, West Street Auction Galleries, West Street, Lewes, E. Sussex BN7 2NJ
Ward & Morris, Stuart House, 18 Gloucester Road, Ross on Wye HR9 5BN
Warren & Wignall Ltd, The Mill, Earnshaw Bridge, Leyland Lane, Leyland PR5 3PH
Dominique Watine-Arnault, 11 rue François 1er, 75008 Paris, France
Wells Cundall Nationwide Anglia, Staffordshire House, 27 Flowergate, Whitby YO21 3AX
Woltons, 6 Whiting Street, Bury St Edmunds, Suffolk IP33 1PB
Woolley & Wallis, The Castle Auction Mart, Salisbury, Wilts SP1 3SU
Austin Wyatt Nationwide Anglia, Emsworth Road, Lymington, Hants SO41 9BL
Yesterday Child, 118 Islington High Street, London N11 8EG

Introduction

The world of collectibles continues to expand almost daily, making it increasingly hard to define just what is likely to be of future value and what isn't. While one expects an early Ming vase or a Chippendale chair to fetch thousands of dollars, the discovery that a 1920s film poster will make $35,000 or a tinplate model fire engine $31,000 may still cause a raised eyebrow or two.

But this is where the fun comes in. Certainly, there are still bargains to be found at the major auction sales. For the average collector, however, fortunes are more often to be made by knowing what to look for at a local flea market or tag sale, and perhaps more especially, recognising its potential when you see it. Not easy, for an increasing number of people are becoming educated in the potential value of their heirlooms/lumber, so you need all the help you can get. And few things will be of more help to you than this book. The title says it all. It identifies hundreds of items, often less well known and downright offbeat, which are well worth snapping up. More than that, it tells you what to look for and why.

A fine Chippendale carved walnut side chair, Philadelphia, circa 1760, with a serpentine crest-rail centered by a shell flanked by foliate boughs and shell-carved ears over fluted stiles, 41³/₄in. high.
(Christie's) **$100,000**

A fine and rare gutty golf ball marker, stamped *A. Patrick*, the hinged handle with leather-covered roller and enclosing two grooved metal rollers, circa 1870. *(Christie's)* **$61,000**

A rare early Ming blue and white jar, painted around the body with two long-tailed phoenixes in flight amidst leafy vines issuing blossoms, above a band of key-fret between double lines at the foot and below a thicker line and larger key-fret band, the spreading neck with a band of overlapping plantain leaves below further double lines, 5¹/₄in. high.
(Christie's) **$95,000**

For example, did you know that a manual golf ball marker dating from the 1870s could be worth $61,000? This is because such hand presses were *'in use'* for only a brief period before the introduction of hydraulic machinery. Or that only three hundred Henry rifles were made with iron frames? Find one of them, and it could be worth $35,000.

Then again, would you know a snowflake stand or a sunburst celebration if you saw them? They are amazing carvings made around 1906 as a retirement hobby by the immigrant German carpenter John Scholl in Germania, Pennsylvania. He created at least 45 of them, and two recently sold for $7,150 and $8,000 respectively. Hang on to your tin toys, too. If you have a George Brown tinplate 'Charles' hose reel, dating from circa 1875, we're talking well over a quarter of a million dollars.

There are plenty more such 'finds' still out there awaiting discovery, and, armed with this book, you stand a much better chance of knowing them when you see them.

Contents

CONTENTS

Navajo Germantown blanket, a Hubbell revival piece, the banded pattern alternating panels of connected stepped diamonds, diamond halves, zig-zags and stripes, in gray-purple, black, white and red, 6 feet 7 inches x 4 feet 9 inches.

(Butterfield & Butterfield) **$11,000**

Washo polychrome basket of flattened hemispherical form, carrying staggered rows of feather tip triangles, diameter 8^1/$_4$ inches.
(Butterfield & Butterfield)

$8,800

Hopi Kachina doll, representing Hututu, standing with arms close to the body, the case mask with domed top, semi-circle ear and one long horn, wearing painted jewelry, sash and moccasins, height 14^1/$_4$ inches.
(Butterfield & Butterfield)

$3,025

Sioux beaded panel from the battle at Little Big Horn, consisting of a trapezoidal hide panel taken from a cradle cover, fully beaded with stepped triangles, diamonds and a roll-beaded edge partially lined with tacks, in translucent green, dark and pale red, yellow, white and cobalt blue on sky blue, length 16 inches.
(Butterfield & Butterfield)

$6,600

Zuni polychrome pottery bowl, the exterior with a wide band of serrated and feathered diagonals, the interior with linear rim band, solid colored parrots in contrasting tones ring a scalloped central device, diameter 11¹/₄ inches.
(Butterfield & Butterfield)

$8,800

Anasazi cradle, Four Mile culture, circa 1375–1450 A.D., consisting of two parallel flat wood slats with plaited foundation, supporting a slightly concave and rounded seat of more plaited fibers, a cloth panel and tubular cane guard fastened across the front, a mass of native cotton twine serving as a pillow, length 30 inches.
(Butterfield & Butterfield)

$4,675

Northwest Coast bentwood box, Northern Coast, the square container painted on opposing sides with elaborate traditional renditions of supernatural beings or animals, complemented by similar floating profiles on remaining panels, the heavy lid with slightly flaring sides, in red and black pigments, height 25¹/₄in.
(Butterfield & Butterfield)

$4,950

Porcelain first appeared in Japan when the discovery of kaolin nearby in 1616 led to the establishment of a ceramic center in Saga prefecture, Hizen, which came to be known as Arita. Early Arita was painted in grayish underglaze blue and primitive red and green enamels. Enameled and blue and white wares with paneled decoration in the later Ming style were brought to the West by the Dutch from the 17th century onwards, often through the port of Imari. Kakiemon and Nabeshima wares were also made at Arita, and production continues there to the present day.

A pair of Arita models of dogs decorated in iron-red, black enamels and gilt with irregular piebald, each seated with its mouth agape, late 17th/early 18th century, each approx. 41cm. high. *(Christie's)*

$125,000

An Arita lobed teapot and domed cover decorated in iron-red, green , yellow, aubergine, black and gilt with ho-o perched among scrolling flowers and foliage beneath a band of stylized leaves to the shoulder, the cover similarly decorated with a flowerhead finial, late 17th century, 13cm. high.
(Christie's)   **$11,500**

A pair of boldly modeled Arita cockerels decorated in iron-red, green, blue-black enamels and gilt with underglaze blue, their elaborate feathers vividly enameled, late 17th/early 18th century, 33cm. high.
(Christie's) **$28,000**

An Arita blue and white rounded octagonal teapot and cover with two shaped panels depicting scenes from O.R. Dapper on a ground of stylized flowers and foliage, the handle decorated with a flowerhead and scrolling karakusa, the domed cover with a band of lappets beneath a finial, Chenghua six-character mark, circa 1700, 26.7cm. long.

The scenes are taken from copper engravings in O. Dapper, Gedenkwaardig Bedriff der Nederlandsche Oost-Indische Maatschappye op de Rust en in net Keizerrik van Taising of Sina, Amsterdam 1670.
(Christie's) **$15,000**

A composite German full armor, of bright steel, comprizing burgonet with rounded one-piece skull with three knurled combs made in one with a short pointed fall, and neck guard with turned and roped edge, pierced with pairs of lining-holes and encircled at the brow and neck with lining rivets.
(Christie's) **$14,600**

Fine lacquered suit of armor, sixty-two plate kabuto with five-lame shikoro, crescent maedate and gold lacquer kuwagata, printed buckskin hiyo-yoita, mabisashi and fukigaeshi wrinkles and five lame neck guard; the do-maru with eight overlapping plates.
(Skinner) **$17,600**

A rare Indian full armor for a man and horse, the former comprising Top, the shallow fluted skull with central plume-holder, adjustable nasal and avantail of small rings, Char Aina of four plates buckled together, and hinged Dastana all finely damascened in gold with scrolling foliage and flower-heads, gorget, shirt and leggings of steel and brass links forming a trellis pattern; the horse armor in four parts, comprising steel chanfron joined by mail to rectangular brass and steel plates with scalloped edges, crinet and peytral of similar construction with additional plates forming lines of bosses, and later crupper of overlapping diamond-shaped brass and steel scales, probably Sindian, partly 17th/18th century.
(Christie's) **$16,500**

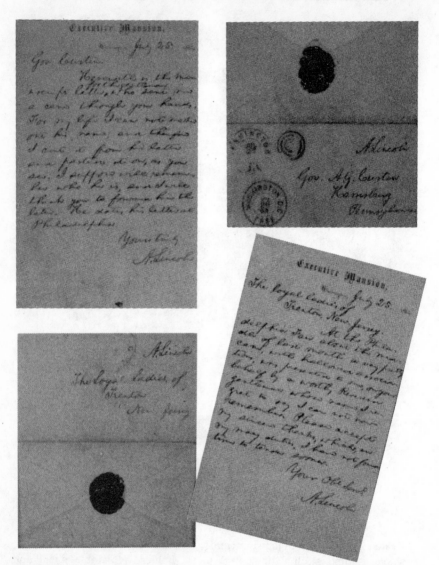

Three Abraham Lincoln autograph letters and a gold handled cane, the letters dated *Executive Mansion Washington, July 25, 1864*. The first letter to Governor A.G. Curtin of Pennsylvania: *Herewith is the manuscript letter for the gentleman who sent me a cane through your hands. For my life I cannot make out his name; and therefore I cut it from his letter and pasted it on, as you see. I suppose you will remember who he is and I will thank you to forward the letter. He dates his letter at Philadelphia*, with Lincoln addressed envelope.
(Skinner) **$66,000**

Sir   Washington Mar. 2 1801.

    I beg leave through you to inform the honorable the Senate of the U.S. that I propose to take the oath which the Constitution prescribes to the President of the U.S. before he enters on the execution of his office, on Wednesday the 4th inst at twelve oclock in the Senate chamber.

    I have the honor to be

        with the greatest respect

            Sir

                your most obedient

                  and most humble servant

                        Th Jefferson

The President pro tempore of the Senate

Thomas Jefferson (1743–1826), an autograph letter signed as President-elect to the President pro tempore of the Senate, Washington D.C., 2 March 1801, preparing to take 'the oath which the Constitution prescribes to the President of the U.S.', one page quarto.
(Christie's)   **$159,500**

An RCA mechanical speaking dog, of painted papier mâché having moveable head and fitted for sound in the rear and the base. Wearing buckled *RCA* dog collar with insignia and marked *His Master's Voice* at base, 39^1/$_2$in. high.
(Butterfield & Butterfield)

$1,650

A very rare early 20th century French electrically-operated life-size Black Boy Magician automaton, in painted papier-mâché, wearing original starched shirt, tailored black cloth waistcoat and jacket, white cotton trousers, and patent leather shoes, the complex mechanism operating his right hand fitted with a vacuum pad to move cards from a tray, his head moving the while and with comic rolling of the eyes beneath waggling eyebrows and grinning mouth, 53^1/$_2$in. high.
(Tennants) **$9,250**

Peasant and baby, a rare composition-headed clockwork musical automaton, modeled as a man seated on the back of a rush chair holding a pig on his left knee and a 'tartine' in his right hand, in original checked trousers, cut velvet jacket, red and white striped shirt, gray top hat and velvet waistcoat, as the music plays he kicks the chair, shrugs his shoulders and closes his eyes and mouth while feeding the pig, who opens his mouth, nods his head and licks the bread, 30in. high by Vichy/Triboulet.
(Christie's)   **$46,613**

A composition-headed standing negro smoking automaton, with moving eyelids and lower jaw and composition hands, in original gray plush top hat, 31in. high, Vichy, circa 1890.
(Christie's S. Ken)   **$9,000**

A Queen Anne ivory double-sided column barometer, circa 1710, the double-sided silvered scales signed on one side *Invented and made by D. Quare, London* and on the other *Faits portatifs par D. Quare à Londres* and numbered *95* on the ivory beneath, calibrated in Quare's usual form for 28–31in., each with two blued steel recorders, the giltmetal hood with profuse acanthus engraving, 36³/₄in. high.

(Christie's) **$70,000**

A William III silver-mounted ebonized siphon tube barometer of royal provenance, circa 1700, the case of oak veneered with ebonized fruitwood, surmounted by an urn applied with silver swags and silver flambeau finial terminating in giltmetal, the concave plinth supported on a reeded half-column with an ebonized carved walnut shell at its base framing the calendar dial with silver date ring and blued-steel hand, the silver register plates signed at the base *D. Quare Lond Fecit*, 39in. high.

Daniel Quare, London, b. 1649, Clockmakers' Company 1671, Master 1708, in partnership until his death in 1724 with Stephen Horseman. He was appointed Keeper of the King's Clocks and was allowed to enter the palace by the back stairs even though he was a Quaker; he was also a maker of mathematical instruments and barometers.

(Christie's) **$603,570**

A George II walnut cased wheel barometer, circa 1740, signed *Jno. Hallifax, Barnsley, Invt & Fecit* after the form and style of a longcase clock, the arched register dial with wheatear-engraved border, engraved spandrels, matted and engraved center, the silvered 'chapter ring' calibrated with concentric scales and with blued-steel hand, 53in. high.

It is natural that, since Hallifax was by trade a clockmaker, he should have housed his barometers in cases modeled on longcase clocks. However, the glazed 'door' covering the register dial in the hood is screwed in position rather than hinged since frequent access to the hand is not necessary.
(Christie's) **$62,300**

An early George III mahogany-cased wheel barometer, circa 1760–72, signed *Geo. Adams, No. 60, Fleet Street –London–Instrut. Maker to his Majesty K.G.III*, the 7¹/₂in. square glazed register dial with plain spandrels, matted center and silvered ring calibrated for 3" in hundreds with simple blued-steel register hand and elaborate pierced giltmetal recording hand with gilt adjustment knob above, 41in. high.

The table for the state of the weather does not quite agree with the scale on the register ring which was engraved to accompany it. However, because of the meterological observations and the unusually wide 0.5in. bore tube, allowing a smooth and accurate movement of the mercury, it has been suggested that Adams intended this barometer more as a scientific than domestic instrument.
(Christie's) **$62,300**

'The Yatman', a half-tester bed, designed by William Burges, the walnut paneled footboard and framework surmounted by an elaborate and ebonized frieze and dentilated cornice, inset with panels of polychrome marble, covered and hung with original fabric, 157.5cm. wide.

In 1858 Burges designed an entire suite of bedroom furniture, including the above, as a wedding present for his friend and patron the Reverend J.A. Yatman of Winscombe, on the occasion of his marriage to Anna Turner. The "Yatman Suite" represents the summation of Burges' early oeuvre in the Jacobean manner.

(Christie's) **$51,000**

A gray and blue-painted Lit A La Polonaise with domed hanging canopy with waved molded rail, centered by flowerheads and foliage and hung with floral chintz, the scrolling end boards carved with flowerheads.
(Christie's)   **$13,000**

A red-painted ebonized and parcel-gilt boat-shaped daybed of Antique Egyptian style, the dished seat covered in black horsehair, the seat-rail painted with a border of anthemia, the prow in the form of a gazelle's head, 76in. wide. *(Christie's)*   **$8,750**

Berlin ceramics date back to the late 17th century, when from 1678 faience and red earthenware was produced. In 1763 the factory came under royal patronage when Frederick the Great purchased it to become the Königliche Porzellan Manufaktur, and production turned to hard-paste porcelain. From the end of the First World War it became known as the Staatliche Porzellan Manufaktur in Berlin.

A Berlin campana-shaped gilt-ground two-handled vase painted with a broad band of garden-flowers including roses, carnations, poppies, hydrangeas, delphiniums and nasturtium on a pale-pink-ground between gilt bands chased with flowerheads, blue scepter mark to plinth, circa 1810, 56cm. high.
(Christie's)   **$15,000**

A pair of Berlin rectangular plaques painted with head and shoulders portraits of young girls facing to left and right, each with long brown hair, one wearing a laced white corsage and gold-embroidered blue velvet waistcoat, impressed KPM and scepter marks, circa 1880, 12³/₄in. x 10¹/₂in.
(Christie's)   **$30,000**

A pair of Berlin armorial oval gold-ground tureens, covers and plinths with linked scroll handles, painted in colors with two putti supporting bronzed swags of fruit hung from satyrs' heads above a band of roundels painted en grisaille with deer, sheep and cattle heads linked by blue scrolling foliage, circa 1820, 45.5cm. wide.
(Christie's)   **$37,600**

A Berlin casket and hinged cover in the form of a commode, the corners molded with foliate scrolls enriched in gilding and surmounted with two cherub heads on the front corners, the white and pale-yellow ground painted on the cover with a cherub seated on a cluster of flower-blossoms within a molded mirror-shaped cartouche of scrolls and trellis-pattern, blue scepter and iron-red KPM and globe marks, circa 1895, 20³/₄in. wide.
(Christie's)   **$11,500**

A German plaque of 'The Interlude' late 19th century, depicting two gypsies, one playing the violin for his slumbering companion, signed *J. Schmidt*, framed 15 x 12in. *(Christie's)* **$17,600**

A Berlin rectangular plaque of Judith finely painted in half-profile wearing a loose white blouse, her sash and skirt embroidered with fruit and flowers, a sword in her left hand and the head of the unfortunate Holofernes in her right, circa 1880, 53cm. by 29cm.
(Christie's)

$20,500

A large and finely painted Berlin plaque of the Holy Family after Raphael painted by Otto Wustlich, signed, the Virgin and St. Elizabeth seated with St. John the Baptist and the Holy Child, St. Joseph standing behind them, a view of a hill town and a lake in the background, 48.5cm. x 39cm., impressed *KPM*.
(Christie's) **$17,000**

Victorian parcel-gilt and turned walnut birdcage, 19th century, the domed rectangular cage with ring-turned columns at the corners, suspended within a ring-turned and molded-arch frame surmounted by turned finials, 6ft. high.
(Butterfield & Butterfield)

$1,650

A late Victorian polychrome and painted tole bird-cage of architectural form, with trefoil-mounted raised turret cresting, the upper canted rectangular level with cusped arches on spirally-twisted columns flanked by later giltwood finials and surrounded by a balustrade, 70^1/2in. wide.
(Christie's)   **$4,950**

Portuguese Colonial carved ivory birdcage, early 20th century, of typical cylindrical form with dragon-carved hanging hook, enclosing carved and painted ivory birds perched on a 'bamboo' rod, 12$^1/_4$in. high.
(Butterfield & Butterfield)

$1,500

Unusual giltwood and red lacquer aviary, late 19th century, the three tiered structure composed of floral carved and pierced panels and columns, set on a platform base raised on four conforming square giltwood legs, 63$^1/_2$in. high.
(Butterfield & Butterfield)

$3,300

It was J. F. Böttger's discovery of red stoneware and porcelain in 1708-9 which gave Augustus the Strong's Meissen factory a lead in porcelain production which it did not lose until after the Seven Years War some fifty years later. Böttger's success as an arcanist was not equalled by his success as a business man, however. He remained under Augustus's close eye almost until his death, and it was not until after that event that the factory reached the period of its true greatness and prosperity.

A rare and attractive Böttger polished stoneware tea canister and cover of hexagonal shape, the vertical panels molded in relief and gilt with birds in flight and perched in trees, against a matt background and within polished borders, 12.5cm. high.
(Phillips) **$16,000**

A Böttger pagoda figure wearing an unusual tall purple hat with deeper purple scrolls and flowerheads between iron-red ribs, with brown hair, eyebrows, eyes and curling moustache and his open mouth with red lips, wearing a loose robe leaving his chest bare, seated cross-legged holding a teabowl and saucer in his right hand, a teapot, another teabowl and saucer and a long pipe in front of him, circa 1715, 13cm. high.
(Christie's) **$13,750**

An extremely rare Böttger polished red stoneware pipe with small funnel shaped bowl, on a long slender cylindrical stem which is in two sections, joined with a silver band and with long silver mouthpiece, total length 27.5cm.
(Phillips) **$20,000**

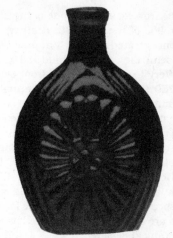

Sunburst flask, mint condition, no wear, medium apricot puce, sheared lip-pontil scar, half-pint, America, 1830–50.

This flask was found in the wall of a 150 year old house.

(Skinner) **$5,225**

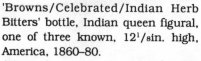

'Browns/Celebrated/Indian Herb Bitters' bottle, Indian queen figural, one of three known, 12¹/₈in. high, America, 1860–80.

(Skinner) **$6,875**

Baltimore/Glassworks Sheaf of Grain pictorial flask, calabash, medium sapphire blue, double collared lip-pontil scar, Baltimore Glassworks, circa 1850.

(Skinner) **$3,960**

The Bow factory was one of the most prolific of the mid 18th century and concentrated mainly on producing 'useful' tablewares in blue and white.

Very few pieces dating from before 1750 survive, and these are mainly painted in vivid famille rose colors against a grayish paste. A selection of items were also produced unpainted but with relief decoration in imitation of Fukien blanc de Chine. The 'quail' pattern derived from Japanese Kakiemon ware is also especially characteristic of the factory as are other exotic bird patterns and botanical designs.

Blue and white production falls broadly into three periods. The first, 1749-54, saw the production of thickly potted, heavy wares painted in a vivid cobalt blue. Decoration was often in the Chinese style with a slightly blurred appearance.

During the middle, and most successful period, from 1755-63, a wide range of products were made, especially sauceboats, center-pieces, mugs, bowls etc. These were less thickly potted, often in powder blue, and favourite designs are 'Image', 'Jumping Boy', dragon, and a harbor scene, all still showing a very strong oriental influence.

From 1764 quality declined both in terms of opacity and painting. Sauceboats and plates remained a speciality, but were now much less elaborate, and after 1770 production fell considerably.

A pair of Bow figures of dancers after the models by J.J. Kändler, he standing before a tree-stump wearing a pale-yellow hat, his blue-lined white jacket applied with blue bows and ribbons in a puce-flowered waistcoat and pale-yellow breeches, his companion holding out her skirt, wearing a pale-yellow bodice edged in puce and with applied blue bows, circa 1758, 19cm. high. (Christie's) $5,500

A Bow figure of the Doctor wearing blue hat, pale-pink cloak, his flowered jacket edged in yellow and blue breeches, standing with his left hand raised, his right hand on his hip, before a tree-stump on a shaped base painted with sprigs, circa 1755, 16cm. high.

(Christie's) **$5,800**

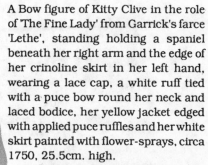

A Bow figure of Kitty Clive in the role of 'The Fine Lady' from Garrick's farce 'Lethe', standing holding a spaniel beneath her right arm and the edge of her crinoline skirt in her left hand, wearing a lace cap, a white ruff tied with a puce bow round her neck and laced bodice, her yellow jacket edged with applied puce ruffles and her white skirt painted with flower-sprays, circa 1750, 25.5cm. high.

The model is taken from an engraving by Charles Mosley published in 1750, based on a drawing by Worlidge.

(Christie's) **$14,750**

A Chippendale inlaid walnut desk-box, Salem, Massachusetts, 1750–1780, the hinged molded rectangular top decorated with stringing and centered by a compass star over a conforming case enclosing an elaborately fitted interior with eleven valanced pigeonholes and eight small drawers and a hinged well with lidless compartments and two additional small drawers above a molded base, on bracket feet, 22¹/₂in. wide.

(Christie's) **$6,000**

Joined oak and yellow pine box, Connecticut or Massachusetts, circa 1700, 27in. wide.
(Skinner) **$12,100**

A nashiji toilet box decorated in takamakie with chrysanthemum beside a rock-lined stream, a woman's travelling-cloak in the foreground, the chrysanthemums inlaid with silver dewdrops, the rocks enriched with kirigane and gilt metal and silver uta-moji forming the first line of a poem, unsigned, circa 1600.

Although the aoimon is usually associated with the Tokugawa family, the version depicted here appears to belong to the Hachisuka, a Daimyo family of Tokushima in Awa province under Toyotomi Hideyoshi in the late 16th century.

(Christie's) **$60,000**

A Vizigapatan ebony and ivory writing-cabinet inlaid overall with foliate scrolls and flowerheads within a foliate border, the sloping twin-flap top enclosing wells, one with compartments, the sides with brass carrying-handles, late 18th century, 16in. wide.
(Christie's) **$4,000**

An early 19th century Continental painted metal coal box, of tapering octagonal form, applied with gilt neo-Classical motifs and shaped ring handles, 2ft. 2in. high, Scandinavian, probably Danish.
(Phillips) **$1,950**

A superb suzuribako decorated with an Imperial ox-carriage in kinji takamakie and hiramakie, silver and aogai on a dark reddish-brown nunome-textured ground, the carriage roof and sides decorated with three bell-crickets on pampas grass, unsigned, 19th century, 4.5cm. high.

The exceptionally fine quality of this suzuribako suggests that it might be the work of Shibaba Zeshin, or alternatively a makie-shi of equal talent and ability.
(Christie's) **$23,100**

A travelling decanter set, the case of plain rectangular form veneered in pollard oak, bound in cut-brass and with recessed brass carrying handles and the lock plate and rising cover inlaid in cut brass with anthemion, the interior containing five decanters and a matching ice pail together with a removable platform containing twelve glasses, 12¹/₄in. wide, mid 19th century.
(Bearne's)   **$1,466**

Carved, turned, painted and gilded Cenotaph, New England, 1800, decorated with green bannerole inscribed *Washington*, 35in. high.

This Cenotaph was first used at the St. James Parish, Great Barrington, Massachusetts in 1800, when a memorial service was held at the first church of the parish soon after the death of George Washington on December 14, 1799. The Parish history, ST. JAMES' PARISH GREAT BARRINGTON, MASSACHUSETTS 1762–1962, by Gerard Chapman, records that 'This urn was placed near the foot of the pulpit stairs to represent the mortal remains of the father of his country while prayers were offered and a suitable sermon preached'.
(Skinner)   **$25,300**

A Vizigapatan ivory workbox
in the form of a house, engraved
with penwork, the hinged lid
enclosing a fitted interior with
side drawer, lacking chimney,
late 18th century, 6³/₄in. wide.
(Christie's)   **$11,600**

A needlework casket, worked in colored silks against an ivory silk ground,
depicting the story of Joseph, the back showing Joseph being thrown down
a well and sold into slavery, the side with Pharoah's dream, the front with
Joseph's brothers, the top with Joseph and Potiphar's wife, the inside lined
with salmon pink silk and watered paper, with a writing set of four glass
bottles, compartments for letters and ink wells, the whole removing to reveal
a bottom compartment lined with padded silk, 5¹/₂in. x 14in. x 10in.,
English 1660. *(Christie's)*   **$159,000**

Hard paste porcelain production began in Bristol in 1770, when William Cookworthy removed his factory there from Plymouth, as a place with a stronger potting tradition. Mugs, sauceboats, bowls, creamboats, coffee cups and pickle leaf dishes were among the items produced, and it is in fact often quite difficult to tell Plymouth from early polychrome Bristol.

Cookworthy and Champion's Bristol factory came to concentrate mainly on tea and coffee services, and while some decoration still shows Chinese influence, Meissen and Sèvres styles predominate.

A rare early Bristol/Worcester cream pot and cover of globular shape with an everted rim and foot, painted in blue in 'Three Dot' painter style with an Oriental landscape, the cover with a pointed finial, 7.5cm. high.
(Phillips) **$9,350**

A Bristol blue and white mug with loop handle, painted with pagodas among trees on a rocky island, Benjamin Lund's factory, circa 1750, 12cm. high.
(Christie's) **$14,500**

French silvered and patinated-bronze and cast brass figural centerpiece, third quarter 19th century, composed of a trefoil-shaped dished tray cast in low relief with three panels of flowers and grapes, applied with three radiating silvered-bronze female therms, raised on the backs of three black-patinated and silvered-bronze blackamoor figures, 8¹/₂in. high.
(Butterfield & Butterfield)
$4,400

Japanese mixed metal vase on stand, Meiji period, signed *Dai Nihon Tei Koku Toyama Ken Takaoki Shi Ohashi San'emon Sei Zo*, formed as rough pottery vase with printed wrapping, iroe-takazogan flowers in copper, 14in. high.
(Skinner)   **$20,000**

A fine French silvered bronze group of a cockerel and hen, cast from a model by Auguste Nicolas Cain, the cockerel rampant on a basket overflowing with vegetables and straw, signed *CAIN SC* and engraved *CHRISTOPHLE & CIE*, second half 19th century, 8¹/₄in. high.
(Christie's)   **$3,000**

A bronze figural group of a fisherman, a basket and double gourd flask hanging from his waist, he holds a large fish attached to a ring in one hand, in the other the stem of a hat in the form of a lotus leaf, worn by a small boy who is dangling a tortoise attached by string, details enriched with gilt, height 13in. overall, signed *Miyao* in a rectangular plaque, Meiji period.

(Bonhams) **$12,000**

Fine gilt bronze figural group of two immortals, Ming Dynasty, the fickle immortal Lu Dong Bin depicted in the clutches of inebriation, supported by a demonic attendant wearing a mugwort skirt and carrying a wine casket on his back, the drowsing bearded sage impeccably dressed in high-belted court robes with trailing sashes, his trusty magic sword slung across his back, the tassels of the hilt precariously resting on his shoulder, $8^5/8$in. high.

(Butterfield & Butterfield)

$9,350

A French gilt-bronze figure of Psyche, cast from a model by Alfred Boucher, shown naked, her long wings falling behind her and held in her right hand, holding her left ankle in the other, 19th century, 18¹/₂in. high.

Alfred Boucher (1850–1934) worked at the École des Beaux-Arts with Dubois and Dumont. He later travelled to Italy, and one of his early works from this period is the figure of Eve. He is renowned for his naturalism, and for his skilful blending of romantic and genre trends, as in the present model of Psyche and the similar figure of 1903.

(Christie's) **$10,250**

Large Korean silver inlaid bronze sacrificial vessel, Yi Dynasty, based on a Koryo Dynasty prototype with a wide everted rim above a deep straight-sided body resting on a high pedestal foot, the sides with similar silver-inlaid Sanskrit characters with ruyi-head defined roundels amid leafy flowering lotus tendrils above a double stiff-leaf border, 8¹/₈in. high.

(Butterfield & Butterfield)

$33,000

A Korean gilt bronze seal, the square base surmounted by a tortoise standing foursquare with head raised and cast with a bulbous snout and incised with fangs, the shell with naturalistic markings chased with areas of shading, the tail swishing to the left, Yi Dynasty, 15th/16th century, 9.6cm. square.
(Christie's) **$20,000**

A pair of patinated bronze and ormolu models of deer, the deer with full antlers lying upon rocky outcrops, possibly North Italian (Piedmontese), 19th century, 13in. high.
(Christie's) **$30,000**

An archaic gold and silver-inlaid bronze axe-head, cast at the angle with openwork dragons biting the blade and gripping the shaft socket, inlaid with patterns of gold and silver (some encrustations), Warring States, 13cm. wide.
(Christie's) **$15,000**

'Valkyrie', a bronze group cast from a model by Stephan Sinding, a spear maiden astride a stallion, on the naturalistic bronze base, 56cm. high.
(Christie's) **$5,300**

An archaic bronze wine vessel and cover, the shoulder cast with a continuous band of spiral scrolls with twelve raised eyes centered at either side, early Western Zhou Dynasty, 33cm. high.
(Christie's) **$55,000**

A fine French bronze figure of Diana Victorious, cast from a model by Albert-Ernest Carrier-Belleuse, the goddess of hunting shown standing, lightly draped, a hunting horn over her right shoulder and a bow in her left hand, late 19th century, 31¹/₂in. high.

The Diane Victorieuse was Carrier-Belleuse's last work. She was first exhibited in plaster at the 1885 Salon; a marble of the same subject was then included in the salon of 1887, the year of the sculptor's death, and finally the bronze was exhibited in 1888. As his last sculpture the Diana Triumphant embodies the culmination of Carrier-Belleuse's art.
(Christie's) **$22,800**

A fine gilt-bronze Bodhisattva seated in dhyanasana, wearing an elaborate triple-tiered crown, compressed scrolls supporting flaming pearls framing the face in meditative reflection and swept up hair tied in a tall chignon, the figure with loose-fitting robes and scarves, further embellished with a tasseled and jeweled necklace trailing to the knees with matching bands on the upper-arm, bracelets and earrings, Five Dynasties/Song Dynasty, 28.7cm. high.

(Christie's) **$85,000**

A French bronze figure of an Aborigine maiden, cast from a model by Cordier, shown dressed only in a grass skirt decorated with shells, a cord necklace around her neck, a pipe inserted into the band of her skirt, her hands raised and clasped about her short curled hair, late 19th or 20th century, 20$^{1}/_{4}$in. high.

The present bronze reveals the influence of Charles-Henri-Joseph Cordier, the celebrated ethnographic sculptor who specialized in Mediterranean peoples from Greece to Africa. This figure, on the other hand, is a study of a different racial type. It is a fascinating study of an Aborigine maiden and an example of bronze in which patination, chiseling and texture are exquisitely worked; particularly in the chasing on the skin and hair, and on the duck-billed platypus.

(Christie's) **$8,700**

'Dancer', a bronze and ivory figure cast and carved from a model by P. Phillipe of a girl standing on tiptoe, her hands outstretched, wearing a short flared dress and jeweled turban, gold and silver patinated with green cold-painted decoration, 64.5cm. high.
(Christie's) **$15,750**

A French silvered and parcel-gilt bronze figure of Sappho, cast by Victor Paillard from a model by Jean-Jacques Pradier, standing pensively beside a column, mid-19th century, 17³/₄in. high.

Pradier's elegant and alluring Sappho was understandably one of the sculptor's most popular works. The founder Victor Paillard cast the model in different sizes and patinas. Paillard exhibited a large silvered bronze Sappho at the 1851 Great Exhibition in London.
(Christie's) **$31,000**

'Salammbô', a gilt bronze bust cast from a design by Louis Moreau, of a young female with long flowing hair, wearing an elaborate head-dress, a revealing dress with central brooch and a necklace, with decoration of cabochon tiger's eye, lapis lazuli and red and black agate, on rock form base with inscription *Salammbo*, signed *L. Moreau*, 74.5cm. high.
(Christie's)   **$8,200**

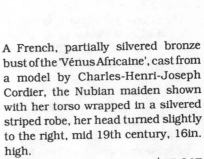

A French, partially silvered bronze bust of the 'Vénus Africaine', cast from a model by Charles-Henri-Joseph Cordier, the Nubian maiden shown with her torso wrapped in a silvered striped robe, her head turned slightly to the right, mid 19th century, 16in. high.
(Christie's)   **$17,347**

Japanese mixed metal vase, Meiji period, finch on a prunus branch, stylized animal base, signed, 13in. high.
(Skinner) **$19,000**

A fine French gilt bronze group of the birth of Venus, entitled 'Venus à la Coquille', cast from a model by Jean-Jacques Pradier, the goddess naked save for a necklace and diadem, seated within a large shell, her legs folded beneath her, a winged putto on either side of the shell, mid 19th century, 9in. high.

Pradier was particularly fascinated by the sea, and therefore the subject of Venus's birth from the sea, was pertinent and allowed him to exploit his equal fascination with the female nude.

The fine chiseling and gilding on the present bronze suggests that this example may well have been cast under Pradier's direction.
(Christie's) **$18,000**

A Regency brass-bound mahogany plate bucket, with brass liner and carrying-handle, the ribbed sides with U-shaped aperture, 15³/₄in. diameter. *(Christie's)* **$5,034**

A mahogany plate-bucket, the octagonal sides pierced with Chinese fretwork bound with brass and with brass carrying-handle, 11¹/₂in. wide. *(Christie's)* **$4,000**

A George III brass-bound mahogany peat-bucket with brass liner, carrying-handles and slatted sides, 15¹/₂in. diameter. *(Christie's)* **$5,000**

An Irish George III mahogany and brass bound peat bucket of ribbed construction, with swing carrying handle, 1ft. 4in. high. *(Phillips)* **$2,500**

Carlo Bugatti (1855–1940) was a Milanese furniture designer and craftsman, who was notable for the originality of his designs. His early pieces, dating from around 1888, often featured diagonal back panels, asymmetrical uprights, tassels, fringes, stamped brass and vellum covered wood. He was also influenced by Japanese styles and decorated his pieces with asymmetrical stylized motifs and floral medallions.

A Carlo Bugatti vellum-covered and pewter inlaid center-piece, the ebonized cross-shaped rotating superstructure inlaid in pewter with oriental motifs.
(Christie's) **$7,500**

A Carlo Bugatti ebonized and inlaid open armchair, the seat-rail covered in beaten copper, above carved supports inlaid with pewter and bone, a circular panel back covered in beaten copper and vellum, on rope supports, above similar upholstered rectangular seat, with elaborately inlaid rectangular armrests.
(Christie's) **$4,500**

A Carlo Bugatti two-seat sofa, the vellum-covered rectangular backrest painted with bamboo and arabic script and decorated with a beaten copper circular medallion, with tassel fringe, the elaborate turned and carved supports and legs partially ebonized and decorated with inlaid brass and pewter designs, the retctangular vellum seat above elaborate carved and fretted apron.
(Christie's) **$5,750**

A black and gilt-japanned bureau cabinet decorated overall with chinoiserie scenes, with arched molded cornice centered by a scallop shell flanked by shrubs, above two arched mirrored doors each with later plate, the reverse painted with figures holding flags, the fitted interior with doors and pigeonholes around a central cupboard with double door flanked by later-decorated columns, 40^1/$_2$in. wide.
(Christie's)   **$52,270**

A George III mahogany bureau bookcase, in four sections, the breakfront central section with arched cornice headed by an acanthus-scrolled cresting surmounted by an anthemion flanked by acanthus scrolls, above a glazed door with gothic quatrefoil glazing bars enclosing four shelves, the side sections each with conforming cresting above open fretwork and glazed door with geometrical glazing bars enclosing three shelves, 112in. high.
(Christie's)   **$9,680**

A Lombardy walnut and ebonized bureau-cabinet inlaid overall in mother-of-pearl with foliate scrolls, the scrolled cresting with brass finials and inlaid with a vase of flowers, above two paneled doors each inlaid with flower vases, the bombé base with hinged flap enclosing a fitted interior above three paneled drawers inlaid sans traverse, on splayed feet, mid-18th century, 45in. wide.
(Christie's)   **$152,000**

A Biedermeier cherrywood and ebonized bureau bookcase, the molded rectangular cornice with two obelisk-shaped finials, above two trellis-filled doors enclosing eight short drawers and one long drawer above two tambour slides each enclosing four drawers and flanking a hinged flap applied with a star, on square tapering legs, first half, 19th century, 47^1/$_2$in. wide.
(Christie's)   **$20,500**

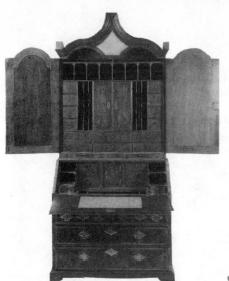

A George I walnut crossbanded and feather strung bureau cabinet, the upper part with an ogee molded cornice and angular arched sides centered by a mirrored panel in the frieze, the interior with pigeonholes, centrally enclosed cupboard with four drawers with pigeonholes and drawers about enclosed by a pair of arched mirror panel doors, 7ft. 6in. high.
(Phillips) **$49,500**

A fine 18th century Mainz walnut fruitwood, tulipwood crossbanded and marquetry bureau cabinet or Schreibschrank of undulating outline, with similarities to the work of Johann Philipp Raab, the upper part with a projecting carved floral and foliate cresting and molded arched cornice, enclosed by a pair of panel doors with a fitted interior, of shelves and nine drawers and paper lining, having a sloping fall enclosing a fitted interior, flanked by pierced canted angles with ionic capital pilasters and pierced scroll volute below, the lower part containing two long drawers applied with neo-Classical handles, 4ft. 8in. wide.
(Phillips)

$243,000

Fine Anglo-Indian etched ivory table bureau cabinet, Vizagapatam, first quarter 19th century, in two parts, the upper part with an interrupted triangular pediment centering a turned finial above four drawers flanked by a pair of cupboard doors, the base with a sloping fall enclosing a fitted interior of pigeonholes and drawers, 23³/₈in. wide. *(Butterfield & Butterfield)*

$23,100

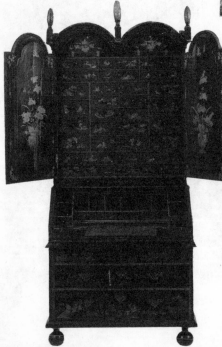

A Queen Anne green and gold-japanned bureau-bookcase decorated overall with chinoiserie, the double-domed cornice with three later cone finials above a pair of fielded paneled doors with warriors amongst pavilions framed by birds, animals and figures within trellis, enclosing a fitted interior of twenty-six various-sized drawers and two arched fall-front panels. *(Christie's)* **$387,000**

A Milanese walnut bureau, banded overall with tulipwood, with stepped rectangular top with a drawer above a hinged flap enclosing a fitted interior, the serpentine front with three long drawers inlaid sans traverse with an oval, with waved apron on shaped bracket feet, 46in. wide. *(Christie's)*

$54,000

A North Italian walnut, ebonized and bone-inlaid bureau, inlaid overall with foliate scrolls, with rectangular top and hinged flap inlaid with an oval of Leda and the Swan, enclosing a fitted interior with slide, on short bracket feet, 47in. wide.
(Christie's)

$21,650

A William and Mary walnut and oyster-veneered cabinet-on-stand, banded overall with fruitwood with molded rectangular cornice, above two doors enclosing eleven drawers around a central cupboard door enclosing five drawers, the stand with one long drawer on spirally-twisted legs joined by waved stretchers, 43in. wide.
(Christie's)

$34,000

A Louis XVI ormolu-mounted mahogany side cabinet with canted rectangular white marble top above one long paneled drawer filled with entrelac pattern above two paneled doors mounted with paterae between fluted angles mounted with chandelles and headed by paterae on later toupie feet, stamped *G. DESTER*, 49in. wide. *(Christie's)* **$100,000**

Miniature painted Chippendale tall chest, made by Jabez Rice, Massachusetts, early 19th century, painted brown, 10¹/₂in. wide.

Paper note attached to back inscribed *This case of drawers was made by Jabez Rice for his little niece.*
(Skinner) **$8,800**

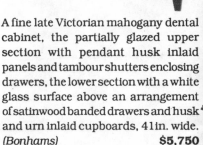

A fine late Victorian mahogany dental cabinet, the partially glazed upper section with pendant husk inlaid panels and tambour shutters enclosing drawers, the lower section with a white glass surface above an arrangement of satinwood banded drawers and husk and urn inlaid cupboards, 41in. wide.
(Bonhams) **$5,750**

A Goanese rosewood, teak and bone-inlaid cabinet-on-stand inlaid overall with stars on concentric circles, the cabinet with rectangular top with eight short drawers and two deep short drawers, the sides with giltmetal carrying-handles, late 17th century, 36in. wide.
(Christie's) **$52,000**

An amusing Scandinavian cabinet on stand, designed by Osten Kristiannson, in oak, modeled as an army officer, his chest set with rows of drawers, his flies opening to reveal a mechanical curiosity, 169cm. high.
(Phillips) **$6,548**

A 'Dieppe ivory' architectural cabinet on stand, carved and engraved all over, the cabinet surmounted by a crenellated cornice and eight tapering finials, fitted with seven concealed drawers, the front centered by an arch carved with beasts, flanked by panels of warriors and numbered busts of worthies, on four square tapering legs, headed with panels of classical emperors, with shaped 'X' stretcher, on block feet, second half 19th century.
(Christie's)

$33,300

A 17th century Flemish ebonised, decorated and tortoiseshell cabinet-on-stand, the hinged rectangular top above a cavetto cornice and enclosed by a pair of ripple molded fielded panel doors, fitted with ten drawers, the interior and reverse of the doors, backs and drawer fronts with paintings, the interior comprising ten drawers around an architectural cabinet door and enclosing an arcaded mirror walled interior and squared floor of tortoiseshell and ivory, 3ft. 2in. wide.
(Phillips) **$20,875**

An important 17th century Italian tortoiseshell, ivory, ebony and gilt bronze mounted architectural cabinet of impressive proportions and accentuated perspective, the whole inset with gilt metal classical relief panels depicting historical and mythological scenes with ripple moldings, the partially balustraded gallery divided by winged putti and surmounted by allegorical figures including the Liberal Arts and Classical gods and goddesses, 6ft. 4in. wide.
(Christie's) **$461,100**

Italian Renaissance-style hardstone, marble and bronze-mounted ebonized cabinet, circa 1860.
(Butterfield & Butterfield)

$93,500

A Flemish silver-mounted parcel-gilt, tortoiseshell, ebony, rosewood and marquetry cabinet-on-stand, the scroll broken cresting carved with the Virgin and Child and Saint John, with molded cornice and ogee frieze above a pair of fielded cupboard doors enclosing an architectural mirror-lined interior with floral and arabesque marquetry panels, on shaped giltwood feet, 76in. wide.
(Christie's)

$121,500

A gold, silver and mother-of-pearl-inlaid brown tortoiseshell table-cabinet inlaid overall with foliate scrolls, with rectangular-coffered hinged lid inlaid with a figure of Plenty holding a cornucopia in a chariot drawn by storks, and with a beehive and flower-basket, with red silk-lined interior, above two paneled doors one inlaid with a pair of doves, the other with a peacock and lion, first half 19th century, probably English, 23¹/₂in. wide.

This cabinet is related stylistically to Augsburg production of the first quarter of the 18th century. *(Christie's)* **$12,870**

A Regency parcel-gilt rosewood side cabinet inlaid overall with boxwood lines, the shaped top with three-quarter pierced brass gallery, the conforming case with five frieze drawers above two pairs of grille-inset doors flanking a mirror-backed open section and interspersed by tapering reeded columns, on hairy paw feet, and a Chinese Kangxi blue and white covered porcelain vase of baluster form decorated in lozenges of flowers and landscapes on a trellis ground, the cabinet 37in. high.

Thomas Sheraton's (1751–1806) patterns for furniture engraved around 1800, illustrate the various features of this 'Grecian' style cabinet, including the concave and convex forms, tapering reeded columns, niche for statue or vase, lion-masks and paws. *(Christie's)* **$174,000**

A very rare 2¹/₄ x 3¹/₄ inch-rollfilm No. 2 Cone Pocket Kodak camera with black morocco leather covered body, collapsible optical finder and sighting arm, sliding three-aperture strip, Eastman Automatic shutter, removable brass film holder, brass film-winding key, red window and two camera-back retaining clips, camera back stamped *Made in U.S.A.* The Cone Kodak is probably the rarest of any Kodak camera of which the No. 2 Cone Kodak is the rarest of the two models made.

(Christie's S. Ken)   **$6,477**

A very rare 35mm. black Leica M2–R camera no. 1248646. This camera dates to 1969/1970 and a batch of Leica M2R cameras numbered 1248201 to 1250200.

Leica M2 camera production began in 1958 and in 1966 Leitz Wetzlar manufactured a US army issue designated the M2S with a rapid loading system. These were later sold by E. Leitz Rockleigh USA to the public after the army canceled their order. The cameras were redesignated as the M2R and sold from 1969/1970 numbers 1248201 to 1250200.

The camera was re-built in the United States with a black chrome top plate and parts supplied by Leitz in Northvale.

(Christie's S. Ken)   **$7,350**

The best known car mascots must surely be Charles Sykes' Spirit of Ecstasy for Rolls Royce, and the wonderful glass offerings by Lalique, quintessentially Art Nouveau in spirit, with their fluid, streamlined forms.

Later, mascots became less concerned with glorifying the speed of the new transport medium, perhaps as it in turn became more commonplace, and reflected the mood of Art Deco by becoming often more whimsical, even impudent in theme.

'Longchamps', a Lalique car mascot, the clear and satin-finished glass molded as a stylized head of a horse, with molded signature *R. Lalique*, 12cm. high.
(Christie's) **$16,000**

Victoire', a good Lalique clear and satin glass 'Spirit of the Wind' car mascot in original Breves Galleries metal mount, molded as the head of a siren-like girl, her eyes blank and staring, with mouth wide open in chant, her long hair wind blown into a stiff geometric flame, 25.8cm. long.
(Phillips) **$14,000**

A carved wood leaping frog
carousel figure, the figure with
whimsical expression and
carved saddle, vest and bow
tie, 38in. high.
(Christie's East)

$17,600

A carved wood stork, the carousel
figure in a striding pose with deeply
carved feathers, saddle with a baby at
cantle and blanket, 67in. high.
(Christie's East)   **$25,300**

Carved and painted carousel bull, late 19th/early 20th century, with horns
and sweeping tail, in a running position, painted white and black, 39in. long.
(Butterfield & Butterfield)   **$1,760**

Castel Durante, in the province of Urbino, is the birthplace of two of the outstanding figures concerned with Italian maiolica, Nicola Pelliparlo, the master of maiolica painting, and Cipriano Piccolpasso, who wrote the definitive work Ltre libri dell'Arte del Vasaio.

The earliest Castel Durante wares can sometimes be attributed to the painter and potter Giovanni Maria, who specialized in grotesque and trophy borders around deep-welled plates containing beautifully drawn heads of girls or youths.

Even in Pelliparlo's earliest works the pictorial painting style is fully developed. In 1519, he painted the d'Este service for the wife of the marquis of Mantua, where every dish and plate, in addition to heraldic arms, bears a different subject from Classical mythology, often taken from slightly earlier woodcuts.

Pelliparlo left Castel Durante about 1527 to join his son in Urbino.

A vaso a palla indistinctly named in Gothic script for *rotag* on an oval yellow cartouche held by mermaids, the reverse with three circular portrait medallions of a young man and two women surrounded by scrolling foliage and flanked by shells, Venice or Castel Durante, circa 1560, 33cm. high.

Although this type of vase is usually given to Venice the shell ornament is known on two documentary albarelli. A Castel Durante attribution should not, therefore, be entirely discounted. *(Christie's)* **$29,000**

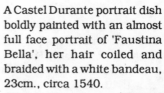

A Castel Durante portrait dish boldly painted with an almost full face portrait of 'Faustina Bella', her hair coiled and braided with a white bandeau, 23cm., circa 1540. *(Christie's)* **$22,000**

A Castel Durante Istoriato dish painted with The Holy Family with St. John resting outside a turreted building with a mountainous lakeside townscape in the distance within a yellow line rim, circa 1525, 31cm. diameter. Known as 'The Virgin with the Long Thigh', the subject is taken from an engraving by Marcantonio Raimondi.
(Christie's)

$135,000

A Castel Durante squat drug jar painted with the naked Fortune arising from the waves on the back of a dolphin, circa 1580, 23.5cm. wide..
(Christie's) **$30,800**

An Istoriato armorial waisted albarello painted with Aurora in her chariot in a continuous mountainous landscape and named for *S°Y.DEFVMO.CON* on a ribbon below, Castel Durante, circa 1563, 30.5cm. high.
(Christie's) **$4,200**

An 18th century North Italian painted sedan chair with restored green and cream panels decorated with vases and baskets of flowers, having flame finials and enclosed by a front glazed panel door, 2ft. 6in. wide.
(Phillips)   **$4,400**

One of a set of ten George III style mahogany "ribbon back" dining chairs in the manner of Thomas Chippendale, with a cartouche-shaped foliate-carved back with a pierced interlacing splat carved with ribbons and serpentine drop-in pad seat with a foliate-molded edge over cabriole legs with foliate scrolling feet.
(Christie's)   **$40,000**

A Charles II oak child's chair with rectangular paneled back carved with a lozenge, the scrolled arms on baluster supports, the solid seat on turned legs joined by square stretchers, lacking finials.
(Christie's) **$8,600**

An early George III mahogany open armchair with rectangular padded back, armrests and serpentine seat covered in yellow moiré silk, the arm-terminals and supports carved with acanthus, the undulating seat-rail similarly carved and centered by a shell, on cabriole legs with scroll feet and shell headings. *(Christie's)*
$33,000

One of a pair of George III giltwood bergères attributed to Marsh & Tatham, each with scrolled padded back, sides and cushion seat covered in ivory damask, the molded frame of the back centered by beading ending in acanthus leaf finials framing rosettes, both stamped *B. Harmer*, the backs 37in. high. *(Christie's)*

$425,000

A 'Napoleon' chair, made by the firm of Aldam Heaton, the upholstered rounded angular back-rest with low scroll leg support, with rectangular seat, on tapering square section legs.

Aldam Heaton produced this model, an example of which he kept in his own home. Sir Edwin Lutyens was much taken with the design which, it is said, he first saw at the Heaton home when he had occasion to rent the house. *(Christie's)* **$7,250**

A Russian ormolu-mounted mahogany bergère with deep curved toprail and high padded eared back, sides and seat covered in green silk damask, the reeded armrests with arched rectangular terminals supported by winged female masks.
(Christie's) **$63,500**

A fine Chippendale carved walnut side chair, Philadelphia, circa 1760, with a serpentine crest-rail centered by a shell flanked by foliate boughs and shell-carved ears over fluted stiles, 41³/₄in. high.
(Christie's) **$100,000**

Chippendale mahogany and walnut easy chair, Southern New England, 1760–90.
(Skinner) **$12,100**

A late Elizabethan oak X-frame chair with waved toprail and rectangular back carved with scrolling foliage within a double-guilloche arch, with molded sides, hipped scrolling arms and planked seat, on frame supports joined by a turned stretcher.

The most famous X-frame chair is the 'Glastonbury' chair at the Bishops Palace, Wells Cathedral.
(Christie's) **$7,160**

One of a set of ten Italian ebonized and parcel-gilt armchairs, the back with giltwood acanthus and flowerhead finials, on square legs with flat stretchers and paw feet, basically 19th century, 60in. high.
(Christie's) **$35,500**

One of a pair of Regency brass-inlaid open armchairs, each with curved toprail and horizontal splat with ebonized balls, on saber legs.
(Christie's) **$9,800**

One of a pair of mahogany library open armchairs of George III style, each with padded waved rectangular back, arms and seat covered in close-nailed floral embroidery, on cabriole legs carved with acanthus and claw-and-ball feet.

(Christie's) **$10,900**

A Federal white-painted and parcel-gilt armchair, Philadelphia, circa 1790, the arching molded crestrail decorated with acorns amid oak leaves over a padded tapering back flanked by reeded baluster-turned stiles above downswept arms with padded rests and acorn and oak leaf ornamentation over reeded baluster-turned supports and a padded bowed seat with molded rails centered by a rosette flanked by acorns amid oak leaves, on turned tapering legs, 36in. high.

According to family tradition, these chairs belonged to Robert Morris, representative to the Continental Congress, and financier of the American Revolution. In 1785 he was awarded a monopoly for the sale of American tobacco to France.

(Christie's) **$52,800**

A pair of George II black and gilt-japanned open armchairs by William and John Linnell, each with stepped rectangular back filled with black and gold Chinese paling, the central uprights decorated in raised gilt with buildings and landscape vignettes surmounted by pagoda-shaped crestings, 40³/₄in. high.

These chairs are part of a set of eight armchairs which formed part of the famous suite of japanned furniture supplied by William and John Linnell to the 4th Duke of Beaufort (1709–1759) for the Chinese Bedroom at Badminton House, Gloucestershire. *(Christie's)* **$292,050**

An Empire mahogany and parcel-gilt bergère, the padded back, drop-in seat and squab cushion covered in close-nailed red velvet, the sides decorated with anthemia, on square tapering legs headed by Roman masks, on paw feet, possibly North European.

This library chair is designed in the Antique manner with curved Klismos crest-rail joined by scrolled bergère arms, embellished with Grecian palmettes and foliage, on winged Minerva therm legs with panther feet. This type of consular or curule chair was popularized by Jacob Frères during the period of Napoleon's consulate.
(Christie's) **$15,200**

A pair of fine early 18th century Chinese carved hardwood dining chairs in the Queen Anne style, the balloon-shaped backs with solid vase splats decorated in relief with interlaced strapwork, arabesques and flowers. These chairs are identical to a well known and documented type distinguished by the oriental timber, peculiarities of construction and highly enriched surfaces simulating carved gesso work on George I period chairs. It is believed they were made in the East by Chinese craftsmen working under European supervision either on the mainland or at a trade center such as Manila and Batavia. *(Phillips)* **$62,000**

A Louis XVI giltwood tabouret de pieds attributed to Jean-Baptiste-Claude Sené, possibly supplied for Royal use at Versailles, the padded back, arms and seat with distressed upholstery, the chaneled beaded frame carved with foliage, the seat-rail with entrelacs on turned stop-fluted tapering legs, with partly obliterated painted inventory mark *VV* on the webbing. *(Christie's)* **$39,270**

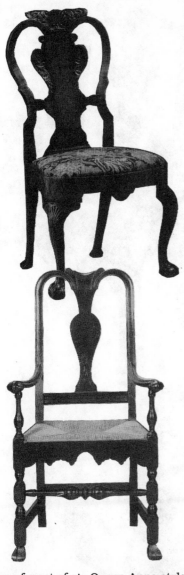

One of a pair of George I walnut chairs with slightly curved backs and solid baluster splats carved with foliage and rosettes, the crestings centered by shells framed by foliate scrolls on a punched ground, the bowed drop-in floral needlework seats with flowers in petit point on a reworked blue gros point ground on plain rails with shell centers and cabriole legs headed by shells and foliage, 40³/₄in. high. (Christie's) **$93,500**

One of a set of six Queen Anne style maple side chairs and an armchair, each with yoked crest above a vasiform splat flanked by molded stiles over a trapezoidal rush seat above an arcaded skirt on block- and ring-turned front legs with paintbrush feet, 43in. high. (Christie's) **$46,200**

A Louis XV grained model fauteuil by Jean-Baptiste Tilliard, with oval padded back and bowed seat covered in red velvet, the frame carved with laurel and entrelac, the arms with leafy terminals on downswept ribbon-tied palm-leaf supports, on turned tapering fluted legs headed by paterae and lotus-leaf feet, stamped *Tilliard*. (Christie's) **$32,000**

A Chippendale walnut armchair, Pennsylvania, 1750–1780, the serpentine crestrail with scrolling ears centering a shell above a spurred vase-shaped splat and serpentine, scrolling arms on deeply molded S-shaped supports, the trapezoidal slip seat fitted to hold a chamber pot frame over a flat arched seat rail centered by a shell on cabriole legs headed by shells on molded trifid feet, 41½in. high.
(Christie's) **$25,000**

A gilt, silver and green-painted grotto rocking chair with back and seat in the form of a scallop shell, with scrolling dolphin arms, supported by seahorse riding on the backs of sea serpents, joined by coral-shaped stretchers.
(Christie's) **$4,500**

A blue-painted Windsor sack-back armchair, New England, late 18th century, the arching crestrail above seven spindles and shaped arms over baluster-turned supports and a shaped plank seat, on baluster and ring-turned legs joined by stretchers, 43^{1}/$_{2}$in. high.
(Christie's) **$10,450**

One of a matched pair of George IV mahogany reading-chairs attributed to Morgan and Saunders, each with yoke-shaped toprail, the back filled with gothic arcading, the back with vertically-and-horizontally-adjustable reading-slope, on ring-turned legs carved with lotus-leaves and with brass caps, lacking upholstery. *(Christie's)*
$24,200

Gustav Stickley five-light wrought iron chandelier, circa 1907, no. 205, square oak frame supporting four suspended heart cut-out lanterns and a central lantern on wrought iron chains, flat black paint, signed on backplate. *(Skinner)* **$3,900**

A brass fifteen-light chandelier with gadrooned baluster shaft with three graduated tiers of scrolling foliate branches with turned nozzles and plain drip-pans, 19th century, 38in. diameter. *(Christie's)* **$50,000**

An Empire ormolu ten-light chandelier with flaming finial and spreading shaft cast with lotus leaves above a band of bees and cornucopia garlanded with laurel wreaths and anthemia, the circular corona with reeded arms, foliate drippans and lotus leaf nozzles flanked and divided by lion masks, with pineapple boss, 41in. wide.
(Christie's)

$76,000

Tiffany two tier turtleback chandelier, dome shade composed of blue iridescent green turtleback tile border above blue shaded to green to gold leaded glass segments arranged in symmetrical geometric progression with gold turtleback at apex; suspended from gilt bronze chain and ball, ornamental drops below ceiling mount embellished with six matching gold favrile shades, total height 24in.
(Skinner)

$22,000

An extremely rare Ottoman chanfron, formed of a single piece of steel with a horizontal flange at the top and shaped flanges around the eyes, low medial ridge and boxed sides at the muzzle, copper rivets with flat circular heads engraved with radiating lines for the side-plates, circa 1517–20, 18³/₄in.

The inscription panels contain the name and titles of the Ottoman Sultan Selim I (1512–1520). The son of Bayazid II and father of Sulayman the Magnificent, he is noted for the conquest of Egypt and Syria in 1517; and his defeat of Shah Isma'il, first of the Safavid rulers of Persia, at the decisive battle of Chaldiran in 1514.

This appears to be the only published example of a chanfron with a datable inscription.

(Christie's) **$96,000**

A very fine Ottoman gilt-copper chanfron (horse armor), formed of a single piece of mercury-gilded copper with shaped flange around each nostril, eye and ear, raised ridge along the nose broadening to a raised central roundel at the forehead and in the center, a raised stylized cypress on a long trunk, engraved and stippled with bold designs of interlaced tulips, second half of the 16th century, 23in. long.

Most of the surviving so-called 'tombak' chanfrons of the sixteenth century are undecorated save for the 'defining' ribs around the nose and eyes. Those with engraved ornament are rare.

(Christie's) **$118,690**

The Chantilly porcelain factory was founded in 1725 by Louis Henri de Bourbon, Prince du Condé, under the direction of Cicaire Cirou. The Prince was an avid collector of Arita pottery and set his factory to manufacture this type of ware. The unique feature of Chantilly is its glaze, which in contrast to the usual transparent lead glaze of soft paste porcelains was an opaque white tin glaze such as that used in the production of faience. The use of this precluded underglaze decoration, but was ideal for painting in the delicate colors of the Kakiemon style typical of Arita ware.

A Chantilly Kakiemon square box and cover, iron-red hunting horn mark, circa 1740, 25cm. high.
(Christie's)   **$29,000**

A pair of Chantilly white wolves naturalistically modeled seated on their haunches looking to left and right, with ferocious looking teeth, pricked ears, long curly coats and bushy tails forming the bases, circa 1740, 21cm. high.
(Christie's)   **$17,000**

The new Chelsea factory, founded in the 1740s, was largely inspired by Nicholas Sprimont, a Huguenot silversmith from Flanders, and it was probably the first of the six or so soft paste factories which sprang up in England by 1750.

Early Chelsea products were very attractive, highly translucent and based on glass ingredients. Pieces from this period often carry an incised triangle and have a strong affinity with Sprimont's silverwork, with particular emphasis on shellwork and scroll motifs. Many pieces were left in the white, although some were colored in Kakiemon style. Figures, often also of oriental inspiration, were made at this time and were invariably left white.

The next, or Raised Anchor Period (1749-53) saw the porcelain becoming more opaque as less lead was used. Figures are now more usually colored, this often being done in the London studio of William Duesbury. While oriental influence remained very strong, many decorations of this period are obviously of Meissen origin. Another interesting decorative development of the time was fable painting on cups, teapots etc., as was the 'Hans Sloane' plant decoration based on the drawings of Philip Miller, head gardener at Hans Sloane's botanical gardens in Chelsea. The range of shapes also widened.

By 1752 a painted Red Anchor Mark was becoming common, and this Red Anchor period, which lasted until about 1758, saw the apogee of Chelsea figure modeling.

A Chelsea 'Hans Sloane' botanical lobed plate painted with a yellow tulip, fern, lilac, a caterpillar and insects, with waved brown line rim, red anchor mark, circa 1756, 25cm. diameter. *(Christie's)* **$4,700**

A Chelsea fable-decorated silver-shaped plate painted in the manner of Jefferyes Hammett O'Neale with the fable of The Fox and the Monkey, the molded border with a loose bouquet and scattered flowers beneath a shaped brown line rim, circa 1752, 22.5cm. diameter. *(Christie's)* **$27,000**

Chelsea ⚓ ⚓

A Chelsea peach-shaped cream-jug, the simple twig handle with opposing leaf terminal, finely painted in the Meissen style with a river landscape scene showing a figure rowing a boat watched by two travelers, the banks with castles, towers and trees, the reverse with a spray of blue flowers and a hairy blue caterpillar, raised anchor mark, 1749–52, 11.5cm. wide.
(Christie's)   **$17,500**

A Chelsea asparagus-tureen and a cover, naturally modeled as a bunch of asparagus enriched in puce and green and tied with chocolate-brown ribbon, one asparagus curled to form the finial to the cover, red anchor and 48 mark, circa 1755, 18.5cm. wide.
(Christie's)   **$6,000**

A Chelsea model of A Little Hawk Owl, its head turned and with pale-yellow, dark and light-brown and black feathers markings, standing astride a tree-stump applied with colored flowers, the rockwork base applied with further flowers, raised red anchor mark, circa 1752, 18cm. high. The source for this model was taken from an engraving in George Edward's Natural History of Uncommon Birds, 1743.

(Christie's) **$20,000**

A Chelsea white chinaman and parrot teapot and cover modeled as a grinning figure of Budai, his loose robe open to reveal his protuberant stomach, seated cross-legged holding a parrot by one wing and its tail, the bird with open beak forming the spout, the entwined branch handle with beech-nut and foliage terminals, his fluted conical hat forming the cover, incised triangle mark, 1745–49, 17.5cm. high.

(Christie's)

$48,000

The relationship between the main Chelsea factory and the Girl in a Swing factory in the mid 18th century is not clear, but it seems certain that many workmen were employed there from Chelsea, and its guiding light was probably the jeweler Charles Gouyn.

The factory was noted between 1749-54 for its scent bottles, but also produced some rare figures, modeled in a unique and dainty style, as well as some dressing table ware.

A 'Girl in a Swing' scent bottle, as a figure of Shakespeare after the model by Scheemakers in Westminster Abbey, and in white, standing against a green rose tree with pink flowers, green bordered column and circular base painted with roses on the underside, 8.2cm.
(Phillips)   **$1,200**

A 'Girl in a Swing' white Holy Family group after Raphael, the Virgin Mary wearing flowing robes seated on rockwork before a tree-stump, her left arm encircling the Infant Christ Child standing leaning across her lap to embrace St. John clad in a lion-skin and kneeling on the lap of the seated figure of St. Elizabeth, circa 1750, 21cm. high.
(Christie's)

$51,700

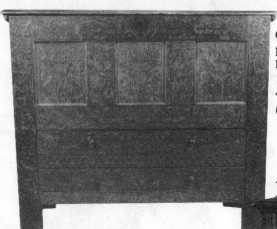

Oak and pine carved and paneled chest over drawers, Hadley area, Massachusetts, 1690–1710, initialed *AC*, 46³/₄in. wide.
(Skinner)   **$10,450**

American Renaissance maple and rosewood chest of drawers, executed by Herter Brothers, 1872 for Thurlow Lodge.
(Butterfield & Butterfield)   **$20,900**

Chippendale mahogany block-front bureau, Boston, Massachusetts, 1760–90, 34³/₄in. wide.
(Skinner)   **$36,300**

Child's whalebone and exotic woods inlaid mahogany chest of drawers, America, 19th century, $21^1/2$in. wide.

This chest was purportedly made for Elizabeth Hill Ryder by her brother, Captain George Indy Ryder of Provincetown, Massachusetts.
(Skinner) **$4,950**

A mid-Georgian mahogany upright chest, the rectangular top above two short and four graduated long drawers on bracket feet, 16in. wide.
(Christie's) **$22,250**

A Chippendale mahogany serpentine chest-of-drawers, Massachusetts, 1760–1780, the thumbmolded rectangular top with serpentine front edge over a conforming case fitted with four graduated long drawers above a molded base, on short bracketed cabriole legs with ball-and-claw feet, 38in. wide.
(Christie's) **$30,800**

Fine pine grained and bird's-eye maple painted apothecary chest, New England, 19th century, the case with rectangular gallery above thirty-two small graduated drawers on shaped bracket feet, the case grain-painted with all drawers in faux bird's-eye maple, 36¼in. wide.
(Butterfield & Butterfield)

$27,500

Chippendale mahogany veneer serpentine chest of drawers, Philadelphia, circa 1789, probably the work of Jonathan Gostelowe (1744–1795), 48in. wide.
(Skinner)   **$23,100**

Carved and painted oak and pine chest over drawer, possibly by Peter Blin (1670–1710). 46" wide.
(Skinner)   **$12,100**

The Saltonstall family Chippendale carved walnut high chest-of-drawers, Salem, Massachusetts, 1760–1780, in two parts: the upper section with molded swan's-neck pediment centering three flame finials above three thumbmolded short drawers, the lower section with mid-molding above one long and three short thumbmolded drawers, on cabriole legs with pad-and-disc feet, $43^1/2$in. wide.

Dr. Nathaniel Saltonstall descended from Sir Richard Saltonstall (1586–1661), one of the original settlers of Massachusetts, an investor in John Endecott's Salem plantation, and founder of Watertown, Massachusetts. Dr. Saltonstall graduated Harvard in 1766, and by 1769 was practising medicine in Haverhill and the surrounding countryside. He married Anna White of Haverhill in 1780, and together they produced seven children; the Saltonstall high chest descended to Nathaniel, the second of their three sons. An inventory of Dr. Saltonstall's estate was filed for probate in 1815, listing a variety of household furnishings.
(Christie's)   **$93,500**

A Wedgwood Fairyland Lustre punch bowl, the interior decorated with The Woodland Bridge pattern, the exterior with the Poplar Trees pattern, 28.5cm. diameter.
(Bearne's) **$3,400**

Anna pottery snake jug, with four snake heads and lower torso of man, with initials *A.M.A.B* and *C2WK Anna ILL 1881*, and initials on base, light beige, 9in., Anna, Illinois, 1881.
(Skinner) **$2,750**

A Capodimonte group of a youth riding a mastiff modeled by Guiseppe Gricci, the youth in peaked pale-pink cap with gilt bow, white shirt and green breeches, holding a gilt lead attached to the mastiff's gilt collar, seated on the back of the dog, his coat marked in brown, 1755–1759, 17cm. high.
(Christie's) **$7,000**

An attractive and brightly colored Musselburgh toby jug with individualistic facial features, seated wearing a chocolate brown coat over a bright yellow waistcoat, black breeches and brick-red stockings, his black shoes with yellow buckles, 23cm. high.
(Phillips) **$2,720**

A George Jones majolica punch-bowl modeled as Mr. Punch lying on his back, being crushed beneath the weight of a large bowl, the surface molded and colored to simulate orange-rind and molded in relief with a wreath of berried holly branches, the smiling figure wearing a white, yellow and blue jester's hat, a green doublet trimmed in white, yellow and claret and with blue leggings and black boots, circa 1874.
(Christie's) **$4,750**

Early 20th century Goldscheider figure of a young seated negro boy, 47in. high.
(Dreweatt-Neate) **$5,450**

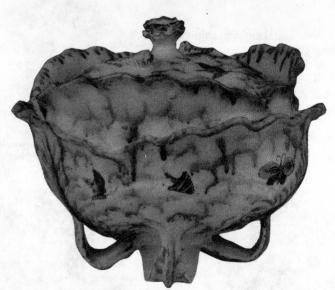

A Brussels cabbage-tureen and cover, the naturally modeled overlapping leaves with waved everted edges and raised midribs, painted in tones of green and with blue, green and yellow scattered moths and bugs, the cover with two root vegetables flanking the open sprout finial, Philippe Mombaers' factory, circa 1770, 30.5cm. wide.
(Christie's)   **$4,650**

A 'Bizarre' Bonjour tea for two designed by Eva Crofts painted in bright colors on a yellow ground with scenes of a Slavonic peasant couple engaged in tea making activities, comprising: teapot and cover, milk-jug, sugar bowl, two cups and saucers, side plate.
(Christie's)   **$9,300**

Paris porcelain American historical pitcher, France, circa 1862, enamel decorated portraits of Grant and Farragut in military dress, 8³/₈in. high.
(Skinner Inc.)

$21,000

A Portuguese faience blue and white tile-picture in the form of a gallant painted in a bright-blue wearing a peruke, long frock-coat with wide buttoned cuffs and tied with a sash and with an embroidered sash across his chest, his tricorn hat beneath his right arm, standing before a rectangular table with scroll and mask legs, flanked by a parrot and a peacock, probably Lisbon, late 17th/early 18th century, 173.5cm. high.
(Christie's)   **$18,000**

A Sceaux faience cabbage-tureen and cover naturally modeled, the outer overlapping gray-green leaves curved and with pale-green midribs and veins, the heart of the vegetable and the cover in a brighter yellow-green, circa 1755, 32cm. wide.
(Christie's) **$12,500**

A pair of Whitman and Roth caricature figures of Gladstone and Disraeli, the former in top hat, buff-colored coat and carrying bag and umbrella, the latter in top hat and chocolate brown coat, both standing on mottled turquoise and brown bases, 40cm. high.
(Phillips) **$6,500**

Paris gilded cup and saucer, the cup shaped as boar's head on oval charger, the oval saucer with raised design of leaves.
(Barbers Auctions)

$2,185

German porcelain monkey band, late 19th century, consisting of eight musicians in 18th century costumes, underglaze blue marks, conductor 7in. high. *(Skinner)*   **$2,420**

Victorian tile panel depicting a scene from a Midsummer Night's Dream, Act IV Scene I. In the wood Titania comforts Bottom (in the form of a donkey), Oberon stands behind, various fairies look on.
(Phillips)   **$5,450**

Important Union porcelain Heathen-Chinee pitcher, Greenpoint, New York, 1876, molded body, the handle formed to represent a bear like animal while the spout is of a sea lion mask, the relief on one side of King Gambrinus offering lager to Brother Jonathon, a goat atop a beer keg, the other side figures of Bill Nye, knife in hand, attacking Ah Sin for cheating at cards, light blue ground background throughout with enamel border and accenting, $9^5/_8$in. high. *(Skinner Inc.)*

$3,500

A finely painted Venetian large oviform jar painted with the forefront of a galloping horse, amongst military and musical trophies, 32.5cm., mid-16th century.
(Phillips) **$48,000**

A Chelsea fable-decorated silver-shaped plate painted in the manner of Jefferyes Hammett O'Neale with the fable of The Fox and the Stork, the molded border with a loose bouquet, scattered flowers and a grub beneath a shaped brown line rim, circa 1752, 23cm. diameter.
(Christie's) **$22,750**

A 19th century Continental cold painted earthenware figure of a seated pug.
(Henry Spencer) **$2,630**

A rare Royal Doulton figure of the Queen of Sheba, HN 2328, designed by P. Davies in a limited edition of 750 in 1982, 9in. high.
(Abridge) **$1,500**

A French faience caricature figure of a brown whippet, seated on its haunches and holding a flowered rectangular tray on his outstretched forepaws, wearing a white shirt, orange bow-tie and waistcoat and an ocher coat, with inset glass eyes and a yellow monocle, circa 1899, 21¹/₂in. high.
(Christie's) **$1,735**

A 'Bizarre' circus teapot designed by Dame Laura Knight, the handle molded as a female acrobat, the finial as two clown's heads, the oviform body decorated with crowd scenes and stars, on four molded feet, printed and painted in colors, 6³/₄in. high.
(Christie's) **$7,000**

A Naples (Real Fabbrica Ferdinandea) figure of a dancing lady, her pale-brown hair tied in a bun, wearing a green and puce striped bodice over a white blouse and blue-dotted skirt and white apron trimmed with gilding, standing with one foot raised looking to her left on a white mound base, circa 1790, 17.5cm. high.
(Christie's) **$9,600**

A Henri van de Velde stoneware two-handled vase, made for the firm of Reinhold Hanke, the rim extending into two curvilinear handles, disc-shaped body, with incised linear decoration, with translucent sang-de-boeuf glaze separating into parts to reveal a beige-colored body, 22.5cm. wide. *(Christie's)*   **$13,937**

Fine tobacco leaf charger, 18th century, of oval form with a scalloped rim, the interior painted overall in vivid shades of yellow, green, turquoise, blue, brown and iron-red with gilt-edged overlapping leaves veined in rose, green or gold superimposed with sprigs of yellow, rose, and iron-red chrysanthemums and peonies with green leaves, 15in. diameter. *(Butterfield & Butterfield)*   **$7,700**

A fine Royal Doulton 'Chang' vase by Harry Nixon, Charles Noke and Fred Allen, 22.5cm., painted mark in black.
(Bearne's)

$3,670

A pair of Siena massive campana-shaped ewers with molded gilt-winged caryatid handles and an applied gilt foliate mask beneath the lip, the bodies painted with Bacchic fauns with a wine-barrel and two wine-jars, one with Cupid in attendance riding a leopard, in wooded rocky landscapes between gilt foliage and blue and gilt gadrooned borders, Bartolomeo Terchi's factory, circa 1730, 63cm. high.
(Christie's)

$32,000

A Wedgwood blue and white jasper 'ruined column' vase, the white fluted columns molded with lichen supported on a solid-blue rectangular base molded with panels of Classical figures at various pursuits, circa 1795, 21cm. wide.

Traditionally the model of these vases is thought to have been executed by William Keeling although there is no documentary proof to support this.

(Christie's) **$10,350**

A Cantagalli charger, possibly by Farini, the central roundel depicting two putti rowing a galleon across choppy waters, 51cm. diameter.

(Phillips) **$1,556**

Important Teco Pottery vase, by Fritz Wilhelm Albert (1865–1940), circa 1906, modeled with twisted iris leaves at top and side, matte green glaze, impressed Teco marks, 14¹/₂in. high.

Fritz Wilhelm Albert was a sculptor educated at the Royal Academy of Berlin. Hired by William D. Gates of Teco Pottery, Albert sculpted architectural terra cotta and garden ornaments as well as Teco pottery.

(Skinner) **$25,000**

Large studio ware ovoid vase, Sumidagawa, late 19th century, the slender ovoid vase applied to the exterior with a continuous band of a horde of monkeys in high relief scrambling over each other on rocky outcroppings and crowding around a cosmetic box and mirror stand, 17³/₄in. high.

(Butterfield & Butterfield)

$2,750

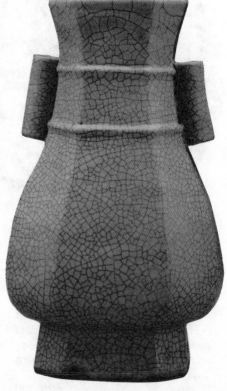

A highly important large geyao octagonal vase, Ba Fanghu, the thinly-potted vase imitating an archaic bronze shape of oblong octagonal section, spreading from a waisted neck applied with two horizontal ribs into a pear-shaped body resting on a high foot slotted at the sides with two rounded rectangular apertures, the neck applied with cylindrical long handles to each side, all under an opaque pale creamy glaze with a dense network of fine black crackles underlaid with a finer network of golden-brown crackles around the mouth and the handles, 10¹/₂in. high.

(Christie's)   **$1,480,918**

A fine blue and white cup, encircled Kangxi six-character mark, finely penciled to the exterior with a continuous mountainous landscape and huts obscured behind willow, the center of the interior with a lone fisherman beside a vertical cliff, 3in. high.

(Christie's) **$43,750**

Ki-Seto model of a Koma-Inu, 19th century, the mythical beast seated on its rear haunches and with its straight forelegs resting to the front of the oval base, its head facing forwards and modeled with humorous features including a wide fanged mouth and oversize eyes, 11⁷/₈in. high.

(Butterfield & Butterfield)

$1,320

A Korean underglaze blue and copper-red kendi modeled in the form of a tortoise on a lotus-leaf-shaped body with the four legs protruding below the shell supporting a double-gourd vase with floral scrolls, the head with bulging features straining from the end of a long neck, Yi Dynasty, circa 1800, 17cm. high.

(Christie's) **$111,000**

The antiquity of Chinese ceramics and their beauty and variety down the ages make their study and collection particularly attractive, and provide scope for every taste.

The earliest unglazed earthenware jars date from as early as 2,000 BC, but it was not really until the Han Dynasty (206BC-220AD) that finer techniques, especially the art of glazing, had been definitively mastered.

The next truly great period was the T'ang Dynasty (618-906AD) when the pottery was characterised by a beautiful proportion and vitality. A lead glaze was revived, which was often splashed or mottled, and many decorative themes reflect Hellenistic influence.

It was during the Sung Dynasty (960-1279AD) that the first true porcelain seems to have been made, and this period too saw the production of some of the most beautiful shapes and glazes of all time. It also saw the beginning of underglaze blue painting, which was to be perfected during the Ming period.

During the Ming Dynasty (1368-1644AD) a more or less standardized fine white porcelain body was developed which acted as a perfect vehicle for brilliant color decoration. Glazes tended to be thick or 'fat'. Colored glazes too were introduced and used either together or singly.

The K'ang Hsi period (1662-1722) marked a further flowering of the potter's art, which continued under his sons Yung Cheng and Ch'ien Lung (Qianlong). The body by now consisted of a very refined white porcelain, thinly and evenly glazed, providing the best possible base for elaborately painted decoration sometimes in the famille rose, famille verte, or famille noire palettes.

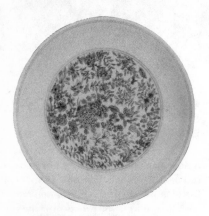 

A pair of Wucai saucer dishes, each painted in blue and enameled in green, aubergine, yellow and iron-red at the center of the interior with a floral roundel of dense torn-off sprays of daisy, magnolia, lotus, prunus, camellia and peony, the underside with five torn-off sprays, 6^1/2in. diameter. *(Christie's)* **$36,900**

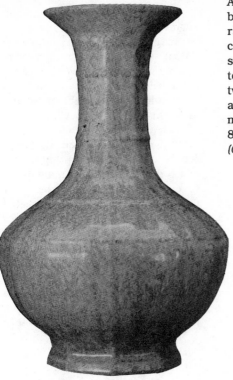

A fine and rare 'robin's egg'-glazed bottle vase of lobed octagonal section raised on a matching foot, the compressed globular body surmounted by a thick cylindrical neck terminating in a flared everted rim, two raised ribs encircling the neck above the sloping shoulder with petal molding within two concentric bands, 8³/₈in. high.

(Christie's)   **$111,000**

A fine and rare blue and white pear-shaped vase, painted around the body in pencil style and brilliant blue tones with the three friends, sanyou, pine, prunus and bamboo, above a band of classic scroll on the slightly-flaring foot pierced at either side with a narrow rectangular aperture, and below a raised band of similar scroll at the neck, 13in. high.

The rectangular apertures pierced through the foot are a conscious imitation of an early bronze shape: it is possible that the Jingdezhen potters were using bronzes from the Imperial Collections at Beijing as their source of inspiration.

(Christie's)   **$284,000**

MING

A rare early Ming white-glazed engraved monk's-cap ewer, Sengmao Hu, the globular body engraved around the mid-section with a single band of Tibetan characters between a border of twelve lotus panels at the base, each containing a lingzhi spray, and an eight-point cloud collar at the shoulder, 7¹/₂in. high.

An important fact has emerged from recent excavations at Jingdezhen which dates these ewers quite firmly to circa 1407. Halima, the most illustrious Lama of the era visited Nanjing in 1407, presiding over services for the Emperor's late parents attended by the Emperor himself. Many of the white wares decorated with the same mantra were almost certainly ordered by Yongle as presentation gifts for the visiting Lama. *(Christie's)* **$222,000**

A rare early Ming blue and white baluster vase and cover, guan, painted around the body in inky tones with 'heaping and piling' to depict a continuous lotus meander between a band of linked ascending and descending cloud-collars enclosing demi-flower-heads around the shoulder, and a border of various floral sprays around the base, the cover of domed lotus pad shape with upturning lobes molded with veins containing flower sprays and surmounted by an elephant finial (the jar repaired, the cover chipped), Yongle, 27cm. wide. *(Christie's)*

$96,000

MING

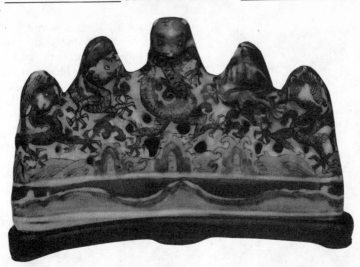

A rare late Ming Wucai brushrest, molded and reticulated with an ascending yellow dragon at the center flanked by four smaller dragons in brown, red, blue and green, all in mid-flight above three rocky islands among cresting waves, the green base molded to simulate a red apron with blue border, 6¹/₂in. wide.
(Christie's)   **$93,677**

A rare early Ming blue and white ewer, the yuhuchun bottle vase with a curved spout, joined to the neck with a cloud-shaped strut opposite a loop handle, both painted with peony scrolls, the pear-shaped bottle with a pair of shaped panels enclosing flowering branches of peach and pomegranate flanked by leafy peony branches above a key-fret band at the footrim and below two continuous scrolls of peonies divided by a band of overlapping upright plantain leaves, 11in. high.
(Christie's)   **$66,500**

A rare early Ming blue and white jar, painted around the body with two long-tailed phoenixes in flight amidst leafy vines issuing blossoms, above a band of key-fret between double lines at the foot and below a thicker line and larger key-fret band, the spreading neck with a band of overlapping plantain leaves below further double lines, 5^1/$_4$in. high.
(Christie's)   **$95,000**

A fine Transitional blue and white brush-pot, circa 1635, painted on the exterior with a scholar seated at a rootwood table shaded by a pine tree, attended by two young boys holding a fan and a cup and stand, all on a rocky terrace, 7^7/$_8$in. diameter.
(Christie's)   **$9,900**

A very fine Ming-style blue and white moon flask, painted to each side in rich cobalt-blue with eight petals, each enclosing one of the bajixiang radiating from a slightly raised boss centered by a stylized flower-head and divided by key-fret and lappet bands, all within a key-fret border, the flat sides painted with a narrow band of leafy scrolls issuing lotus blossoms, 19^1/$_4$in. high.
(Christie's)   **$192,500**

MING

A Ming 'Green and Yellow' dish, jiajing six-character mark and of the period, the exterior painted with eight ruyi surmounted by 'Precious Objects' and surrounded by leafy stems, the interior with a further five ruyi connected by a leafy vine, 6³/₄in. diameter.
(Christie's) **$5,000**

A fine early Ming blue and white 'dice' bowl, the heavily-potted rounded sides painted to the exterior with a leafy peony scroll above a band of upright lotus panels, the foot with a scroll of pinks, the rim with double lines above the unenclosed nianhao, the biscuit of the foot burnt around the edges to bright orange, 11³/₈in. diameter.
(Christie's) **$241,000**

A fine early Ming blue and white dish, the medallion painted with a ribboned bouquet of lotus flowers, leaves, a seed pod, sagittaria and aquatic plants, encircled by three concentric rings below a composite floral scroll with pairs of camellia, hibiscus, peony, gardenia and lotus blooms, Yongle, 40.3cm. diameter.
(Christie's)

$256,000

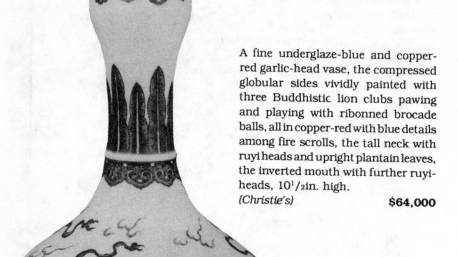

A fine underglaze-blue and copper-red garlic-head vase, the compressed globular sides vividly painted with three Buddhistic lion clubs pawing and playing with ribonned brocade balls, all in copper-red with blue details among fire scrolls, the tall neck with ruyi heads and upright plantain leaves, the inverted mouth with further ruyi-heads, 10¹/₂in. high.
(Christie's)   **$64,000**

A fine and rare 'green dragon' baluster jar and cover, crisply painted in underglaze-blue around the body with two five-clawed dragons, muzzles agape and with long whiskers, each grasping at a large flaming pearl ahead of it, and striding in mutual pursuit, the shoulder with Buddhist Emblems above a ruyi band, the flat-topped cover with a single dragon and pearl, 8³/₈in. high.
(Christie's)   **$64,000**

SONG

It was during the Song or Sung period, from 960-1279 AD, that potters became established as respected craftsmen on a par with the bronze worker and the jade carver, and the pieces they produced were strongly impressionistic and naturalistic in style.

Their wares were made in the simplest ways with little painting or embellishment. Most were wholly undecorated or enhanced by molding, stamping, the application of clay reliefs or etching. All these processes were carried out while the clay was still unfired. The glaze was added and the whole was then subjected to a single firing.

Song glazes tend to be thick and hard, and any crackle is positive and well-defined.

A Cizhou slip-decorated pillow, the concave headrest of ruyi shape, the design of a seated cat with ears erect wearing a floral scarf painted in a brown slip with details incised through to the white ground, Northern Song/ Jin Dynasty, 32cm. wide.
(Christie's) **$150,000**

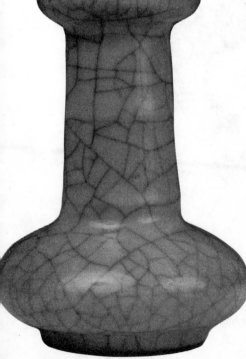

An important Jiaotan Guanyao bottle vase, Southern Song Dynasty, the compressed globular body rising to a tapering cylindrical neck with two slightly-raised horizontal bands, the broad cup-shaped mouth with flattened everted rim, all under a rich pale gray-blue glaze with irregular light brown crackles stopping neatly above the wedge-shaped dark brown foot, $4^5/8$in. high.
(Christie's) **$355,000**

113

A rare green and chestnut-glazed pottery figure of a horse, anding four-square on a rectangular base, the head lowered below the powerfully arched neck with ears pricked, nostrils flaring and mouth open, predominantly glazed in green washes, Tang Dynasty, 56.4cm. high.
(Christie's London)

$100,000

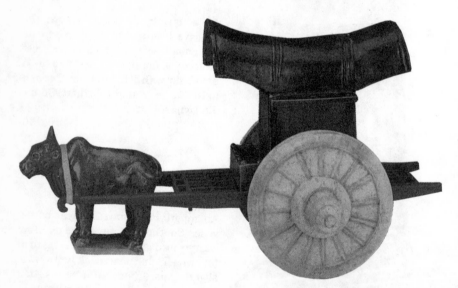

A Sancai pottery model of an ox and cart, the cuboid cart with an arched roof, the back pierced with a rectangular door, the front incised with thin vertical 'planks', supported on two unglazed large wheels with bulbous hubs, the ox standing four-square on a rectangular base, swishing its tail up to one side, Tang Dynasty, the cart 23cm. long.
(Christie's)

$8,800

TANG

A Sancai pottery figure of a horse, standing foursquare on a rectangular base, well modeled with strongly contoured flanks and facial features, caparisoned with ornamental harness suspending tassels, saddled and bridled, its body under a straw glaze with details in mustard and green glazes, Tang Dynasty, 50.5cm. high.
(Christie's)   **$21,350**

Of the many figurine artists who emerged during the years following the First World War one of the most important was Dimitri (Demetre is the Gallicised form) Chiparus. Chiparus was a Rumanian who came to Paris to study under A Mercié and J Boucher. He started exhibiting at the Salon des Artistes Français in 1914, when he received an Honorable Mention, and continued to do so until 1928.

His figures include realistic reproductions of nudes and women in everyday clothes, as well as columbines and pierrots, and dancers, some in amazing postures and obviously influenced by the Ballets Russes.

'Les Amis de Toujours', a bronze and ivory group, cast and carved after a model by Demetre Chiparus, modeled as a lady flanked by two borzoi, the lady with ivory face and hands, wearing a jeweled bodice and long dress, on stepped brown onyx base, engraved *Chiparus*, 11in. high.
(Christie's)   **$9,648**

'The Squall', a bronze and ivory figure of a wind blown woman, cast and carved from a model by D. Chiparus, she is depicted with muff held to her face, her skirt blowing about her knees. *(Phillips)* **$2,000**

A large Art Deco bronze and ivory figure, cast and carved from a model by Demetre Chiparus, as a female dancer influenced by the Ballets Russes, 71cm. long. *(Phillips)* **$44,000**

'Starlight', a bronze and ivory figure, cast and carved from a model by Demetre Chiparus, she wears a long-sleeved top and pointed helmet-hat and flared pleated skirt cut on a star-like bias.

(Phillips) **$10,700**

'Ballets Russes', a parcel-gilt and cold-painted bronze and ivory group of three dancers, by Demetre Chiparus, 24in. high.

Sergei Diaghilev's Ballets Russes were a revelation to the Parisian public when they were first seen in 1909. Bold and colorful, these had a great influence on the worlds of art and fashion. This group is a good example of Chiparus's ability to immortalize the actors in these exotic spectacles.

(Christie's) **$88,000**

'Dancer of Palmyra', a gilt bronze figure cast from a model by D.H. Chiparus, of a dancing girl standing on tip-toe with one foot pointing forwards, her arms stretched upwards, wearing a silver-patinated jeweled headdress, bodice and tassel-skirt, on stepped brown marble plinth, 68.5cm.
(Christie's) **$9,500**

A stylish bronze and ivory figure, cast and carved from a model by Demetre Chiparus, she wears an elaborate beaded costume with a layered and hooped skirt, the golden costume has silvered detailing in places, and she poses on tiptoe above a stepped brown onyx base, 33.5cm. high.
(Phillips) **$12,000**

'Patience', a bronze and ivory figure cast and carved from a model by Demetre Chiparus, the barefooted young lady stands in her nightgown her hands clasped, her eyes averted modestly downwards, presumably waiting, 37.5cm. high.
(Phillips) **$10,400**

An amusing German enameled cigarette case, depicting in naturalistic colors a gentleman and his female companion, both with cigarettes in their mouths, each smouldering where one touches the other.
(Phillips) **$700**

A German chromium plated metal aeroplane smoker's set, modeled as a bullet shape aeroplane, the body with cigar compartment, lighter and ashtray interior, the wings lifting to reveal cigarette compartments with cigar cutter propeler, raised on twin wheel supports, 24cm. long.
(Phillips) **$1,500**

A German Art Nouveau silver and enameled cigarette case, depicting in naturalistic colors a Mucha-style girl, her hair dressed with roses, she inhales the scent of a rose held in one hand, against a red ground over engine-turned surface, 8.5cm. long, maker's marks for Heinrich Levinger, London import marks for 1896.
(Phillips) **$1,500**

The legendary Clarice Cliff was born in 1899 in, perhaps inevitably, Staffordshire, where she started work at 13 in one of the local potteries, painting freehand onto pottery.

Her formal training comprised a year, when she was 16, at the Burslem School of Art, and a later year at the Royal College of Art, where she studied sculpture . At 17, she had gone to work at the firm of A.J. Wilkinson, and she remained with them, and their subsidiary the Newport Pottery, for the next two decades, ending up as Art Director and marrying the boss, Colley Shorter, when she was forty.

A 'Bizarre' single-handled Lotus jug decorated in the "Blue W" pattern, painted in colors between orange borders, large rubber stamp mark, 11^1/$_2$in. high.
(Christie's S. Ken)   **$4,425**

A pair of Clarice Cliff teddy bear book ends decorated in the 'Red Flower' pattern, painted in colors, 6in. high.
(Christie's S. Ken)   **$8,000**

A good Clarice Cliff 'Age of Jazz' figural group, modeled as a two-dimensional pianist and banjo player in evening dress, painted in black, red and brown against a cream ground and raised on a stepped rectangular base.
(Phillips) **$6,000**

A pair of Bizarre bookends, modeled as a pair of parakeets with green plumage on checkered base, 7in. high.
(Christie's) **$1,771**

An 'Applique' octagonal plate by Clarice Cliff decorated in the 'Caravan' pattern, painted in colors, painted mark, 11in. diameter.
(Christie's S. Ken)

$4,400

A Clarice Cliff Applique-Lucerne lotus jug, painted with an orange roofed chateau perched on the side of yellow and green hills, 29.5cm. high.
(Phillips London) **$10,000**

A 'Bizarre' grotesque mask designed by Ron Birks, covered in a dark blue Inspiration glaze, the features picked out in red.
(Christie's S. Ken) **$2,300**

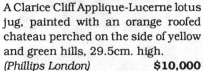

An 'Appliqué Bizarre' conical jug decorated in the 'Lugano' pattern of farmhouse in alpine landscape, 9¹/₂in. high.
(Christie's S. Ken) **$6,750**

A Clarice Cliff Sliced Circle pattern 'Lotus' jug, the vessel with twin handles and painted in bright colors, 29cm. high.
(Phillips London) **$4,725**

A small ebony silver-mounted striking bracket clock, circa 1708, the case with cast and chased silver mask and acanthus mounts to domed top with typical acanthus lyre form handle, silver bolection molding framing the dial and sides with well cast scrolling acanthus sound frets centered with Apollo's mask, acanthus-engraved squab feet, the back door with pierced wood soundfret, the $4^3/4$ x $5^1/4$in. dial signed *Tho: Tompion & Edw: Banger London* to the top within foliate engraving and flanked by subsidiary rings for strike/silent and regulation, the silvered chapter ring with mock pendulum aperture to the matted center, 9in. high.

(Christie's) $1,012,440

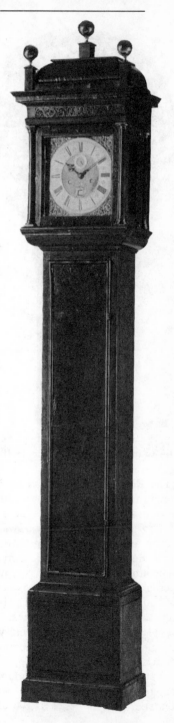

An early silver-cased, minute repeating, perpetual calendar, astronomical traveling timepiece with alarm, London 1823, 6in. high, by James Fergusson Cole (1799–1880). *(Christie's)* **$273,311**

A fine Queen Anne burl walnut longcase clock, Thomas Tompion, no. 486, the sides and plain plinth inlaid with ebony stringing, later skirting, the trunk with plain molded door, convex molding below the caddy top hood with plain corner columns with gilt capitals supporting molded and pierced frieze, brass ball finials, the eleven-inch dial, signed at VI o'clock with double screwed Indianhead spandrels, the silvered roman chapter ring enclosing seconds ring, circa 1710, 92in. high. *(Christie's)* **$181,500**

A George III 'Act of Parliament' clock, signed Justin Vulliamy, London, the molded circular dial painted with Roman chapters, pierced brass hands, the trunk door with chinoiserie landscape, the timepiece movement with tapered rectangular plates, last quarter 18th century, 58in. high. *(Christie's)* **$9,350**

The Egyptian temple gate clock, 1927, by Cartier.

The Egyptian revival has been a constant source of inspiration to jewelers and their associated craftsmen. The Art Deco period was as strong as any in reflecting this and some designers became known for their imaginative use of Egyptian motifs. Charles Jacqueau who worked for Louis Cartier was inspired by both Egyptian and Oriental themes. The Egyptian temple gate clock was completed by the master horologer Maurice Couet in 1927. His knowledge and skill set the highest standard of inspired craftsmanship. *(Christie's)* **$1,540,000**

A fine silver/gilt and enamel minute repeating timepiece by European Watch & Clock Co., for Cartier, in red leather traveling case, 2^{13}/₁₆in. high. *(Christie's S. Ken)* **$11,000**

A fine chased gilt Grande Sonnerie carriage clock with moon phase, calendar, thermometer and winding indicator, the movement stamped *H.L.* in lozenge punch, probably made for A.E. Bourdin, Paris. The silvered platform with counterpoised straight line lever escapement, uncut bimetalic balance, the unusual movement with backplate cut to reveal intermediate wheels pivoted in V-strap planted on backplate, striking grande/petite sonnerie and quarter repeating on two nested bells, the under dial work incorporating bimetalic strip for thermometer fixed to reverse of dial plate, the dial with gilt mask profusely engraved with leafy scrolls and strapwork, signed on the reverse, *Droz*, circa 1860, 8in. high. *(Christie's, New York)*

$22,000

A William and Mary floral marquetry longcase clock, on bun feet, the plinth and trunk door inlaid with panels of flowers and birds, convex molding below the flat top rising hood with twist columns flanking the 9¹/₂ inch square dial, signed *Wm. Cattle in Fleet Street Londini fecit* at VI o'clock, 1680s, 78¹/₂in. high.

(Christie's) **$19,800**

An automaton wall clock, English, early 19th century, the shaped copper plate face with painted figure of a rotund boy holding the circular painted dial, the pendulum and weight driven movement enclosed within wood frame, operating rolling eyes and protruding tongue, 15in. high.

(Bonhams) **$1,600**

A Victorian carved walnut shelf-clock by Seth Thomas Company, Thomaston, Connecticut, circa 1890, of violin form carved with foliage centering a glazed cupboard door painted in gilding with musical motifs and opening to a white-painted dial with Roman chapter ring over a molded base on ogee bracket feet, 29in. high.
(Christie's) **$4,180**

A Louis XVI ormolu-mounted verde antico, griotte and portor marble mantel clock, the later glazed circular enamel-chaptered dial with later movement set within the plinth of a spreading obelisk surmounted by a silvered globe and mounted with a figure emblematic of rain with a pitcher among clouds, on a stepped square base with a draped figure of a river god and a winged putto seated on rocks, 32¹/₄in. high.
(Christie's) **$37,500**

A rare chased gilt carriage clock with singing bird automaton, signed *Japy Freres & Cie*, on shaped polygonal base concealing the bird mechanism, the molded case with cast and chased foliate scrolls and flowers at the angles, surmounted by glazed virtrine with rising handle displaying the bird perched within realistic silk and feather foliage, circa 1860, 12³/₄in. high. *(Christie's)* **$18,700**

An ormolu mounted George III Turkish market musical small bracket clock, Markwick Markham Perigal, London, within a domed case profusely mounted with ormolu scrolls, flowers, shells and flambeau finials, similar pierced mounts to the sides, leaf capped, swag draped buttresses to the corners over double scroll leaf capped feet, the arched silvered dial engraved with flowers and vines, champlevé enameled in blue and green, the triple fusée movement with verge escapement, striking the hour on bell and playing one of the four tunes on eight bells with 12 hammers, mid 18th century, 17in. high. *(Christie's)* **$27,500**

A unique wall clock, designed and executed by Margaret Gilmour, the square tin body decorated in repoussé with Celtic entrelac designs on a hammered ground, inset with oval lozenge of turquoise, the pendulum and two cylindrical weights with similar repoussé decoration, the circular dial with incised arabic chapters, 45.7cm. square.
(Christie's)　　　**$23,474**

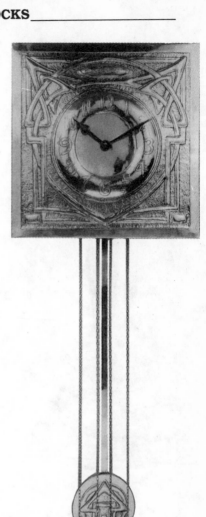

A Charles II ebony Dutch striking small bracket clock, Joseph Knibb, London, within a phase III case with gilt foliate scroll escutcheons to the door and foliate mounts to the caddy top, restored carrying handle, the signed six inch square dial with silvered chapter ring sometime reversed but now returned to show its original surface enclosing calendar aperature and winding holes in the matted center, circa 1680s, 11in. high.
(Christie's)　　　**$46,200**

A gilt metal figural stackfreed clock, the molded circular base chased with strapwork, flowerheads and fruit above band of gadrooning and below band pierced with C-scrolls, the figure, in classical armor, standing next to an engraved shaft supporting a wreath and scroll mount to silver time ball engraved with Roman chapters and signs of the zodiac, the bell concealed within base of clock, circa 1580, 11³/₄in. high.

(Christie's) **$11,000**

A fine inlaid walnut grande-sonnerie Lanterndluhr with calendar, the waisted glazed case with ebony moldings, tapered rounded drop and sliding hood fitted with gilt bezel enclosing the white enamel dial with roman chapters, subsidiary seconds, day and date rings, blued-steel hands, the glass enclosed 8-day three-train movement with knife edge suspended steel rod pendulum incorporating pallets to dead beat escapement, 57in. high.

(Christie's) **$74,800**

A good George III mahogany bracket clock, the arched case surmounted by a spire and urn finial and flanked by reeded scroll supports with carved floral mounts, on a shaped rectangular base, the circular enamel dial signed Grant, Fleet Street, London, the circular twin fusée movement signed in a floral cartouche on the backplate and with anchor escapement, 1ft. 7in. high.

(Phillips) **$7,160**

Mahogany carved tall case clock, Benjamin Willard, Grafton, Massachusetts, 1770, brass dial, engraved with *Benj Willard, Grafton Fecit 1770*, pendulum bob is marked *John Morris 1770*, 89in. high.

(Skinner) **$48,400**

A Victorian parcel-gilt and silver-mounted carriage timepiece, the case with large baluster finial to fish-scale pierced molded top with two amorous angels seated above, gilt three-quarter Corinthian columns, urn and foliage engraved sides, the base with two recumbent putti, the trellis and foliate-engraved silvered dial signed *Hunt & Roskell*, the base stamped *MORTIMER & HUNT, 1842*, 8¹/₂in. high.
(Christie's) **$15,000**

A Louis XVI ormolu-mounted Paris porcelain musical automaton clock, the glazed circular enamel dial signed *Ardiot* with ribbon-tied laurel-swag cresting and pierced giltmetal hands with indirect drive from the bridgecock vergé movement mounted beneath the musical frame with chain fusée driving the bellows, cam-and-rod drive through a composition tree to an automaton bird atop flapping its wings.

The movement is thought to be Swiss and probably by Pierre Jaquet-Droz (1721–90), a specialist in this field in the second half of the 18th century. He had already perfected a mechanical canary bird by 1758 and on a promotional tour in Europe that year, he sold to Ferdinand VI of Spain a bracket clock known as Le Berger fitted with a canary which sang eight tunes and moved its beak and body.
(Christie's) **$18,500**

One of a pair of massive cloisonné chargers decorated in vibrant colored enamels and various thicknesses of wire, with dense profusions of flowers and foliage including irises, hydrangeas, peonies, tiger-lilies, chrysanthemums, wild pinks and morning glories, late 19th century, 92.5cm. diameter.
(Christie's) **$19,250**

A Hayashi Kodenji cloisonné vase decorated in various colored enamels and thicknesses of silver wire on a deep blue ground with sparrows, the foot and neck with formal lappets and tendrils, signed *Nagoya Hayashi saku*, late 19th century, 31.5cm. high.
(Christie's) **$8,085**

A pair of cloisonné enamel turquoise-ground standing duck vessels, looking to the left and right, their plumage detailed in wire, the backs set with tubular stoppers, Qianlong/Jiaqing, 21.5cm. long.
(Christie's) **$7,500**

One of a pair of cloisonné and gilt-bronze horses and riders, the riders seated on saddle cloths, wearing long cloaks and wide brimmed hats, 12¹/₂in. high, 19th century.
(Bonhams) **$7,450**

Pair of massive cloisonné enamel vases, Meiji period, each of slender ovoid form tapering slightly above the base and surmounted by a tall waisted neck flaring towards the rim, the body featuring a pair of peacocks perched on the trunk of a flowering cherry tree entwined with blossoming wisteria vines extending to either side, 35¹/₈in. high.
(Butterfield & Butterfield) **$9,900**

A large Sino-Tibetan cloisonné enamel qilin, standing boldly foursquare on a draped waisted rectangular base decorated with shou characters, swastikas, floral scrolls and lotus panels, the dark-blue-ground animal with fur-like cloisons and flame-scrolls, snarling to expose gilded fangs and tongue, with a detachable horn and bushy green tail, Qianlong, 61.8cm. high.

(Christie's) **$14,000**

A cloisonné enamel and gilt-bronze pear-shaped vase, the body decorated with flowering and fruiting sprays of finger citrus, pomegranate and peach issuing from rockwork above a band of lotus panels, Jingtai four-character mark, 17th century.

(Christie's) **$5,750**

A cloisonné enamel and gilt-bronze recumbent mythical lion, crouching looking to its right, the rich black body set with white, yellow, turquoise and iron-red details on the muzzle and back and a green tail, 18th century, 18cm. long.

(Christie's) **$4,350**

An early Tudor iron-bound ash coffer bound overall in rectangular geometric pattern, the hinged domed top enclosing an interior with false floor and till, the sides with carrying-handles, 34^{1}/$_{2}$in. wide.
(Christie's) **$9,045**

An important large roironuri ground domed seventeenth century export coffer decorated in gold, silver and black hiramakie, takamakie, nashiji, hirame with a central lobed panel depicting stags beside rocks and autumnal flowers, the cover with two similar panels, depicting figures and attendants in a formal fenced garden beneath a plum tree, and a village beside a lake among pine trees, 2nd quarter of 18th century, 138cm. wide.

Towards the end of the seventeenth century the rich shell-inlaid coffers of the Momoyama period were gradually replaced by a more restrained and elegant style with carefully placed gold lacquer decoration on a plain black lacquer ground. The demands of the Dutch, who exported lacquer chests, coffers and panels, together with much porcelain, from their trading station at Nagasaki, meant that much of the lacquer had to be produced to a fixed price and time; as a result, their thin coats of black lacquer often became gray and oxidized after years of exposure to sunlight, and were sometimes 'refreshed' by a western japanner, using a shellac-based 'lacquer'.
(Christie's) **$298,375**

Joined and paneled oak and pine chest, Connecticut, 1670–1710, 55^1/2in. wide.

This chest was included in the second Wallace Nutting collection and in the Ironworks House at Saugus, Massachusetts. This collection was purchased from Mr. Nutting about 1918, by Morris Schwartz who sold it to Sacks, an antique dealer of Boston. Mr. Sack sold it to a customer for $250.00.
(Skinner) **$3,025**

A large Momoyama period rectangular coffer with domed hinged cover, the front and top with two mokkogata foliate panels each, decorated in gold and brown lacquer and aogai with a tiger, a peacock, oxen and geese among a variety of trees and flowering shrubs, circa 1600, 131.2 x 55 x 64.4cm. high.
(Christie's) **$282,000**

A giltmetal-mounted walnut coffer, banded overall with ebony, the repoussé mounts with birds among flowerheads and foliage, the hinged domed top enclosing a red velvet-lined interior, with later base stenciled *A.W.L. 161*, the back previously mounted, Flemish or North German, late 17th century, 24in. wide.
(Christie's) **$7,000**

A Momoyama period small rectangular wood coffer and domed cover decorated with panels of mandarin orange trees, magnolia and cherry in gold lacquer, brown and aogai, contained within lozenge and check borders in gold lacquer and aogai, with gilt metal hinges, late 16th century, 15.6cm. high. *(Christie's)* **$13,000**

A United States gold ten-dollar piece or 'Eagle', 1795. The illustration is of the obverse, showing a capped bust of Liberty with the date below. 1795 was the first year in which the United States struck gold coins, and very few examples of this coin have survived. *(Christie's)* **$115,500**

A Phoenician silver tetradrachm Panormous, Sicily, circa 400 B.C.

The coins of Panormous were mostly copied from those of other Sicilian cities, notably Syracuse, Gela and Segesta. The obverse of this, with Nike crowning a charioteer, and the reverse, showing the head of the Syracusan nymph Arethusa surrounded by four dolphins representing the sea, depend on dekadrachms of Syracuse engraved by the artist Euainetos. *(Christie's)* **$36,900**

1915 Panama-Pacific Exposition commemorative set. *(Butterfield & Butterfield)* **$59,400**

A 1954 bronze penny which is thought to be the only one in existence. No pennies of this date were struck for circulation but a number were made for die-testing purposes and according to Royal Mint records all were destroyed, along with the reverse die. However, one must have escaped as it was found in change in 1956. *(Spink's)* **$36,750**

A Louis XV style ormolu-mounted tulipwood and kingwood parquetry commonde a vantaux, circa 1900, after Antoine Gaudreaux, with a serpentine molded rouge royal marble top, above a conforming ormolu edge and two conforming doors, each applied with foliate scrolled mounts suspending a medallion depicting classical scenes, coins and foliate drapery, on ormolu cabriole legs with scroll feet headed by ram's masks, 36³/₄in. high, 67¹/₄in. wide. *(Christie's)*   **$21,000**

A German amaranth and marquetry small bombé commode by Abraham and David Roentgen, the serpentine top inlaid in natural and green-stained woods with three pierced rococo scrolled brackets entwined with trailing flowers and supporting musical trophies, circa 1765–1768, 35in. wide. This commode with its rare marquetry of musical trophies and flowers was probably 'Eine Commode mit Blumen und musicalischen Tropheen einglelegt', advertised as seventh prize in the 1769 lottery organized in Hamburg by David Roentgen. *(Christie's)*

$197,000

A harewood, mahogany-banded, marquetry and gilt metal-mounted demi-lune commode in the style of Mayhew and Ince, the brass bordered top with concentric marquetry bands of bellflowers, radiating bands, trailing foliage and ribbon-tied swags above a frieze drawer with classical urns and husk festoons with three drawers below flanked by guilloche inlaid uprights and cupboard doors, on foliate molded brass feet, 43in. wide. *(Christie's)* **$77,600**

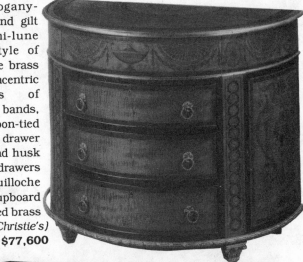

A Louis XVI ormolu-mounted mahogany commode by David Roentgen with slightly coffered rectangular top and a frieze drawer centered by a beaded roundel above three graduated long drawers edged with beading and mounted with drapery swag handles between fluted pilasters, 52in. wide.

The elegant restrained style of this commode with its finely figured veneers embellished with ormolu beads, flutes and ribboned medallions reflects the French Grecian style adopted by David Roentgen (1743–1807) after his appointment as ébéniste-mécanicien to Louis XVI and his admittance as a maître to the Parisian ébéniste's guild in 1780.

(Christie's) **$233,750**

Hans Coper (1920-1981) trained as an engineer in his native Germany, but fled to England in the late '30's. During the war, he met another refugee, Lucie Rie, and went to work in her studio. They started making ceramic buttons, then graduated to domestic ware and in the evenings Coper could experiment with his own designs.

His biggest 'break' came when Basil Spence commissioned two candlesticks from him for Coventry Cathedral. His work is now established among the foremost modern pottery with prices to match.

A stoneware buff cup form by Hans Coper, on a conical base surmounted by a manganese disc, the rim of the cup, manganese merging into heavy texturing, circa 1970.
(Bonhams)   **$2,650**

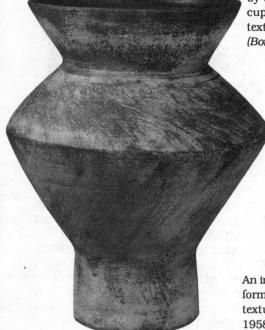

An important early stoneware 'thistle' form pot by Hans Coper, with diagonal texturing, impressed *HC* seal, circa 1958, 12^1/$_4$in. high.
(Bonhams)   **$13,000**

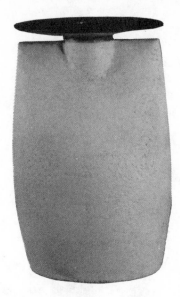

A fine stoneware sack form by Hans Coper, white with bronze disk top, impressed HC seal, circa 1970, 7^1/$_2$in. high.
(Bonhams) **$15,000**

A beautiful stoneware 'hour-glass' vase by Hans Coper, white and brown with distinctive white inlaid lines round the base, the slender central section heavily textured, the interior dark brown, impressed *HC* seal, circa 1963, 12in. high.
(Bonhams) **$19,200**

An outstanding stoneware pot by Hans Coper, white with a deep manganese band at the rim merging into a textured surface, the cylindrical base with an incised spiral, impressed *HC* seal, circa 1966, 7^1/$_4$in. high.
(Bonhams) **$16,000**

A brass lantern in the form of a pierced owl, a hinged opening to one side, late 19th/early 20th century, 13in. high. (Christie's) **$5,600**

An Art Deco patinated copper globular vase by Claudius Linossier, decorated around the upper body with a band of silver and black patinated lozenges against a ground shaded with red, ocher, black and tints of mauve, 17cm. high. (Phillips) **$8,500**

A copper electrotype model of the Vendôme column cast with a continuous spiraling relief of military maneuvres, second quarter, 19th century, 52in. high.

A reproduction of the column (143 feet high) in the Place Vendôme which was designed by Bergeret and made of the metal from Russian and Austrian cannon. It commemorates the campaigns of 1805–1807 and was constructed by Denon, Gondouin and Lepère in 1806–10.
(Christie's) **$15,850**

A very fine gilt-copper pear-shaped ewer and cover, 16th century, probably circa 1550, modeled after a Near Eastern metalwork shape, relief cast with petal-shaped panels at either side depicting dignitaries beside plantain and prunus, above a band of mythical animals and rockwork among wildly breaking waves at the flaring foot, 11⁷/₈in. high.

The shape is closely related to porcelain vessels of the period; notably blue and white wares, and the rare ewers in kinrande palette made for the Japanese market.

(Christie's) **$31,250**

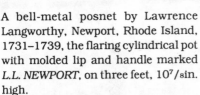

A bell-metal posnet by Lawrence Langworthy, Newport, Rhode Island, 1731–1739, the flaring cylindrical pot with molded lip and handle marked *L.L. NEWPORT*, on three feet, 10⁷/₈in. high.

Lawrence Langworthy is recorded to have worked in Newport as a pewter, brass and iron founder from 1731 until 1739. He was admitted a freeman of the town in 1735.

(Christie's) **$6,600**

147

A gold harp corkscrew, Holland, 19th century.
(Christie's) **$4,916**

A fire steel and corkscrew combination, 19th century.
(Christie's) **$11,755**

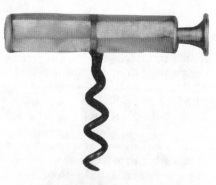

A Thomason corkscrew, 19th century.
(Christie's) **$13,251**

A two-part travelling corkscrew with mother-of-pearl casing, 19th century.
(Christie's) **$1,966**

A gentleman's sleeved waistcoat of linen, the borders worked with exotic leaves in corded and knotted work, with small ball-shaped self-embroidered buttons to the hem, circa 1690.
(Christie's S. Ken) **$4,246**

A rare pair of lady's mules of pale blue satin embroidered in white thread partly wrapped in silver with sunbursts trimmed with sequins, with square toes, circa 1665.
(Christie's S. Ken) **$23,350**

A rare hoop of blue, pink and gray striped cotton with three bamboo hoops, 47in. wide, mid-18th century.
(Christie's S. Ken) **$8,000**

A gentleman's nightcap of linen worked in cutwork with vines, the cuff also edged with lace, English, circa 1610. *(Christie's)* **$6,625**

A gown of ivory silk, printed with undulating bands of pink columbines against seagreen and lilac heart shaped leaves, the sleeves and hem trimmed with lilac ruched ribbon in the Regency manner.
(Christie's) **$7,750**

A gentleman's linen nightcap, embroidered in colored silks, gilt and silver gilt threads, with a repeating pattern of Tudor roses and pansies framed by gilt coiling stems, also with strawberries and leaves, English, circa 1600.
(Christie's S. Ken) **$27,600**

A pair of ladies' shoes of ivory silk applied with ivory silk braid, the tongue lined with blue silk damask, with white kid rands, English, early 18th century.
(Christie's)   **$6,102**

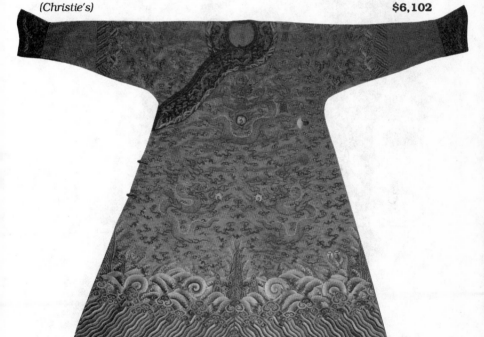

A Chinese imperial dragon robe, of canary yellow silk, finely embroidered in colored silks and gilt threads, with nine dragons chasing flaming pearls amongst cloud scrolls, bats and shou symbols, also with the twelve symbols of authority, over a turbulent sea-wave border, second half of 18th century.

The twelve imperial symbols of authority relate to the sacrificial obligations of the Emperor.
(Christie's)   **$26,500**

A 1950's bathing outfit comprising a one-piece bathing suit in black cotton decorated with P.V.C. polka dots, boned and draped bodice and flying panel, a belt, ribbon and a wrap of white cotton decorated with black P.V.C. polka dots and an ivory sequined bathing cap in the form of a flower, with handwritten labels stitched inside, inscribed *M. Monroe – designed by William Travilla and Charles Lamaire for the film There's No Business Like Show Business, Twentieth Century Fox, 1954*. This costume was used for publicity purposes but was not included in the final cut of the film. *(Christie's)*   **$22,000**

An open robe, with sack back, and petticoat of yellow silk woven with silvery white sprays of honeysuckle and roses, trimmed with scalloped flounces and edges with ivory silk fly braid, with Milanese lace added at the cuffs, English, circa 1760.
(Christie's)

$26,500

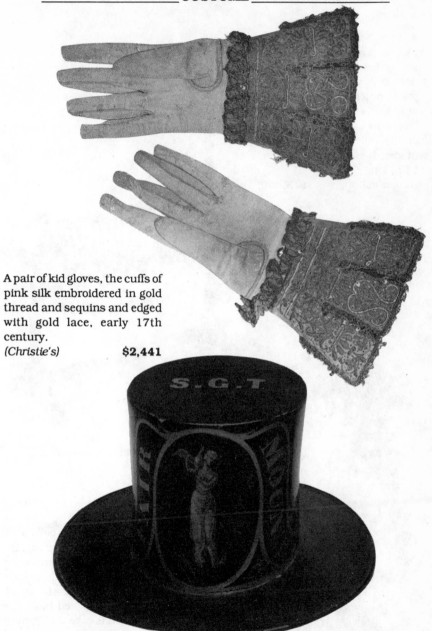

A pair of kid gloves, the cuffs of pink silk embroidered in gold thread and sequins and edged with gold lace, early 17th century.
(Christie's) **$2,441**

Painted and decorated parade fire hat, Philadelphia, circa 1854, decorated with a central medallion depicting William Rush's figure 'Water Nymph and Bittern'.
(Skinner Inc.) **$8,500**

A rare Napoleon I ormolu-mounted mahogany cradle of slatted boat-shape suspended between two turned uprights joined by a matching stretcher studded with ormolu stars, the foot of the basket and the head of the taller post with well-modeled swan-head finials, 52in. long.

(Tennants) **$13,500**

A Venetian giltwood cradle, the canopy hung with bells with feathered cresting, the scrolled headboard carved with foliate trails and strapwork with dished base, the ends carved with putti with feather head-dresses, first half 18th century, 24in. wide, 33in. high. *(Christie's)*
$6,000

A Regency brass-mounted mahogany cot, the arched canopy hung with orange silk, on four spreading turned supports each with vase-shaped finials, the slatted sides around a blue-silk draped cushion and two buttoned cushions, on turned tapering legs and brass caps, stamped *BUTLER'S PATENT*, 57in. wide.

Thomas Butler (1787–1814), cabinetmaker and upholsterer of 13 and 14 Catherine Street, Strand, London, specialized in patent furniture. He made use of a patent no. 1483 granted to his former business partner Thomas Waldron on 4 June 1785. This patent was for the construction of bedsteads without the use of nuts and bolts for easy assembly and traveling.
(Christie's) **$4,840**

An Italian baroque giltwood cradle in the form of a shell carved with flowerheads, each end with a putto, one leaning over the edge, the other seated and holding a garland of flowers, enclosing an iron swinging basket with tole liner on four scrolling supports, carved with putti and C-scrolls and hung with swags of flowers, probably Roman, early 18th century, 61in. wide.
(Christie's) **$20,000**

Creamware was developed by Josiah Wedgwood in response to the huge middle class demand for tableware which would be both durable and attractive. It was first introduced in 1761, at which time the glaze was not very resilient, and could be easily scratched. Nor could it withstand boiling water, which made it unsuitable for tea and coffee pots. By 1764, however, Wedgwood had solved all these problems. The final result was pleasing and modestly priced, and moreover was well suited to mechanical decoration.

A late 18th century creamware coffee pot and cover, 10¹/₄in. high. *(Dreweatt-Neate)* **$8,200**

A creamware model of a bird perched on blue and green rockwork, with light-brown body, yellow head and its incised wing and tail feathers enriched in blue, olive-green and light brown, perhaps Yorkshire, circa 1790, 20cm. high.
(Christie's) **$3,350**

A Staffordshire creamware model of a water-buffalo of Whieldon type naturally modeled and covered in a streaked manganese glaze, leaning against a cream tree-stump applied with berried foliage, on a shaped flat base, probably 18th century, 25.5cm. long.
(Christie's) **$7,480**

A George III mahogany bedside cupboard attributed to Thomas Chippendale with three-quarter galleried rectangular top with hinged and upward-folding paneled shutter, the sides with gilt-lacquered brass carrying-handles on tapering paneled legs, 18in. wide.

Although there is no direct parallel to this exceptionally neat and elegant bedside table in Chippendale's documented oeuvre, every one of its decorative details appears on pieces from his best known commissions. *(Christie's)* **$58,500**

A giltmetal-mounted tortoiseshell and ebony boulle bibliotheque basse with breakfront rectangular top above a paneled door inlaid with foliate scrolls and mounted with a figure of Poloma flanked by musical trophies, with label indistinctly inscribed in ink *Mrs W.P. Lomas.* A series of bibliotheques basses of this form with central panel mounted with mythological figures and flanked by glazed doors have been attributed to Boulle. *(Christie's)* **$390,000**

A Charles II walnut, elm and ash hanging-cupboard, the rectangular top with later molded cornice and bolection-molding frieze above a pierced door with baluster spindles flanked by triple-pierced baluster panels flanked and divided by turned pilasters and columns, the lower section inlaid with boxwood and bogwood geometric banding, 31in. wide.

(Christie's) **$7,160**

A walnut and parcel-gilt lit en bateau with paneled ends between column angles with bands of foliage and gadrooned ball feet, the shaped concave side edged with ribbon-tied reeding and scrolls carved with laurel foliage, with box-spring and mattress covered with pink, ivory and yellow striped taffeta and two bolsters, early 19th century, probably German, 82in. long.
(Christie's) **$28,000**

A fine vintage Dursley Pederson bicycle in full working order.
(Russell, Baldwin & Bright) **$2,275**

A Benelli 175 Monza motorcycle, chassis no. 281, with 175 cc single shaft
engine, three speed gearbox, 1927.
(Finarte) **$15,000**

Auguste (1853–1909) and Antonin (1864–1930) Daum were French glass craftsmen who were much influenced by Gallé and became members of the Ecole de Nancy. They made great use of cameo glass enameling and later also worked in pâte de verre. Acid etched pieces are also common. Their lamps are highly characteristic for their frequent use of the mushroom shade. Stems are also of glass, and these are decorated to form a uniform whole with the shade.

A Daum carved, acid-etched and applied vase, the mottled yellow, red and blue glass overlaid in similar colors and areas of green with grape laden vine branches, 19cm. high.
(Christie's) **$39,000**

A Daum acid-etched, wheel-carved and enameled vase, the cylindrical form of pointed oval section, the clear and acid-textured glass mottled with pink and green, decorated in relief with heavily carved polychrome field mushrooms in the rain, a distant landscape beyond, 21.5cm. high.
(Phillips) **$18,600**

William Frend de Morgan (1839-1917) was an English ceramic designer, perhaps now particularly remembered for his tiles. His designs were much influenced by his friend William Morris and include, birds, fish, flowers and mythical beasts. He established his own pottery in Chelsea in 1872, producing his own tiles, and experimented with lustre decoration in an attempt to reproduce the red lustre of maiolica painted in Gubbio. He also designed dishes in cream earthenware decorated in red lustre, and the Sunset and Moonlight suites decorated in gold, silver and copper. With Morris at Merton Abbey he continued to make tiles and dishes, and also established a factory at Fulham with Halsey Ricardo producing tiles and murals. He retired in 1905 and the factory closed in 1907.

A good William de Morgan 'Persian-style' circular wall plate, painted by Charles Passenger, depicting in the sunken center, a pair of dolphins, encircled with stylized floral and scale borders, 43.5cm. diameter.
(Phillips) **$9,000**

A William De Morgan tile picture comprising four tiles with polychrome underglaze decoration depicting two fruit trees and two dragons on garden wall, impressed mark, 20^1/2 x 20^1/2in.
(Andrew Hartley)

$10,638

When Chinese porcelain arrived in the West, Europe was literally dazzled. Nothing of such beauty and brilliance had ever been manufactured there, and the indigenous pottery industries now had to compete with the flood of imports. Majolica had been made in small workshops throughout Holland by potters who were experienced yet open to new techniques. A result of this was delft, a decorated, tin-glazed earthenware, known elsewhere as faience. It first appeared in the early 17th century and the next 120 years were to see the steady development of both technique and quality.

A Brislington delft Royal portrait charger, painted predominantly in blue with a half portrait of Queen Mary, the monarch wearing a yellow, manganese and blue crown and yellow necklace, flanked by the initials Q,M., diameter 9¹/₂in., circa 1690.
(Bonhams) **$20,500**

An English delft blue and white drinking vessel modeled as a spurred boot, inscribed beneath the flared rim *OH. MY HEAD* above a wide blue band and painted with scroll, triangular and semi-circular ornament, the foot with line and dash ornament, Southwark, circa 1650.
(Christie's) **$21,650**

A London delft blue dash Royal Coronation charger, painted in blue, manganese and yellow, portraying King William III and Queen Mary in their Coronation robes, he holding the orb and scepter, she a fan, circa 1690.
(Bonhams) **$45,000**

A London delft blue dash Royal equestrian charger, painted with a monarch wearing a crown, and holding a baton, riding a prancing stallion, flanked by two-tiered trees with green foliage on a stippled brown ground, edged by concentric double blue lines and within a yellow and blue line and blue dash rim, circa 1690.

(Bonhams)

$31,705

A London delft plate, painted in manganese and blue, with a half portrait of King George III wearing the Royal Garter flanked by *GIIIR*, diameter 9in.

This plate, circa 1760 and presumably manufactured to mark the Coronation of George III, would appear to be British Royalty's last appearance on English tin glazed earthenware. At present only three examples of this plate are known to be recorded.

(Bonhams)   **$28,000**

An 18th century English delft puzzle jug with printed flower decoration and inscribed *J.J. 1730*, possibly London, 7^1/$_4$in. high.

(Andrew Hartley)   **$7,000**

An English delft plate, painted in blue with a half portrait of George I wearing coronation robes and crown, holding the orb, flanked by the initials 'K G' within a double line border and blue dash rim, diameter 8³/₄in., circa 1714. *(Bonhams)*

$20,500

A rare and important English delft wine bottle dated 1644 of onion shape with a loop handle, inscribed in blue with the crowned monogram of Charles 1st, 15.5cm. high. *(Phillips)* **$59,500**

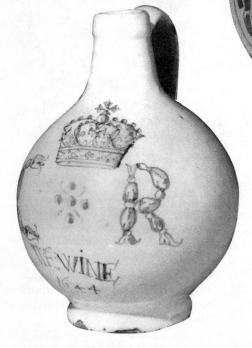

A Lambeth delft charger, painted in green, orange, red and blue with a head and shoulder portrait of King George I, flanked by the initials 'G.R', within a wide dusted manganese band, the border with stylized scrolled foliage and floral pattern, diameter 13in., circa 1714. *(Bonhams)*

$31,700

A rare English delft plate, painted in blue with the dispossessed King Charles II hiding in the Boscobel Oak, his visible face encircled by three yellow enamel crowns, diameter $9^1/4$in., circa 1745.

In September 1651 following his defeat at Worcester, the 21-year-old Charles II is chronicled as having spent one night hiding from Cromwell's troops up an oak tree at Boscobel in Brewood forest. The Boscobel Oak quoted later became a well represented Jacobite symbol and this romantic motif appears on Delft and Chinese export pieces supporting the Stuart cause during both the 1715 and 1745 rebellions.

(Bonhams) **$16,785**

A very rare London delft teapot and cover of globular form with loop handle and straight spout, painted in blue, iron-red and green with whorl and lozenge-shaped motifs.

(Phillips) **$39,000**

Porcelain making in Derby commenced around the mid 18th century and has continued there ever since. During the early period, from 1750 onwards, production concentrated mainly on figures, with the result that, in contrast to most other factories of the period, comparatively few 'useful' wares were made. Emphasis from the beginning was on decoration, which was always very fine, even if some pieces of the pre-1760 period appear rather primitive and thickly potted. When more functional pieces were produced these still had decorative themes, with openwork baskets, pot pourris and frill vases featuring largely in the output. Fine tea and coffee wares were often painted with Chinese figure subjects.

William Duesbury, the London porcelain painter, became a key figure from 1756. He bought the Chelsea factory in 1770 and finally moved to Derby in 1784, where he was succeeded by his son, William II, in 1786.

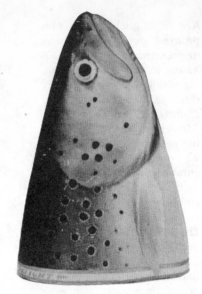

A Derby trout's head stirrup-cup naturally modeled and colored, the rim reserved and inscribed in gilt *THE ANGLER'S DELIGHT* between gilt lines, Duesbury & Kean, circa 1800, 10.5cm. high. *(Christie's)*   **$2,000**

A Derby group of two lovers and a jester after the model by J.J. Kändler, the lovers seated before white flowering bocage, he in iron-red-lined puce jacket, flowered waistcoat and green breeches, his companion in yellow bodice, striped skirt and puce underskirt reserved with flowers and flowerheads, the jester standing beside offering a tray with two cups, Wm. Duesbury & Co., circa 1765, 29cm. high.
(Christie's)   **$6,500**

166

Late 18th century puce marked Derby porcelain bough/crocus pot with twin ram's head handles and removable pierced liner, 5^1/$_4$in. high.
(Bigwood) **$8,000**

A Derby yellow-ground botanical dessert-service painted in the manner of John Brewer with specimen flowers, named on the reverses in Latin and English, the wells gilt with stylized pendant ornament, within bright yellow borders between gilt lines, circa 1800.
(Christie's) **$100,000**

A Derby two-handled chocolate cup, cover and stand, painted on one side, probably by George Complin, with two finches perched amongst fruit, including grapes, a peach, a pineapple, cherries, gooseberries, within a basket, set on a pedestal, within a gilt edged oval-shaped panel. The cup has double twist handles, the cover a gilt acorn knop and gilt leaf border, the stand a similar border, 15.5cm. high, 1789–95.

(Phillips) **$18,350**

A pair of Derby Mansion House dwarfs, wearing brightly colored striped and flowered clothes, Robt. Bloor & Co., circa 1830, 17.5 and 17cm. high.
(Christie's) **$3,465**

A Derby cabaret set, each piece painted, probably by Zachariah Boreman, with named Derbyshire views reserved with simulated pearl borders, all with blue painted crown, batons and D mark, circa 1790.
(Phillips) **$17,500**

A carved and painted wooden doll, with rouged cheeks, dark enamel eyes, stitched brows and lashes, carved ears and adolescent figure, circa 1740 (arm missing, two fingers broken, leg detached), 18in. high.
(Christie's S. Ken)   **$16,500**

A fine bisque swivel-headed bébé doll, with closed mouth, fixed brown yeux fibres outlined in black with pink shaded lids, 20in. high, impressed *BRU Jne 7*, circa 1880.
(Christie's S. Ken)

$22,500

Bisque bébé doll, incised as follows, head, *Bru Jne 9*, left shoulder *Bru*, right shoulder *N9*, wardrobe consists of corset cover, bloomers, $1/2$ slip and two dresses, paperweight eyes, closed mouth, and human hair wig, 24in. high.
(Butterfield & Butterfield)

$23,100

169

A bisque headed bébé doll with blue lever-operated sleeping eyes, pierced ears, two rows of teeth, blonde skin wig and jointed wood composition body, 17in. high, marked Ste A 1, Steiner, circa 1880.

(Christie's S. Ken) **$5,600**

A bisque headed bébé doll, with closed mouth, fixed blue eyes, blonde wig, and composition body, 14in. high, stamped in red, Depose Tete Jumeau Bte.

(Christie's S. Ken) **$5,200**

A very rare bisque-headed googlie-eyed doll, with round blue sleeping eyes, closed disgusted down-turned water melon mouth, short blonde wig and toddler body in original green and mauve racing colors, 14in. long, impressed *Heubach Koppelsdorf 319.3*, circa 1920's.
(Christie's)   **$7,300**

A bisque-headed bébé, with open/closed mouth, fixed blue eyes, blonde mohair wig, pierced ears, bisque shoulder-plate and arms, and gusseted kid body, original pale blue satin dress, cotton drawers, later shoes and hat, 19in. high, circa 1880.
(Christie's)   **$26,103**

The first ever hot air fan with 2 stroke hot air motor driven by a copper petroleum lamp, on a richly decorated cast metal tripod stand with 2 wooden carrying handles, 113cm. high, only known example, circa 1860.
(Auction Team Koln) **$4,200**

The Napier patent coffee machine, circa 1845, the apparatus comprising of copper flask, condensing tube and beaker of up-turned bell form, glass spirit burner, the whole suspended and housed within gilt metal frame, upon a ceramic base plate edged with gilt, 13in. high.
(Bonhams) **$735**

A lockstitch sewing machine, No. 164, with original instruction leaflet and invoice, by C. McQuinn, 1878.
(Christie's) **$6,704**

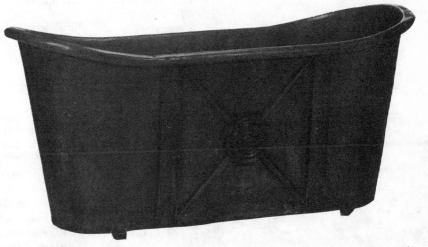

Empire tin-lined zinc baignoire, circa 1820, with rounded tapering and slightly arched ends, the sides with intersecting tapering cylindrical rods centered by a circular embossed disk flanked by plain pilasters, 5ft. 4in. long.
(Butterfield & Butterfield) **$1,100**

Doucai, or Tou t'sai, means literally 'contrasting color' and refers to a decorative technique consisting of a pattern outlined in a thin, penciled, underglaze blue, infilled with translucent, enameled overglaze colors, principally red, yellow and green.

Examples exist from the early Ming Dynasty, and the technique seems to have been perfected in the Chenghua period.

Imitations and new-style wares were made under Yung Cheng and Ch'ien Lung and the 18th century saw the period of greatest output in this style.

A fine Doucai ogee dish, Qianlong seal mark and of the period, painted to the center of the interior with a full-faced flower-head with overlapping petals, encircled by four peach and four stylized lotus-blossom scrolls, the rim with the eight Daoist emblems, 7⁷/₈in. diameter.
(Christie's) **$25,000**

A fine large Doucai jardinière, Qianlong seal mark, the thickly potted sides rising to a wide rim, finely painted to the side with five medallions filled with lotus flowers and feathery foliate, interspersed by elaborate interlaced ruyi-heads and feathery leaves, all between lotus panels above the foot and a band of interlocking quatrefoils enclosing chrysanthemum and lotus flower below the rim, 13in. diameter.
(Christie's)

$284,000

Dr Christopher Dresser (1834–1904) was a Glasgow born botanist, designer and writer. He studied first at the London School of Design before training as a botanist and becoming a lecturer at the Department of Science and Art. The two strands of his training combined happily when he started to design silver in the early 1860s. His work was characterized by the simplicity of its design and the careful adaptation of form to purpose.

Dresser was also an enthusiastic collector of Japanese arts, and the influence of the Japanese style is often clear in his own pieces. He designed for leading silver manufacturers such as Hukin and Heath and for J Dixon.

A Hukin & Heath electroplated metal and glass 'crow's foot' decanter, designed by Dr. Christopher Dreser, stamped *H&H*, and with registration lozenge for 1878, 24cm. high. *(Christie's)* **$25,575**

A Hukin & Heath electroplated 'Tantalus' designed by Dr. Christopher Dresser, the open rectangular square-section frame with sliding and locking front stretcher, the perpendiculars supporting shelf with square wells, the hinged cover with ebonized bar handle supported on arched brackets, with three new square-section decanters, with registration lozenge for 1879, 28cm. high. *(Christie's)* **$10,670**

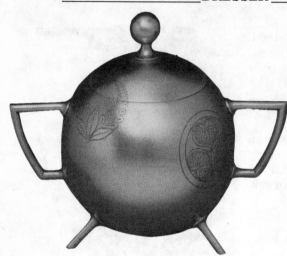

A Hukin and Heath electroplated biscuit barrel, designed by Christopher Dresser, of spherical form on three feet with two angular handles and a knopped hinged cover, 20cm. high.
(Phillips) **$5,000**

An Elkington & Co. electroplated barrel-shaped metal teapot, designed by Dr. Christopher Dresser, with ebonized curving wooden handle, stamped with a variety of Elkington & Co. marks and *16594*, 17cm. high.
(Christie's) **$6,150**

An Elkington & Co. electroplated toast rack, designed by Dr. Christopher Dresser, with a tall central 'T" base and three low triangular shaped supports on either side of it, stamped *Elkington* and with facsimile stamped signature *Dr. Christopher Dresser*, 13.5cm. high.
(Christie's) **$13,250**

A Hukin & Heath plated soup tureen, cover and ladle, designed by Christopher Dresser, the deep sided vessel supported on three prong feet, having two ebonized rod handles, the flat cover with ebonized finial, 21cm. high, the matching ladle with ebonized rod handle, 32cm. long.
(Phillips) **$17,100**

A Hukin & Heath electroplated and glass 'crow's feet' decanter, designed by Christopher Dresser, the clear glass amphora shaped body supported on three metal feet having an angular metal handle with a metal rim and cover, 24cm. high.
(Phillips) **$8,200**

A Hukin & Heath electroplated metal three-piece tea-set, designed by Dr.
Christopher Dresser, comprising: a tea-pot, milk jug and two-handled bowl,
each piece on four short curly feet, registration lozenge for 1878, 8.5cm.
height of teapot.
(Christie's) **$9,200**

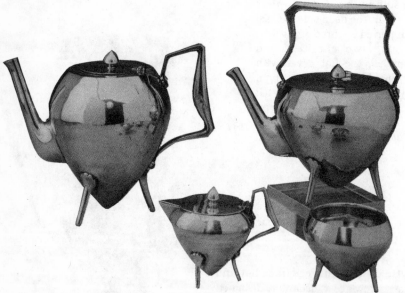

A James Dixon four-piece electroplated metal tea-set, designed by Dr.
Christopher Dresser, comprising: a teapot, kettle, sugar basin and milk jug,
each piece supported on three spike feet, conical bodies, angular spouts,
each with stamped *JD* monogram, facsimile signature, and registration
lozenge for 1880, 23cm. height of kettle.
(Christie's) **$21,483**

A James Dixon & Sons electroplated claret jug designed by Dr. Christopher Dresser, with angled handle, the conical body with tapering cylindrical neck and triangular spout, the flat hinged cover with ball finial, the body with a circular panel and friezes of finely engraved decoration, 21.7cm. high.

(Christie's) **$21,340**

A Hukin & Heath electroplated metal tureen, designed by Dr. Christopher Dresser, with bone finial and cylindrical bar handle, on three spike feet, glass liner, with registration lozenge for 1880, 25.5cm. high.
(Christie's) **$12,275**

A 19th century Viennese enamel and ormolu mounted model of a coach, the pink ground painted with reserves of figures in landscapes, 8in. long.

(Christie's) **$2,574**

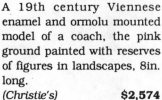

An etui, circa 1760, one side painted with the portrait of a woman, the reverse with a couple out walking, 10cm.

(Lawrence Fine Art) **$2,700**

A fine South Staffordshire rectangular blue ground enamel tea caddy, the cover painted with three herdsmen and their cattle by a river before an architectural background in a raised gilt scroll and rocaille cartouche, circa 1770, 8¹/₂in. long.

(Christie's) **$31,680**

A tall 'Façon de Venise' goblet with a shallow flared bowl, the stem formed as three hollow pear-shaped knops divided by mereses and short plain sections, on a folded conical foot, Liège, perhaps Bonhomme glasshouse, 17th century, 25cm. high.
(Christie's) **$6,800**

A Façon de Venise serpent-stemmed goblet, the flared funnel bowl supported on a merese, the stem with a coiled section enclosing brick-red and opaque-white threads and applied with turquoise pincered ornament, 17th century, 18cm. high.
(Christie's) **$8,000**

A 'Façon de Venise' latticinio goblet, the compressed oval bowl with a band of verto a retorti between white threads, the rim with a band of granular gilding, supported on a tapering oviform stem molded with lion's masks alternating with escutcheons between bands of gadrooning, South Netherlands, second half of the 16th century, 13cm. high.
(Christie's) **$11,650**

A 'Façon de Venise' flute, the slender funnel bowl supported on a merese, the stem with a wrythen-molded section with opposing pincered flanges and a spirally incised coil resembling a seahorse applied with a turquoise flange, above a short plain section and folded foot, The Netherlands, 17th century, 26.5cm. high.
(Christie's) **$14,850**

A 'Façon de Venise' latticinio goblet and cover in vetro a retorti with allover marvered thread and gauze decoration, the deep funnel bowl with everted rim supported on a clear merese above a spreading folded foot, Venice or Low Countries, late 16th/early 17th century, 27cm. high.
(Christie's) **$30,000**

A Hall-in-Tyrol 'Façon de Venise' large goblet, the flared funnel bowl lightly molded with an allover 'beech-nut' pattern, supported on a hollow compressed knop molded with vertical ribs and with traces of gilt enrichment, the high conical foot with folded rim, perhaps workshop of Sebastian Höchstelter, 16th century, 26cm. high. *(Christie's)* **$31,845**

A 'Façon de Venise' latticinio silver-mounted table-bell, the flared trumpet-shaped bowl in vetro a retorti with spiral gauze cable alternating with marvered threads terminating in a ball knop with clear collar, the contemporary silver mount surmounted by a gadrooned hollow knop with rattle enclosed within four curved arms, South Netherlands, second quarter of the 17th century, 18cm. high.
(Christie's) **$10,200**

It was the Italian city of Faenza, situated between Bologna and Rimini, that was to give its name to the tin glazed earthenware which came to be known as faience. From the late 14th century it had been associated with maiolica manufacture and from the mid 15th century developed a very distinctive style. Apart from the usual drug pots, fine baluster vases decorated with heraldic devices, contemporary figures or gothic foliage, were produced.

Later some large pieces in full relief were attempted. By the 16th century several Faenza painters were engaged in painting in the style now associated with Urbino, and referred to as istoriato.

Pair of Bough pots, the ribbed bodies decorated 'Al Garofano' in iron red, blue and green, Faenzà, 18th century, 21cm. high.
(Finarte) **$3,200**

Two faenza waisted albarelli decorated in the workshop of Virgiliotto Calamelli and named in Gothic script for Diagalangi and Diaprunis. Simp on a central ribbon with a half-length figure of a girl tied to a tree and a portrait of a girl in profile to the left named *CAMILLA*, circa 1525, 27cm. high.
(Christie's)

$37,600

A Faenza circular tondino of Cardinal's hat form, circa 1525, 25cm. diameter.
(Christie's) **$25,000**

Large Faienza oviform wine jar, 18th century, painted with a roundel of leaves and fruit enclosing a cherub's head with halo and blue and green wings below, reserved on a yellow ground painted overall with scrolling foliage in blue, $22^{1}/_{4}$in. high.
(Butterfield & Butterfield)

$1,650

A maiolica group of the Virgin and Child seated holding the Christ Child on her knee, her features enriched in blue, wearing an ocher veil and ocher-trimmed blue cloak, yellow dress tied with a green sash and yellow shoes, the Christ Child wearing a blue flowerhead pendant and with yellow hair, resting on his mother's left knee, most probably Faenza, circa 1540, 40cm. high.
(Christie's) **$27,000**

Pierre le Faguays was a native of Nantes in France. A member of the Société des Artistes Français, he exhibited at their salons, where he gained an Honorable Mention in 1926. He was also a member of the La Stèle and Evolution groups, where artist craftsmen exhibited bronzes, ceramics, lamps and other decorative objects.

Le Faguays worked in the 'stylised' mode, which combined elements from many contemporary influences.

'Bacchante', a bronze green and brown patinated figure, cast from a model by Pierre Le Faguay, of a nude female kneeling on one leg, the other bent forward, her upper body and head reclined, clasping grape bunches to her head, with a cloth draped over her arm, falling to the ground in folds, on a rectangular bronze base, signed in the bronze *Le Faguay*, with founder's mark, 66.5cm. high.
(Christie's) **$11,748**

'Diana', a bronze figure, cast from a model by Pierre Le Faguay, modeled as a lithe young woman wearing a short classical tunic, 66.5cm. high. *(Phillips)* **$2,189**

A silvered bronze figure of a dancer, cast from a model by Pierre Le Faguays, the young woman wearing a pleated dress with paneled skirt, 1920s, 65cm. *(Bonhams)* **$2,300**

'Fawn and Nymph', a bronze sculpture, cast from a model by Pierre Le Faguay, the stylized group depicting a fawn in pursuit of a naked nymph, mounted on rectangular wooden base, 46.5cm. high. *(Christie's)* **$12,500**

Famille rose is a style of decoration based on Chinese porcelain painting introduced during the Yongzheng period around 1730. A deep rose pink enamel derived from gold features strongly in the palette and by mixing this with white a variety of pinks and deep rose colors were now obtainable. It was much in demand for tableware produced for the nouveau riche of the Industrial Revolution.

A famille rose Canton enamel and gilt-bronze model of a jardinière, the knobbly bonsai tree with gilt branches, set with metal and hardstone leaves and blossoms, all in a blue-ground hexafoil jardinière cast with gilt fretwork containing six floral panels, Qianlong/Jiaqing, 58cm. high.
(Christie's)   **$5,900**

A rare famille rose long-necked oviform vase, iron-red Xianfeng six-character mark and of the period, enameled on the broad body with two clusters of flowering chrysanthemum, peony and magnolia, above bands of key-pattern and formal scrolling flowers reserved on a violet-blue-ground at the foot, 12in. high.
(Christie's)   **$18,500**

A fine famille rose bowl, the steeply-rounded sides enameled with a continuous scene of Immortals and scholars variously engaged in dispute or relaxation within a simple landscape, 6³/₄in. diameter.
(Christie's) **$20,000**

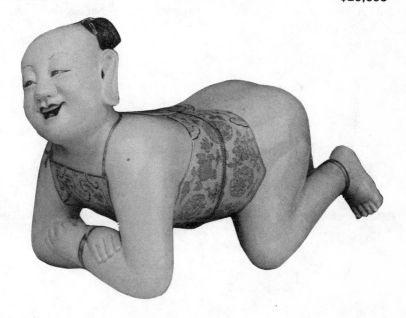

A rare large famille rose kneeling boy pillow, the plump infant crouching on all fours with a smiling face raised to the left and his feet in the air, his black-painted hair tied in two bangs, wearing around his waist a typical child's garment enameled with blue sprays and roundels of fruit and foliage at the back and a large dragon at his stomach on a paler ground, 15in. long.
(Christie's) **$39,000**

A fan, the leaf with a landscape after Meindert Hobbema by Giuseppe Prosdocimi, the sticks by Jorel, made for Count Demidoff, circa 1875, 11in. *(Christie's)* **$7,715**

An early 18th century Flemish fan, portraying the scene of Jupiter appearing in a shower of gold coins to Danae reclining on a cushion, 28cm. long, circa 1720. (Phillips) **$1,400**

A fan, the leaf with the arrival of Queen Maria Leszczynska at Versailles, French, circa 1750, 10in.
(Christie's)   **$20,207**

'The twentieth birthday of Le Grand Dauphin', a rare unmounted fan leaf painted in bodycolor with Louis XIV, seated beside the Queen, Marie Thérèse, whilst a figure dressed in blue decorated with gold fleurs de lys showers a basket of gold coins at the feet of Le Grand Dauphin, their son, dressed in blue stands beside them. There are few prints of Louis XIV's offspring when young but the Dauphin's portrait compares closely with the mezzotint published by Charles Allard.
(Christie's S. Ken)   **$20,240**

Pair of French 19th century bronze firedogs, a seated poodle and long haired cat respectively, seated on tasseled cushions, polished, on rectangular bases, the outset corners set with paterae and vitruvian scroll moldings, 1ft. 4in. high.
(Russell Baldwin & Bright)   **$5,600**

Fine pair of Louis XV ormolu and patinated bronze chenets, mid-18th century, in the form of a black patinated boar rising to its feet or a reclining stag, each resting on foliage between an oak branch and scrolling stylized foliage in high relief, 19in. long.

The design of the boar is based on a reproduction of the monument after the antique in the Mercato Nuovo in Florence.

This was a popular model and a number of virtually identical examples are recorded, including a pair of chenets in the Dauphin's bedchamber at Versailles.
(Butterfield & Butterfield)   **$16,500**

Pair of large patinated bronze figural andirons of American Indians, by Louis Potter, first quarter 20th century, Roman Bronze Works, New York, each depicted as a kneeling male figure bending forward slightly and looking downward, possibly preparing to drink from a stream, 22in. high. *(Butterfield & Butterfield)*

$4,950

A pair of Chippendale brass andirons, American, late 18th century, each with a ball-and-flame finial over a baluster and ring-turned support and hipped arched legs, on ball-and-claw feet, 21$^{1}/_{2}$in. high. *(Christie's)* **$9,350**

Pair of Italian baroque style patinated bronze grotesque andirons, second half 19th century, each in the form of a serpent-tailed many-breasted long-necked chimera, with furled wings, rearing backwards with a snarling head, 28in. high. *(Butterfield & Butterfield)*

$5,225

A pair of Louis XVI ormolu and bronze chenets with recumbent lions upon draped shaped rectangular plinths with pine-cone finials and foliate panels on acanthus-headed toupie feet, 15³/₄in. wide.

Designed in the French neo-classical or Grecian manner with bacchic ornament comprizing a lion regarding a pine-cone on a pedestal, couchant on a draped tabouret embellished with acanthus foliage and supported on fluted toupie feet.

(Christie's) **$10,850**

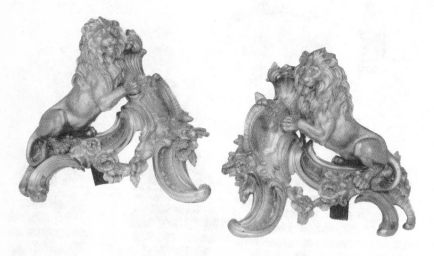

A pair of early Louis XV ormolu chenets of scrolled outline, cast with C- and S-scroll rockwork and flowerswags rising to a cartouche engraved with a later *JW* monogram below a Continental Viscount's coronet, supporting a rearing lion, 15in. wide.

(Christie's) **$18,700**

A Modernist glass and chrome metal fish tank, the clear glass tank with polished copper column supports at each corner, with four detachable chrome metal vases, on two column supports joined by two amber-tinted glass rods on polished steel base inset with topaz-colored glass, 130.5cm. high.

(Christie's)   **$8,600**

A George III mahogany gold-fish bowl stand of triangular outline, the top with raised circular center and gadrooned border, fitted with a cupboard door between fluted chamfered angles on cabriole legs carved with acanthus ending in scrolled feet, now associated with a glass fishbowl with compressed ovoid body and spreading foot, the stand 26¹/₄in. high.

(Christie's)   **$19,500**

A Louis XIV carved and gilded frame, the corners and centers carved with anthemia and ovals with flowers flanked by interwoven c-scrolls, sumptuous foliage and flowers running to cartouches centered with flowersprays on a cross-hatched ground, $31^7/_8$ x $36^1/_2$in.
(Christie's) **$24,500**

A Fabergé silver-mounted birchwood imperial photograph frame containing a signed photograph of Tsar Nicholas II, dated 1915, St. Petersburg, 1908–17, $17^1/_2$ x $14^3/_4$in.
(Christie's) **$19,000**

An Anglo-Dutch carved frame, circa 1660, the top with overlapping leaves, foliage and clusters of flowers running to a laurel wreath centered with a coat of arms and surmounted with scrolling acanthus leaves, the sides covered in high relief with putti holding shields, overall size $26^1/_2$in. x $22^1/_4$in.
(Christie's S. Ken)

$6,750

When Louis XV, ever jealous for his Sèvres protegé, refused Paul Hannong a licence to continue making porcelain at Strasbourg in 1755, Hannong took his know-how across the Rhine to Frankenthal, where the Elector Carl Theodor allowed him to set up in some disused barrack buildings.

Hannong quickly set to work, and within a few months was producing pieces of a standard high enough to be used as court gifts. He subsequently returned to Strasbourg, leaving his elder son, Charles-François-Paul as director at Frankenthal. Charles died in 1757, however, whereupon his younger brother Joseph Adam took over, and in 1759 bought the factory from his father. In 1762, the Elector himself bought it out, and it continued in production until 1800.

A Frankenthal figure of a girl emblematic of Spring after the model by Karl Gottlieb Lück, her hair in a white and gilt snood, wearing a white bodice with yellow bows, white apron and puce striped and flowered skirt with a gilt fringed hem, circa 1765, 14cm. high.
(Christie's)   **$1,750**

A Frankenthal baluster ewer and cover probably painted by Jakob Osterspey with Bacchus and Venus reclining beside him scantily clad in brown and pink drapes, a pair of billing doves on a rock behind, above a molded and gilt feuilles-de-choux band, sprays of flowers flanking the scroll handle with puce shell thumb-piece, blue rampant lion mark, impressed *I* and *IH* for Joseph Hannong, circa 1758, 23.5cm. high.
(Christie's)   **$17,000**

Emile Gallé was born in 1846 and started his career as a ceramicist. In 1874 he established a small workshop in Nancy, where during the 1890s he was to become the inspiration for what became known as the Ecole de Nancy, a group of French Art Nouveau artists who followed his techniques and decorating style. He made earthenware and later also experimented with stoneware and porcelain. His pieces were decorated with heraldic motifs and plant designs, and featured flowing, opaque glazes.

In the early 1870s he also started experimenting with glass, and this is the medium with which he is now most associated. In fact, he revolutionised its manufacture by going completely against the traditional ideal of crystalline purity and aimed instead for an opaque, iridescent effect. He experimented with the addition of metal oxides to the glass melt, coloring glass in imitation of semi-precious stones, and also even exploited the impurities to give glass the quality of a fabric or the suggestion of mist or rain.

Gallé signed all his creations, and after his death in 1904 a star was added to the signature. His factory continued in operation until 1931 under his friend and assistant Victor Prouve.

'Vase à Pekin', a Gallé carved, acid-etched and fire-polished bronze-mounted vase, of baluster form, the jade-colored glass overlaid with purple lotus flower, on a bronze base with scrolled and splayed foot, the glass with carved signature *Gallé*, 26.5cm. high.

(Christie's) **$21,450**

A Gallé mold-blown cameo glass vase, of oviform with flared neck, the amber-tinted body overlaid with mauve-blue and reddish-amethyst glass mold-blown and acid-etched with pendant fuchsias and foliage in relief, 30cm. high.
(Phillips) **$18,350**

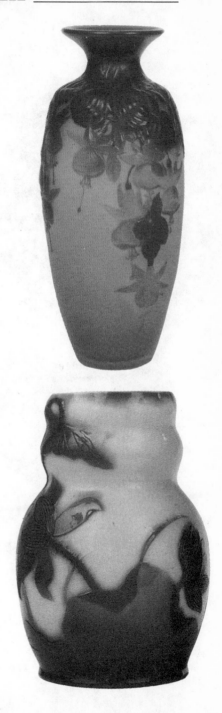

A good Gallé cabinet, on four scroll legs, the walnut frame enclosing a cupboard above two horizontal drawers, having ebony and ivory handles, the front, top and sides inlaid in fruitwoods with sprays of irises, 130cm. high.
(Phillips) **$6,548**

'Vase à Pekin', a Gallé carved and acid-etched fire-polished vase, of ovoid form with double-ribbed neck, the jade-colored glass overlaid with purple lotus flower, with carved signature *Gallé*, 21cm. high.
(Christie's) **$11,798**

'Paysage Vosgien', a Gallé carved and acid-etched double overlay landscape vase, of flask form with boat-shaped neck, the pale amber glass overlaid in purple and blue with a farm in a wooded mountainous landscape, with carved Gallé signature, 43.5cm. high. *(Christie's)* **$77,000**

A Gallé enamel painted, acid-etched and gilded two-handled jardinière, swollen form with everted neck and applied lug handles, the smoky-green tinted glass with polychrome enamel painted decoration of grasshoppers, a butterfly and a cicada amongst foliage and mushrooms, with gilt highlights, the base with elaborate carved signature Emile Galle depose del ft and mushroom, 31.2cm. diameter.
(Christie's) **$40,000**

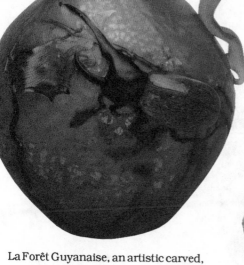

A Gallé carved and acid-etched double-overlay plafonnier, the opaque yellow shade overlaid with lilac-colored flowers and green foliage, with metal mounts, carved signature *Gallé*, 15³/₄in. diameter.
(Christie's) **$13,200**

La Forêt Guyanaise, an artistic carved, applied, marquetry and internally decorated glass jug, signed by Emile Gallé, 7³/₄in. high.

This vase is the only known variation on La Forêt Guyanaise shaped as a jug. It reflects Gallé's superb manipulation of glass and his close affinity with nature.
(Christie's) **$1,250,000**

A French faience cat, in the style of Gallé painted in colors with floral patterned pink ground coat, lace headscarf and locket with canine portrait hung on a chain, 12³/₄in. high.
(Christie's) **$4,250**

A Gallé enameled jug, of swollen form pinched at sides, with pulled lip and applied handle, the amber tinted glass with polychrome enameled wild flowers and praying mantis, 18.2cm. high.
(Christie's) **$7,000**

A Gallé intrecalaire, intaglio carved 'verrerie parlante' vase, the clear glass decorated internally with mottled green, yellow and amber oxide striations, overlaid in red, with intaglio decoration of a seahorse among various seaweeds, 11cm. high.
(Christie's) **$55,000**

A Gallé carved, acid-etched, applied and fire-polished vase, flared at base with trumpet-form neck, the acid-textured butterscotch ground with gold foil inclusions overlaid with amber heavily carved sunflowers, applied flower centers with purple and green foil inclusions, with elaborately carved signature *Gallé*, 35.2cm. high.
(Christie's) **$18,200**

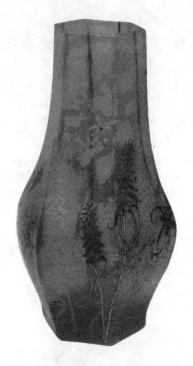

A Gallé carved acid etched triple overlay landscape vase, 50.5cm. high.
(Christie's) **$10,824**

A Gallé internally decorated martele enamel painted vase, of bombé hexagonal form, internally decorated with silver foil inclusions, the glass shading from pink at the base to a milky color, areas of which are splashed with iridescence, some areas martele, with enamel painted and carved decoration of wild orchids, the base engraved *Emile Galle* with a floral emblem, 30.5cm. high.
(Christie's) **$14,000**

A Gallé faience model of a cat, the creature sits back on its haunches and gazes with glass eyes and whiskered grin, its yellow body decorated in blue and white with heart shapes and roundels, 34cm. high, signed *GR* for Gallé Reinemer and with Cross of Lorraine.
(Phillips) **$2,600**

Roman brown basalt relief of an erotic scene, 2nd–3rd century A.D., the naked copulating couple carved in high relief, she rests her elbows on a dial and faces front, 12¹/₂in. wide. *(Butterfield & Butterfield)*

$3,300

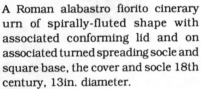

A Roman alabastro fiorito cinerary urn of spirally-fluted shape with associated conforming lid and on associated turned spreading socle and square base, the cover and socle 18th century, 13in. diameter.
(Christie's)   **$16,850**

A fine English lead figure of Acis, attributed to the workshops of John Cheere, the young faun clad in a tightly-fitting bacchic goat-skin with curling hair and painted ears, leaning against a tree-trunk, indistinctly signed *William C...*, circa 1770, 52in. high.

The present figure of Acis is based on an antique marble original, now at Holkham Hall, Norfolk, known as The Holkham Faun. This was acquired from Rome by the Coke family in about 1750. It has been suggested that John Cheere (1709–1787) acquired reproduction rights to the distinctive Coke Collection from about 1760, as other lead figures copied from Holkham statues began to appear after this time.
(Christie's)   **$37,000**

One of a set of ten carved stone urns, each with an egg-and-dart rim, the circular body carved with four ring handles and hung with drapery, the lower part decorated with foliage, late 18th/early 19th century, 29in. high. *(Christie's)* **$61,000**

Louis XVI terra cotta figure of a maiden, depicted with flowers in her upswept hair, wearing a laced bodice and long skirt and holding her apron in her right hand, her left hand held to her chin, 43in. high. *(Butterfield & Butterfield)*

$17,600

An early Orrefors 'Ariel' glass vase designed by Edvin Ohrström, of heavily wrought globular shape of aquamarine tone and internally decorated with air bubbles of abstract forms, one resembling a seahorse, 15cm. high. *(Phillips)* **$7,800**

Dale Chihuly Macchia Series Studio glass vase, large freeform dynamic vessel of opaque to translucent sky-blue, decorated in molten state with horizontal striping and random white spots enhanced by colorful specks of yellow, blue, red, amber and gold, 17in. high.
(Skinner Inc.) **$6,000**

A Gabriel Argy-Rousseau pâte-de-verre circular box and cover, of pale amber glass, the cover molded with yellow and purple stylized petals radiating from a central clump of yellow stylized flowerheads, framed within a purple geometric border, the body also molded with stylized petals and a geometric border, 11.2cm. diameter.
(Christie's) **$5,400**

A J. & L. Lobmeyr large circular dish engraved by Karl Pietsch with 'The Marriage of Neptune and Amphitrite', the center with a running figure of Bacchus holding a goblet and flowing drapery beside a leaping panther, the well with bands of scroll, flute and key-pattern ornament, 1878–1881, 42.5cm. diameter.

The design for this dish, inspired by an antique frieze at that time exhibited in the Munich Glyptothek, was made by August Eisenmenger (1830–1907), the well-known Viennese painter, in close conjunction with Ludwig Lobmeyr, second generation owner of Lobmeyr. Karl Pietsch (1828–1883) of Kamenicky Senov who executed the engraving on this dish was one of the foremost engravers of the period whom Lobmeyr employed for very special commissions.

(Christie's) **$74,000**

The English glasshouse of Thomas Webb & Sons was established at Stourbridge, Worcs. It is well known for its fine engraved glass and for its cameo glass, dating from the late 19th century. From 1902, Burmese glass, an American art glass shading greenish yellow to delicate pink, in matt or glossy finish was made, and was much used for lamp production. The firm continues in production today.

Webb gem cameo glass vase, designed and hand carved by George Woodall, flared conical footed vessel of deep sapphire blue and blown out neck ring, layered with sky blue and white, hand carved overall with apple blossoms and buds on leafy tree branches in high relief with extraordinary detail, 8¹/₂in. high.

(Skinner) **$23,000**

A fine Georgian air-twist glass candlestick.
(Russell, Baldwin & Bright)

$4,000

Large dark blue Peking glass bottle vase, 19th century, of compressed globular form with a tall cylindrical neck and resting on a ring foot, the glass of a translucent violet-blue tone throughout, 15^1/$_8$in. high.
(Butterfield & Butterfield)

$4,675

An important A S.A.L.I.R. 'vaso Veronese', designed by Vittorio Zecchin, the traditional Venetian shape pierced with elaborate and intricate acid-cut fretwork of a hunting scene against a stylized background with cellular pattern composed of irregular pentagons, topaz colored glass, 51cm. high.
(Christie's) **$47,000**

An engraved decanter and a stopper, for BEER, of club shape and named within a quatrefoil cartouche issuant with hops and barley and suspended by chain ornament from the shoulder, with a facet-cut spire stopper, circa 1770, 36cm. high overall.
(Christie's)   **$6,800**

'Amor and Alcestis;. a Morris & Co. stained glass panel designed by Edward Burne-Jones, from Chaucer's Legend of Goode Wimmen, 48cm. high, 54.5cm. wide. *(Christie's)*   **$23,474**

A pair of Regency Cary's globes, the celestial globe adapted to 1800, the
terrestrial globe with additions to 1825, each on circular walnut stand with
turned legs, joined by X-shaped stretchers, 28in. diameter.
(Christie's) **$33,000**

A magnificent pair of gilt-metal globes, terrestrial and celestial, bearing the
Tughra and Latin inscription of Sultan Murad III, diameters 29.6cm., overall
height 40cm., overall width 38cm., unsigned, attributed to the workshop of
Gerald Mercator at Duisburg, dated 1579.
(Christie's) **$1,636,800**

A blacksmith-made iron club head with cut-off nose and curved sole, 5in. hosel, late 17th/early 18th century. *(Christie's)* **$76,000**

A scared-head long-nosed Thornwood playclub by Hugh Philp, the head stamped *H. Philp*, the sole inscribed in ink *Strath and W. Bl ...*, circa 1820.

Hugh Philp (1782–1856) was born in Fife. In 1812 he began repairing golf clubs and 1819 was appointed to the Society of St. Andrews, later the Royal and Ancient, as club maker. *(Christie's)* **$26,400**

A fine and rare gutty golf ball marker, stamped *A. Patrick*, the hinged handle with leather-covered roller and enclosing two grooved metal rollers, circa 1870.

The first gutta percha golf balls were smooth and it was soon realized that they flew better only after being 'cut'. Thereafter gutty balls were produced by hand hammering the exterior to improve flight. For a very brief period various hand-operated devices were produced to mark the gutty ball before the advent of hydraulic machinery. *(Christie's)* **$61,000**

An unusual feather-filled golf ball by Allan Robertson, stamped *Allan* and numbered *28*, circa 1840.

Allan Robertson (1815–1859) was by common consent the supreme golfer of his era and with his assistant, Tom Morris, he manufactured feather golf balls of the highest quality.

(Christie's)   **$19,000**

A rare long-nosed scared-head baffing spoon by Mungo Park, the head stamped *M. Park* (Mungo Park, Open Champion, 1874).

(Christie's)   **$18,000**

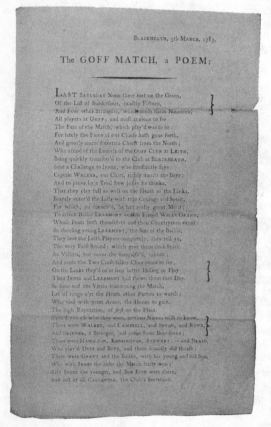

The Golf Match, A Poem, Broadsheet (Edinburgh or Leith), Blackheath, 5th March 1783.

This un-recorded and probably unique printed copy refers to a match between the Members of Leith and Blackheath. The captain in 1782 was John Walker and most of the names mentioned in the broadsheet are mentioned in the Blackheath Club cash book for the year 1787.

(Christie's)   **$16,000**

The Hagenauer workshop flourished in Vienna between 1898 and 1958. A definite house style began to emerge after the proprietor's son Karl joined the enterprise in 1919, and from the 1920s onward they produced figures, often either sporting or with a sporting motif, in metal and/or wood.

These were given a highly stylized, abstract, often whimsical interpretation, and their unique style makes them easily identifiable.

A Hagenauer brass bust of a young woman, lightly beaten textured surface applied with brass strips to form the flowing hair and features, with beaded necklace, 47cm. high.
(Christie's) **$9,000**

'Man and Woman', a Hagenauer brass sculpture, of two stylized male and female figures, standing arm in arm, with curled strips at their feet in the form of grass, mounted on a triangular base, *Made in Austria*, 98cm. high.
(Christie's) **$10,200**

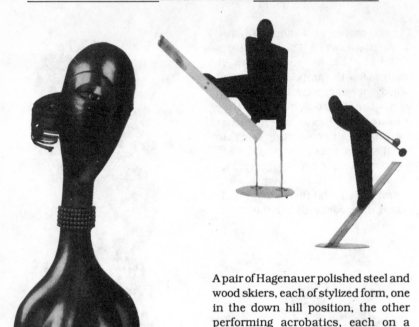

A pair of Hagenauer polished steel and wood skiers, each of stylized form, one in the down hill position, the other performing acrobatics, each on a circular base, with stamped marks *wHw, Hagenauer, Wien, Made in Austria,* 33cm. high.
(Christie's) **$2,350**

A Hagenauer brass and copper bust of a woman, the stylized figure with lightly hammered surface, with applied beads to neck and curled and cut copper strips forming hair, applied glass and enamel forming the eyes, *Made in Austria,* 60.5cm. high.
(Christie's) **$10,750**

Hagenauer figure of a piano player, nickel-finish flat stylized representation, impressed with Wiener Werkstatte mark *Made in Vienna, Made in Austria, WHW,* 8^1/$_2$in. high.
(Skinner) **$1,100**

An Italian haliotis veneered and gilt painted bowl, with an everted rim edged with cabochon, on a pinched socle and acanthus draped shaft with spreading circular base, 17^1/$_4$in. high. *(Christie's)* **$5,700**

A pair of English bluejohn urns, each with stepped turned finial and on turned socle and stepped fluorspar and black marble base, 19th century, 13^1/$_2$in. high. *(Christie's)* **$6,195**

A porphyry cistern with molded rectangular top and bowed tapering body on instepped block feet, 17th century, possibly reusing an earlier and perhaps Ancient piece of porphyry, 36in. wide. *(Christie's)* **$45,000**

A close-helmet with one-piece skull with high roped comb, pointed visor with single vision-slit and lifting peg, fitting into the upper-bevor, the latter with circular breaths on the right and pivoted at the same points as the bevor, two pivot-hook catches on the right, and two gorget-plates at front and rear, the main edges with sunken roped borders, circa 1560, probably Italian, 11³/₄in. high.

(Christie's)   **$13,695**

A German foot-combat close-helmet with one-piece skull with low file-roped comb, brass plume-holder, bluntly pointed visor and upper and lower bevors pivoted at the same points on either side, the visor with cusped upper-edge and pierced with trefoils, centrally divided sight and turned brass lifting peg combined with a locking catch, the upper bevor symmetrically pierced with trefoils and hearts, brass locking hook and stud, two gorget-plates at front and rear, the lower one with turned rope edge and a central circle of brass-headed rivets, and struck with the Nuremberg mark and a maker's mark, the main inner edges bordered by a double line and brass-headed rivets throughout, circa 1630, 12¹/₂in. high.

(Christie's)   **$11,500**

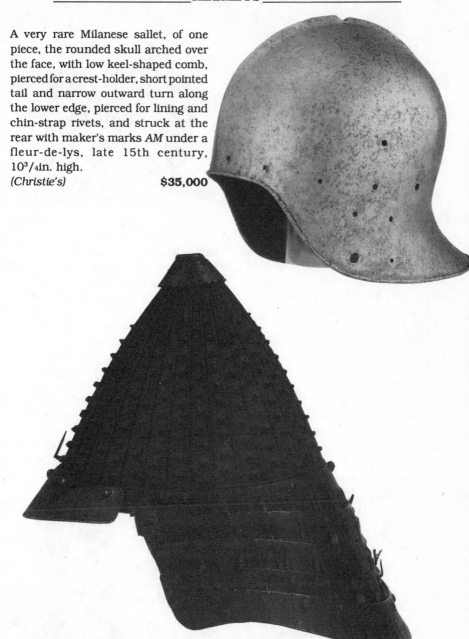

A very rare Milanese sallet, of one piece, the rounded skull arched over the face, with low keel-shaped comb, pierced for a crest-holder, short pointed tail and narrow outward turn along the lower edge, pierced for lining and chin-strap rivets, and struck at the rear with maker's marks *AM* under a fleur-de-lys, late 15th century, 10³/₄in. high.
(Christie's) **$35,000**

An unusual Hoshi-Bashi kabuto of conical form, constructed of thirty-two plates each with ten upstanding rivets, late Momoyama or early Edo Period.
(Phillips) **$13,500**

A French close-helmet, the one-piece skull with high roped comb, brass plume holder, pointed visor with single vision slit, fitting into the upper-bevor, the latter with circular breaths on the right, circa 1570, 12in. high.
(Christie's) **$6,300**

A rare Saxon Electoral Guard comb-morion of one piece with roped comb and brim, the base of the skull encircled by sixteen gilt-brass lion-masks capping the lining rivets, each with a ring in its mouth, the surface decorated with gilt etching against a later black-painted ground, comprising narrow bands of foliated scrollwork encircling, on each side of the skull, figures respectively of Mutius Scaevola putting his hand in the flames, and of Marcus Curtius leaping into the gulf, and on each side of the comb, respectively the arms of Saxony and the insignia of the Arch Marshalcy of the Holy Roman Empire, struck on the brim with the Nuremberg mark, circa 1580, 11¹/₂in. high.
(Christie's S. Ken) **$16,000**

A burgonet by Caremolo Mondrone of Mantua, made in one piece with roped comb of medium height, upturned pointed fall and similar, but shorter neck-guard, the main edges turned and roped and with recessed borders, circa 1540, 9¹/₂in. high.

Caremolo Mondrone was born in Milan in circa 1489 and is recorded as working for Federigo II Gonzaga, Duke of Mantua from 1521 until his death in Mantua in 1543. His patrons also included the Emperor Charles V.
(Christie's) **$4,400**

The New Frontier, Republic, 1935, one-sheet, linen backed, 41 x 27in. *(Christie's)* **$5,720**

The Oregon Trail, Republic, 1936, one-sheet, linen backed, 41 x 27in.

Westerns became the life and livelihood of actor John Wayne, but of the over one hundred he made in his long and celebrated career, few movie posters were as memorable as his films. Featured here is a poster from The Oregon Trail, highlighted by a full painted image of The Duke, his striking portrait a perfect likeness. *(Christie's East)* **$10,450**

The Jazz Singer, Warner Brothers, 1927, 24-sheet, linen backed, 9 x 20 feet.

When Warner Brothers was ready to introduce its first partial-sound movie it needed a proven commodity and turned to Broadway's top star, Al Jolson. It produced a romanticized version of Jolson's own life, The Jazz Singer, that allowed him to sing many of his trademark songs, including "Mammy".

Remarkably, a billboard-sized poster has survived, a massive head of Jolson in black-face dominating the poster.

(Christie's East)   **$18,700**

The Old Dark House, Universal, 1932, 41 x 27in. The critical and box office success of Boris Karloff, as the monstrous creation of Dr. Frankenstein, convinced Universal Studios to quickly produce other films of this genre, created specifically for the multi-talented actor. The Old Dark House reunited Karloff with his Frankenstein director, James Whale, and features an impressive supporting cast of up-and-coming stars such as Charles Laughton and Melvyn Douglas.

(Christie's)   **$48,400**

The Phantom of the Opera, Universal, 1925, paper backed, 41 x 27in.
(Christie's) **$38,500**

Dracula, Universal, 1931, insert, 36 x 14in. The first major sound horror film was Dracula in 1931. The film has since spawned scores of sequels and remakes, but Bela Lugosi's portrayal of Dracula has become a permanent fixture in American popular culture.

Three years later, Lugosi played Chandu the Magician in a serial, The Return of Chandu. Perhaps capitalizing on his acclaim as Dracula, the poster artists depicted a sinister image of Lugosi, when in fact he played the film's hero.
(Christie's) **$33,000**

Blonde Venus, Paramount, 1932, one-sheet, linen backed, 41in. x 27in.

Hollywood glamour is synonymous with the face of Marlene Dietrich. Producers of her films knew this well, dominating her posters with her likeness. Blonde Venus is a remarkable film for its time, where Dietrich, while married, has an affair and becomes a prostitute but still maintains the sympathy of the movie audience.
(Christie's East)   **$7,480**

A Dog's Life, First National, 1918, one-sheet, linen backed, 41in. x 27in.

The history of the comedy film was deeply influenced by Charlie Chaplin. He was at the peak of his career when he released A Dog's Life. Three years later he released The Kid, his first feature, a beautiful film that made a star of Jackie Coogan.
(Christie's East)   **$17,600**

The Cabinet of Dr. Caligari, Goldwyn, 1921, one-sheet, linen backed, 41in. x 27in.

In 1919, Robert Wiene directed a film in Germany that changed the face of the cinema. The film not only broke all the rules, but forever changed the rules by which films were made. The Cabinet of Dr. Caligari is told from the perspective of its lead character, revealed in the final reel to be a madman. The film had a strong impact on such great German directors of the twenties as Fritz Lang, Paul Leni, and G.W. Pabst, and influenced many American directors as well. In 1921, a daring Sam Goldwyn brought the film to the United States. The unusual sets and direction and the memorable performance of Conrad Veidt still fascinate audiences today.
(Christie's East)   **$37,400**

King Kong, RKO, 1933, three-sheet, linen-backed, 81 x 41in.

An innovative form of early animation was used in the mid-teens by Willis O'Brien, who created a series of short films using a process known as stop-motion photography. He used this technique to great effect in the 1919 film, The Ghost of Slumber Mountain, which brought animated models of dinosaurs to life.

Fourteen years later, O'Brien created the special effects for King Kong, and not only gave the giant ape life', but gave him a distinct personality. The three-sheet depicts Kong in his most memorable pose, grasping the frightened Fay Wray while perched atop New York's Empire State Building. (Christie's)

$57,200

The Unknown, MGM, 1927, one-sheet, linen backed, 41in. x 27in.

Lon Chaney was the Man of a Thousand Faces, but he labored in films long before becoming a star. Although he had been in films seven years before making Outside the Law, he was still billed second to Priscilla Dean. By 1927 he was supported by a new young actress with flashing eyes, Joan Crawford, in The Unknown.
(Christie's East)   **$12,100**

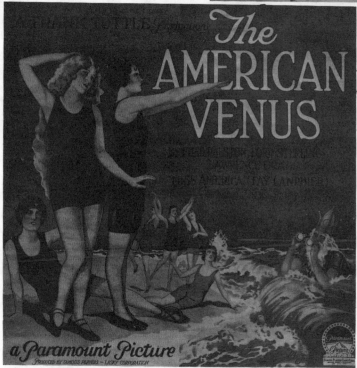

The American Venus, Paramount, 1926, six-sheet, linen backed, 81 x 81in.
Few posters from any of Alfred Hitchcock's pre-1940 films are known to exist. The Woman Alone combines classic Hitchcock suspense elements: a woman in distress and an unknown, menacing villain.
(Christie's East)   **$3,740**

The Wizard of Oz, MGM, 1939, three-sheet, linen backed, 81 x 41in.
(Christie's East) **$25,300**

The Adventures of Robin Hood, Warner Bros., 1938, three-sheet, linen backed, 81 x 41in.

Errol Flynn was the epitome of the swashbuckling hero. His elegant wit and flirtatious charm were used to their best in The Sea Hawk and The Adventures of Robin Hood, posters from which are among the very best created for adventure films. These two films are sound remakes of silent film classics.
(Christie's East) **$19,800**

Scottish staghorn and ivory inkstand, 19th century, the shaped rectangular stand mounted with an antler pen holder, a sander, inkwell and small dished tray, the cylindrical sander and well each decorated in relief with carved ivory figures of a stag and a deer, 7¹/₂in. high.
(Butterfield & Butterfield)

$935

One of a matched pair of American horn open armchairs made up of joined links each with crescent cresting and arched back, the padded seats and arms covered in differing pale blue material, late 19th century.

The manufacture of furniture in America from the horns of the Texas longhorn steer follows directly in the tradition of antler furniture made in Europe, particularly in Austria, in the 1830s and 1840s. Wenzel Friedrich (1827–1902) of San Antonio, Texas, was a first generation immigrant from Bohemia and he manufactured these chairs from circa 1880–1890. By the early 1890s longhorn cattle had been superseded by a shorthorn breed less suitable for chair-making.
(Christie's) **$3,350**

Rhinoceros horn libation cup, 17th century, pierced and carved with pines on a rocky landscape, extending into the interior and across the base of the foot, 5in. high.
(Skinner) **$14,300**

The most notable prints of the Art Deco period more often than not have distinctly erotic overtones, and the artist who most immediately springs to mind in this connection is the Frenchman Louis Icart. His sinuous female figures in their drifting skirts, often accompanied by equally sleek grayhounds, have a fantasy quality. Often his message is less subtle and on occasion borders on the pornographic, reflecting the hedonism and decadence of the times.

'Winter Warmth' by Louis Icart, etching and drypoint, printed in colors, signed lower right, numbered 44/100, framed, 20 x 27.5cm.
(Christie's)   **$2,000**

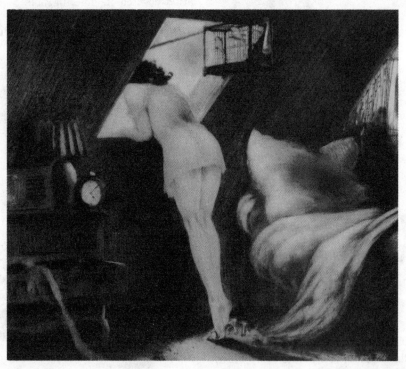

'Attic Room', by Louis Icart, etching and drypoint, printed in colors, signed lower right, with artist's blindstamp © *Copyright 1940 by L. Icart Paris New York*, framed, 37.5cm. x 44cm.
(Christie's)   **$9,000**

'Coursing II', by Louis Icart, etching and drypoint, printed in colors, signed lower right with artist's blindstamp, *Copyright 1929 by L. Icart Paris*, 41cm. x 65cm.
(Christie's) **$16,643**

'Leda and the Swan', by Louis Icart, etching and drypoint, printed in colors, signed lower right with artist's blindstamp, *Copyright 1934 by L. Icart Cty*, N.Y., 52cm. x 80cm.
(Christie's) **$18,600**

'Orchids' by Louis Icart, etching and drypoint, printed in colors, signed lower right, with artist's blindstamp, © *Copyright 1937 by L. Icart Sty. N.Y.* 71.5 x 50cm.
(Christie's) **$9,250**

'Papillon II' by Louis Icart, etching and drypoint, printed in colors, signed lower right, with artist's blindstamp, © *Copyright 1936 by L. Icart Sty N.Y.,* 18.5 x 24cm.
(Christie's) **$9,450**

'Smoke' by Louis Icart, etching and drypoint, printed in colors, signed lower right with artist's blindstamp, numbered 111, © *Copyright 1933 by Les Graveurs Modernes, 194 Rue de Rivoli, Paris,* 38.1 x 51.5cm. *(Christie's)* **$6,500**

'My Model' by Louis Icart, etching and drypoint, printed in colors, signed lower right, with artist's blindstamp, artist's proof, © *Copyright 1933 by L. Icart Sty. N.Y. Gravure Garantie Originale,* 55.6 x 43.5cm. *(Christie's)* **$7,000**

The name Imari derives from the port through which the porcelain of 17th century feudal Japan was exported. It has been adopted to describe the palette of underglaze blue and overglaze iron red and gilt of the Arita export wares. Most 17th century Japanese porcelain was blue and white and, due to fluxing of the cobalt with the glaze, the blue decoration characteristically bleeds into the surrounding area. It was to overcome this fault that early workmen painted iron red and gold onto the glaze to conceal the blurred edges.

An ormolu-mounted Imari coffee urn and cover, the fluted sides with a continuous design of ho-ho birds among flowering and fruiting boughs, the cover similarly decorated, late 17th century, overall height 30.5cm.
(Christie's) **$23,000**

An Imari large jar and cover decorated with a continuous decoration of ho-ho birds perched in the boughs of a blossoming tree or on woodwork, the vase and cover Genroku period (1688–1703), the stand 19th century, overall height 104cm.
(Christie's) **$35,000**

An Imari koro and cover modeled as a seated karashishi decorated in iron-red, green, black enamels and gilt on underglaze blue with spotted fur details, the head detachable, late 17th/early 18th century.
(Christie's) **$11,000**

An Imari gin-cask modeled as a bijin seated on a stylized cart, her kimono decorated with stylized flowerheads and foliage including paulownia, late 17th-early 18th century, 38.5cm. high.
(Christie's) **$30,300**

Lacquer single-case inro, inscribed and sealed *Zeshin*, in the form of a worn inkstone with archaic script and musical instruments in relief, a single drawer compartment, incised signature, 3in. long.
(Skinner) **$22,000**

A three case shibayama inro in the form of a tied bag, decorated with a ho-o bird among flowers and foliage beside a biwa on the reverse with a kabuto filled with peonies suspended from a cherry tree, both late 19th century, 10cm.
(Christie's) **$13,475**

A large kinji ground two-case oval inro, in the shape of Daikoku's treasure bag, decorated in Shibayama style with Ebisu with a abacus seated before an account book and Daikoku counting coins watched by a mouse, unsigned, 19th century.
(Christie's) **$16,450**

A fine four-case inro decorated in hiramakie on a hirame ground with a flock of cranes among pine trees beside a waterfall, others alighting on the reverse, signed *Toyo saku*, with red lacquer seal, with a fundame manju netsuke lacquered with fruits and chestnuts, and a red glass ojime, 19th century, 8.3cm,
(Christie's) **$14,000**

A three-case hirame inro decorated in silver, gold and gray hiramakie with three red-capped cranes on the reverse cypress saplings, signed *Koma Yasutada saku*, 19th century, 7.3cm. high.
(Christie's) **$8,150**

A sheath inro, the outer case in gold hiramakie, takamakie nashiji on a kinji ground, with two panels of irises, waterplants, peonies and chrysanthemums, silver rims, bordered by aogai decorated in iroe hiramakie with floral roundels, the inner three-case section decorated in iroe togidashi on a nashiji ground with fans, all 19th century, inro 8.3cm.
(Christie's) **$17,000**

A four case kinji ground inro decorated in shibayama style with a cockerel on a mortar beside a pestle, the reverse with a hen and a chick, nashiji interior, signed on an inlaid tablet *Ryoshu*, late 19th century.
(Christie's) **$10,588**

A three-case kinji ground inro finely decorated in shibayama stle with hanging flower baskets, an arrangement of flowers in a Chinese style vase on the reverse, metal surrounds engraved with flowers and scrolling foliage, unsigned, late 19th century, 10.2cm. long.
(Christie's) **$17,325**

A fine single case inro decorated in iroe hirazogan and takazogan on a kinji ground with gold and silver nashiji and hirame, depicting Ariwara no Narihira on horseback and attendants, signed Shinkokusen, 19th century.
(Christie's) **$7,315**

A three case inro decorated in iroe togidashi on a roironuri ground with Masatsura at the tomb of Go-Daigo, signed *Toyo*, with Kakihan, late 19th century, 8.5cm. high.

The scene depicts Masatsura engraving a poem over the temple door with an arrow, translated reading, "Should I return not, I leave my name among others killed by bows".
(Christie's) **$80,000**

A five-case inro decorated in gold and silver togidashi on a roironuri ground with a spider weaving a long thread beside his web spun above flowers and grasses signed *Shunsui Ganshosai* with ojime and a wood netsuke of a bat with a spider, eyes inlaid in dark horn, late 19th century, 7.8cm inro.
(Christie's) **$32,000**

A three-case double gourd-shaped inro decorated in gold and silver hiramakie on a kinji ground, nashiji interiors with rats preparing the wedding feast, with scenes of musicians and dancers, others arranging flowers in a large basket, late 19th century, 11cm. high.
(Christie's) **$14,000**

A George III watch alarm by W. Gossage complete with the original box and instructions.
(Russell, Baldwin & Bright)

$1,000

A rare American kaleidoscope, G.C. Bush, Providence, Rhode Island, on baluster base with four molded feet with textured pasteboard tube and brass collar incorporating object case filled with colored glass, last quarter 19th century, the tube $10^{1}/_{4}$in.
(Christie's) **$1,980**

A Wimshurst-pattern electrostatic plate machine, with six segmented glass contra-rotating plates, copper brushes and brass conductor combs attached to conductor cylinders raised on insulated columns with chains from four Leyden type jars, 27in. wide.
(Christie's) **$5,482**

238

An unusual late 14th (?), 15th (?), or early 16th (?) century brass astrolabe, from France or the Low Countries, with quatrefoil ornamentation on the rete and a dedication dated 1522, unique amongst known astronomical instruments in featuring 'Chaldean' or 'Astrologers' numerals.

The unusual throne resembles a conifer in cross-section, the shackle is simple and supports a thin circular ring. The scale of the rim is divided for each 5°, subdivided into degrees, and the hours are labeled in ciphers 1–12 and again 1–12.

(Christie's)   **$85,140**

An exceptional Crookes' phosphorescent 'Bouquet' tube of large size, the finely modeled copper flowers each applied with phosphorescent material giving beautiful natural colors, 18in. high.

(Christie's)   **$4,699**

A fine brass universal equinoctial ring dial, the pivoted horizon ring engraved with 24-hour Roman chapters graduated at five-minute intervals, probably English, late 17th century, 15cm. diameter.
(Christie's New York)

$3,520

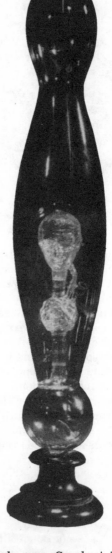

A fine early 19th century twin pillar duplex action vacuum pump, the rack gearing contained within the two lacquered brass pillars with pediment supported in two tapering columns with urn finials, $10^3/_4$in. long.
(Christie's) **$1,175**

An extremely rare Crookes' 'Man Smoking a Pipe' tube, the figure in pale green, the pipe spiral twist brown, on ebonized stand, $14^1/_2$in. high.
(Christie's) **$4,500**

A George III pocket chronometer by John Arnold, circa 1785, with 1³/₄in. diameter enameled dial, now in later mahogany case as a boudoir clock, 7in. high.
(Bearne's) **$8,460**

A very rare decoratively engraved spy camera in the form of a finger ring, reputedly used by the Russian KGB.
(Christie's) **$20,812**

A Döbereiner lamp by Foster and West, London, early 19th century with mahogany base and cover, glass cylinder, gilt brass and lead, 21in. high.
(Christie's) **$8,232**

A universal rectilinear dial, Prague, circa 1590, signed, gilt brass, by Erasmus Habermel (late 16th century), 8⁷/₈ x 5⁷/₈in.
(Christie's) **$288,124**

A fine Neo Classical steel and cast iron serpentine fronted fire grate, the polished and engraved steel facade of waisted outline, surmounted by acanthus chased urns, the beaded top rail above twin collared rails, within a 'U' shaped border with applied bosses, flanked by square tapering uprights with canted angles interlinking with the cast iron grate, 43in. wide.
(Christie's S. Ken) **$9,150**

A 17th century iron strongbox, of Armada design, the hinged top with nipple studs to release the key cover to a twelve shutter locking device with pierced scroll cover, the front with architectural and acanthus leaf ornament, with carrying handles to the sides, 58cm. wide, probably German.
(Phillips) **$1,591**

Cast iron garden ornament in the form of a Newfoundland dog, America, mid 19th century, 55in. long.
(Skinner) **$23,100**

Phrenology head inkwell, milk glass head and font, cast iron frame, patented 1855, America.
(Skinner) **$2,750**

Cast-iron painted blackamoor tether, American, 19th century, the standing figure dressed in a white shirt and black pants with out-stretched right arm holding a tether ring on a yellow square plinth, 44in. high.
(Butterfield & Butterfield)

$1,650

'Le Cigognes d'Alsace', an Edgar Brandt wrought iron and bronze decorative panel, embellished in gilt bronze with three storks amid wirework clouds, within a wrought iron octagonal panel with granulated rim and foliate scrolls, and applied with a sunburst of radiating bands.

Antique American wood and iron candle mold, designed for twenty-four candles, 22in. wide.
(Eldreds) **$633**

Replicas of Brandt's original 1922 panels were installed in the interiors of the lifts at Selfridges in 1928.
(Phillips) **$8,185**

One of a pair of Regency wrought iron garden seats with scroll feet.
(Russell, Baldwin & Bright) **$15,000**

Lobed oval jadeite bowl, carved to the well with a pair of carp encircling a fronted blossom amid further blossoms and leafy tendrils, the exterior carved with panels of spiky lotus surrounded by leafy vines and four evenly spaced ruyi-head handles dangling loose rings and resting on four short supports, 13^1/$_4$in. wide.
(Butterfield & Butterfield)

$27,500

A very fine white jade table screen, carved according to the theme of Lanting Tsu by Wong Xizhi, to the front with scholars gathered along the bank of the winding stream, cups of wine being conveyed on floating carriers, all beside a pavilion before distant rocky landscape, the reverse with an incised imperial inscription of the original corresponding text within a squared-spiral border, 9^5/$_8$in. high.
(Christie's) **$170,680**

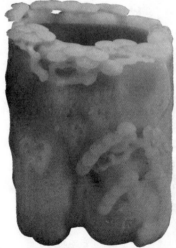

Fine nephrite brushpot, late 18th/ early 19th century, carved in the form of a hollow tree trunk to simulate the natural pitting and knotting of wood enveloped with boughs of pine carved to one side and around the oval rim, 7^1/$_2$in. *(Butterfield & Butterfield)*

$59,400

A pale celadon jade figure of a camel naturalistically carved and detailed with a thick mane, bushy tail and thick hair on the top of the humps and legs, Qing Dynasty, 19cm. wide.
(Christie's) **$5,750**

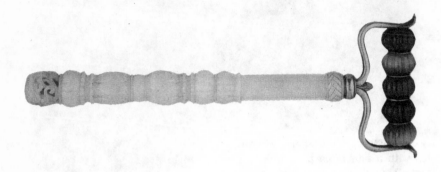

A celadon jade back massager with a pale celadon jade handle ornately carved with stylized buds and petals and an openwork lingzhi cluster at one end, mid Qing Dynasty, 26.5cm. long.
(Christie's) **$8,500**

A gray and russet jade bull, carved recumbent with its legs tucked into its body, turning slightly to the right with naturalistically detailed openwork horns curling back to its neck, its incised tail sweeping its hindquarters, the stone of mottled gray tone with scattered deep russet inclusions, Ming Dynasty, 13.5cm. long, wood stand, fitted box.
(Christie's) **$12,000**

A Russian diamond, sapphire, ruby and plique-a-jour enamel moth brooch, St. Petersburg maker's mark J.V.
(Lawrence Fine Art)

$16,600

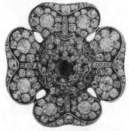

A mid-19th century gold, ruby and diamond flower brooch, with four petals, pavé-set with old-mine brilliants, centering in a larger oval ruby.
(Bearne's) $13,000

An antique diamond aiguillette, circa 1850. One of the aiguillettes from the French imperial jewels made for the Empress Eugénie by the house of Bapst.
(Christie's) $123,585

A sapphire, diamond and enamel cicada brooch, circa 1890. The late 19th century was a time of transition with classical themes becoming more stylized with the popularity of Plique-à-jour enamel. This cicada shows the transition very well, with the figurative image used in a fresh and unusual way. Although not signed it bears an indistinct maker's mark which is probably that of Frédéric Boucheron.
(Christie's) $63,360

A Guild of Handicrafts Ltd. silver and enamel brooch designed by C.R. Ashbee, London hallmarks for 1907, 7.8cm. long.
(Christie's) **$16,250**

A Victorian gold and shell cameo brooch, last quarter of the 19th century, the oval plaque carved as two female profiles, an owl and a dove, within a gold beaded border.
(Lawrence Fine Art) **$2,400**

A Belle Epoque diamond brooch, circa 1910.
(Christie's) **$87,780**

An Edwardian sapphire and diamond pendant, circa 1910.
(Christie's) **$171,380**

A fancy color and colorless diamond scroll brooch.
(Christie's) **$1,320,000**

An enamel and diamond orchid brooch, circa 1900 by Duval et le Turcq.
(Christie's) **$16,302**

A 19th century sapphire and diamond frog brooch, set in silver and gold.
(Dreweatt Neate) **$6,358**

A mid 19th century enameled gold and seed-pearl hinged bangle.
(Bearne's) **$2,400**

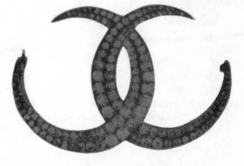

An Art Deco yellow and colorless diamond spray brooch by Cartier, circa 1920.
(Christie's) **$47,948**

A large interlaced 'C' brooch set with a double row of diamonds (approximately 14 cts.)
(Woolley & Wallis) **$11,000**

There is a charming tradition that Sakaida Kizai-emon, an Arita potter, made an ornament in the form of twin persimmons (kaki) for his feudal overlord, who was so pleased with it that he conferred on him the honorary name of Kaki-emon. Sakaida adopted this as his family name and it was thus that the porcelain got its name. Sakaida worked for a merchant named Toshima Tokuyemon, who had learned the secret of enameling in colors, and together they mastered the art to commence one of the most important ceramic productions.

A kakiemon model of a seated bijin decorated in iron-red, turquoise, aubergine, blue, yellow and black enamels and gilt, her kimono with a design of scattered flowersprays and leaves, her undergarment with splashes of color interspersed among flowerheads and cloud-pattern, seated with her kimono falling in folds behind her, late 17th century, 27cm. high.

The model displays the early Edo change in the use of armrests (soku), which were originally a rich man's prerogative used only by the members of the Imperial Court and feudal lords. During the Edo period (1614–1868), they came into widespread use in the entertainment quarters and among the newly rich middle-class merchants. *(Christie's)* **$288,000**

An early enameled kakiemon style teapot decorated in iron-red, blue, green, yellow and black enamels, with two shaped panels depicting ho-o birds swooping down upon the flower and vegetation-filled ground, late 17th century, 15cm. long. The enameling suggests a small kiln active possibly during the third quarter of the 17th century. *(Christie's)* **$43,000**

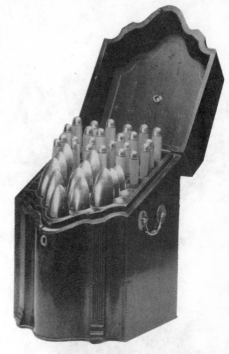

A George III cutlery box of serpentine form, veneered in mahogany, with parquetry stringing and silver handles and lock plate, 14½in. high, 26oz.
(Bearne's) **$2,540**

A pair of George III mahogany, kingwood banded and herringbone strung knife boxes, with sloping lid, the front of projecting broken outline flanked by simulated pilasters and having original matrix, on later feet, 38cm. high.
(Phillips) **$4,875**

A spherical tripod koro and cover, decorated in Shibayama style on a gold lacquer ground, the body with birds on a blossoming branch and two oni at kubi-hiki represented in shippo, mother-of-pearl, coral, stained ivory, tortoiseshell, shell and other materials, signed *Gyokukendo*, late 19th century, 19cm. high.

(Christie's) **$13,500**

A pair of carved red lacquer armchairs carved in mirror image, the high back with three panels, the center depicting the Queen of the West in a pavilion surrounded by attendants, the eight Immortals and their attendants outside on a terrace, the flanking panels with Daoist figures and mythical beasts amidst clouds and pavilions, 18th/19th century.

(Christie's) **$25,600**

A pair of cylindrical gold lacquered wood vases decorated in gold and silver takamakie, hiramake and kirigane and inlaid with wood and ivory with Fukurokuju and Daikoku standing under blossoming boughs with attendants, late 19th century, 52cm. high.
(Christie's) **$16,250**

A large Export lacquer medallion, the oval plaque decorated in gold hiramakie on a roironuri ground with a bust portrait of Pieter Brueghel the Elder, 18th century, 22.5cm. high.
(Christie's) **$3,450**

A gold fundame and nashiji ground suzuribako in the shape of takarabune, a treasure boat, the cover decorated in gold hiramakie with inlays of coral, malachite, mother-of-pearl, chased metal and gilt metal with a boat full of jewels, coins, scrolls, Daikoku's hammer, kakuremino, kakuregasa, potted plum, tachibana and coral trees, unsigned, 18th century.

(Christie's) **$36,575**

A fine lozenge-shaped gold lacquer vase, the sides decorated in gold hiramakie, takamakie, okibirame, kirikane, kimpun, hirame and Shibayama style with Shoki searching for oni in the stream, an oni perched on a willow tree whose image is reflected in water, the reverse with a hanging flower basket of hydrangea, chrysanthemums and lilies suspended from a tree, unsigned, 19th century, 18.5cm. high.

(Christie's) **$19,000**

A matching bundai and suzuribako, the bundai depicting the Uji river and bridge, in the distance the Byodo-in Temple with ho-o roof finials, in togidashi, hiramakie, okibirame and other techniques, the bridge post caps inlaid in metal, the corners and shaped legs with silver kanagu decorated with peony and karakusa on a nanako ground, 19th century, with lacquer fitted boxes each inscribed *Uji meisho makie.*
(Christie's) **$97,000**

A fine carved red lacquer dish, the front carved through to a buff ground to depict a brace of pheasant perched and fluttering among a dense field of blossoming peony, incised with naturalistic feathery and floral details, the reverse carved with a continuous frieze of peaches, Ming Dynasty, 29.5cm. diameter.
(Christie's) **$17,000**

A fine lacquer vase and cover decorated in gold and silver hiramakie, takamakie, hirame, gyobu-nashiji and fundame with two panels elaborately decorated in shibayama style alternately cherry blossoms and Shoshi and Sangyoku, the foot and shoulder with silver lappets decorated with cloisonné enamel depicting various floral designs, signed *Sadatoshi*, late 19th century.
(Christie's) **$34,650**

Good gilt lacquer decorated kodansu, Meiji period, the rectangular chest with a pair of small sliding doors ornamented with a flock of cranes amid pine and above a small hinged double-door compartment featuring recessed panels of minogame reversed by flowering peony bushes to the interior and on the stack of three small interior drawers to the right.
(Butterfield & Butterfield)

$9,900

A gold lacquer skull attended by three ivory oni, the threee demons with stained detail and decorated with accoutrements in Shibayama style, unsigned, 19th century, overall height 20cm.
(Christie's) $14,500

An important seventeenth century ewer and basin decorated in gold hiramakie, hirame, nashiji and kirigane on a black lacquer ground with subjects connected with water, including views of Kiyomizu-dera, formerly known as Seisui-ji, the Otowa-no-taki waterfall at the foot of Okuno-in, and people relaxing on bamboo platforms built over a stream to benefit from the air cooled by the water, 17th century, the basin 53cm. diameter.
(Christie's) $182,875

Réne Lalique (1860–1945) was one of the most versatile designers of the Art Nouveau/Deco periods, working in the varied media of jewelry, glass and silver.

As an apprentice in 1876 he studied at the École des Arts Décoratifs in Paris and became a leading Art Nouveau jeweler, receiving his first important commission from no less a person than Sarah Bernhardt. He became a freelance designer, and worked for Cartier and Boucheron. His favorite motifs were flower and insect forms, and he produced pieces using semi-precious stones, glass, gold, ivory, horn and enamel.

His interest in glass dated from the 1890s, when he first started to incorporate it into his jewelry. By 1914 he had all but abandoned jewelry and moved on to glass as his major medium. His work was strongly influenced by Gallé, and he experimented with unpolished statuettes and vases. In 1908 Coty commissioned him to design a range of perfume bottles, and shortly after this he acquired a glass factory. The 1920s and 1930s marked the period of his greatest success.

'Bacchantes', a Lalique gray and amethyst tinted vase with bronze mount, flared cylindrical form, the satin-finished glass molded in relief with nude dancing maidens, the bronze base cast with fronds of seaweed, 32cm. high.
(Christie's)   **$35,250**

'Oranges', a Lalique clear glass and back enameled vase, globular with thick everted rim, molded with oranges amongst overlapping enameled long, pointed leaves, with molded signature *R. Lalique* and engraved signature *R. Lalique France*, 28.5cm. high.
(Christie's)   **$51,128**

'Tourbillons', a Lalique yellow glass vase, of bucket form the thick walled body molded in deep relief with abstract scrolling, 8in. high.
(Christie's) **$17,000**

'Alicante', a Lalique electric-blue glass vase, oviform with short cylindrical neck, the satin-finished glass molded with three pairs of budgerigars in profile amongst ears of millet, 25.5cm. high.
(Christie's) **$68,500**

'Source de la Fontaine, Doris', a Lalique clear and frosted glass luminaire, modeled as the statuette of a young woman, her watery robe falling to her ankles, clasping a writhing fish to her bosom, her eyes cast downwards, 24¹/₂in. high.
(Christie's) **$25,700**

'Suzanne', Lalique opalescent glass figurine modeled as a naked girl, her arms outstretched to reveal a cascade of loose fitting drapery, she stands posed on one leg on shaped rectangular base, 23cm. high.
(Phillips) **$27,250**

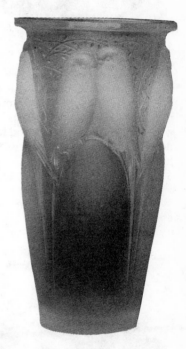

'Ceylan', a Lalique opalescent glass vase, molded with four pairs of budgerigars perched amid foliage, blue staining, 24.2cm. high.
(Christie's) **$4,778**

'Bacchantes', a Lalique blue-stained vase, the flared cylindrical body molded in relief with nude female dancing figures, 24.5cm. high.
(Christie's) **$18,915**

'Languedoc', a Lalique emerald green vase, slightly compressed globular form with short neck, the satin-finished glass molded with bands of overlapping stylized leaves, with engraved signature *R. Lalique France*, 22cm. high.

(Christie's) **$20,999**

'Gobelet six figurines', a Lalique clear glass vase, of flared form intaglio molded with six vertical panels, each with maiden in long robes and head-dress, clasping a floral bouquet, 19cm. high.

(Phillips) **$1,650**

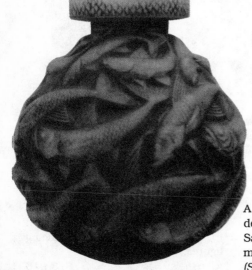

A large blue stained glass vase decorated with fish in relief in the Salmonides pattern with an impressed mark *R. Lalique France*.

(Stride's) **$34,000**

'Hirondelles', a Lalique wall-light, the semi-circular wall plaque with molded decoration of five swallows in flight, above a hemispherical satin-finished shade, mounted on a circular gilt-painted backplate, 47.5cm. diameter.
(Christie's) **$16,000**

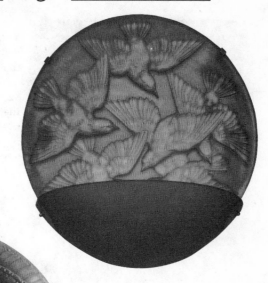

'Escargot', a Lalique amber glass vase, the milky-amber glass molded with a spiraling shell motif, with molded and engraved signatures *R. Lalique*, 25.5cm. high.
(Christie's) **$16,650**

Acid etched, frosted red glass, molded fish design vase 'Poissons', by René Lalique, 9in. high.
(Du Mouchelles)
$12,750

'Oran', a large Lalique blue-stained vase, slightly flared form, heavily molded with chrysanthemum flowers and leaves, with wheel-carved signature *R. Lalique France*, 26.8cm. high.
(Christie's) **$12,750**

'Suzanne au Bain', a Lalique amber glass figure, molded as a nude girl standing, her arms outstretched supporting a drape, on flared plinth, with molded signature *R. Lalique*, 23cm. high.
(Christie's)
$43,000

'Penthièvre'. a Lalique blue vase, globular with flat circular collar rim with molded decoration of four bands of stylized angel fish, with engraved signature *R. Lalique*, 27cm. high.
(Christie's) **$23,738**

The Pairpoint Manufacturing Co. started out as electroplaters in New Bedford Mass. in 1880. In 1900, they merged with the Mount Washington Glass Co. to become the Pairpoint Corp., making glass only.

Their products were not much influenced by the innovations of Tiffany and Frederick Carder of the Steuben Glassworks, and they continued producing Victorian inspired floral designs.

Pairpoint blown-out puffy lamp, squared molded Torino glass shade with rippled exterior surface design overall, reverse painted interior with puffy red, yellow, pink and green blossoms, buds and leaves at each end upon deep cranberry red background, embellished with colorful medallions of flower-filled cornucopia, raised on four-arm support, quatri form silvered and gilt metal shaft and base with molded floral motif, 21¹/₂in. high. *(Skinner)*   **$13,200**

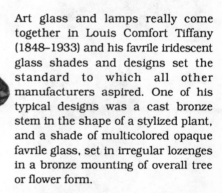

Art glass and lamps really come together in Louis Comfort Tiffany (1848–1933) and his favrile iridescent glass shades and designs set the standard to which all other manufacturers aspired. One of his typical designs was a cast bronze stem in the shape of a stylized plant, and a shade of multicolored opaque favrile glass, set in irregular lozenges in a bronze mounting of overall tree or flower form.

Tiffany bronze and favrile blue dragonfly lamp, conical tuck-under shade of seven mesh-wing dragonflies with blue bodies and jewel eyes against blue and green mottled and striated glass segments, 22¹/₂in. high. *(Skinner)*   **$22,000**

A Gallé carved and acid-etched double-overlay lamp, with three-branch mount, the base of elongated baluster form, on circular foot, with mushroom-cap shade, the yellow glass overlaid with purple and blue marguerites, 39.2cm. high. *(Christie's)*

$55,000

Tiffany bronze and turtleback glass table lamp, nineteen iridescent green tiles bordered above and below by mottled green square and rectangular favrile glass segments, mounted on original matching urn-form bronze base with medial band of twelve green turtleback tiles, 24in. high. *(Skinner)* **$23,000**

A Gallé carved and acid-etched double-overlay table lamp, with three-branch mount, the base of flared cylindrical and shouldered form, on broad circular foot, with mushroom-cap shade, the yellow and red-tinted glass overlaid with red stylized flowers and fruit, both shade and base with carved signature *Galle*, 55.5cm. high. *(Christie's)*

$68,000

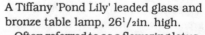

A Tiffany 'Pond Lily' leaded glass and bronze table lamp, 26¹/₂in. high.

Often referred to as a flowering lotus, this model is listed in the 1906 price list published by the Tiffany Studios as a 'Pond Lily'.

(Christie's)   **$440,000**

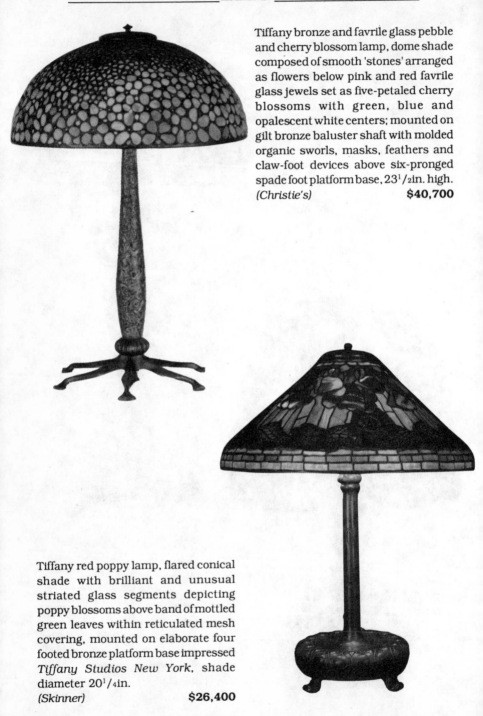

Tiffany bronze and favrile glass pebble and cherry blossom lamp, dome shade composed of smooth 'stones' arranged as flowers below pink and red favrile glass jewels set as five-petaled cherry blossoms with green, blue and opalescent white centers; mounted on gilt bronze baluster shaft with molded organic sworls, masks, feathers and claw-foot devices above six-pronged spade foot platform base, $23^1/2$in. high. *(Christie's)* **$40,700**

Tiffany red poppy lamp, flared conical shade with brilliant and unusual striated glass segments depicting poppy blossoms above band of mottled green leaves within reticulated mesh covering, mounted on elaborate four footed bronze platform base impressed *Tiffany Studios New York*, shade diameter $20^1/4$in.
(Skinner) **$26,400**

The brothers Henri and Desiré Muller, who were active during the first third of the 20th century, trained under Gallé at Nancy, before setting up their own businesses in Luneville and Croismare in 1895. Their vases and lamps, which often combine up to seven layers of glass, are usually beautifully carved. They also developed the technique of fluorogravure, using hydrofluoric acid to bite into glass painted with deep colored or iridescent enamels.

A Muller Frères carved and acid-etched cameo landscape table lamp, with three-branch mount, the slender baluster base on flared foot, with mushroom-cap shade, the orange and white glass overlaid in dark amber with a wooded river landscape and deer, 48cm. high.
(Christie's) **$17,160**

Tiffany bronze and favrile lotus bell lamp, mottled green and white glass segments arranged in bell form geometric progression, mounted within adjustable harp frame on ribbed cushion base with four ball feet, 21in. high.
(Skinner) **$26,250**

The Handel Company was established by Philip Handel at Meriden, Connecticut around 1885, and from 1900–1930 a branch also operated in New York City. The company produced Art Nouveau and other styles of art glass vessels, but came to be known principally for their leaded glass shades for gas and electric lighting. Many styles closely followed the designs of Tiffany, but were very much less expensive.

Handel interior-painted glass and patinated bronze floral lamp, 1st quarter 20th century.
(Butterfield & Butterfield)

$15,400

Early Tiffany blown-out bronze and favrile Tyler lamp, shaped dome shade of leaded glass segments arranged as twelve green swirling swags above repeating green border elements against white and mottled yellow background, raised on bronze oil lamp base with green favrile glass blown-out body and ball feet, 24in. high.
(Skinner) **$44,000**

Daum cameo glass table lamp, mushroom dome shade and baluster shaft base of mottled yellow glass with green and red shadings, the top layered in green and black cameo cut and wheel finished in a broad seascape with sailing vessels, the base cut back in stylized full-length floral design over, 26^{1}/$_{2}$in. high.
(Skinner) **$15,000**

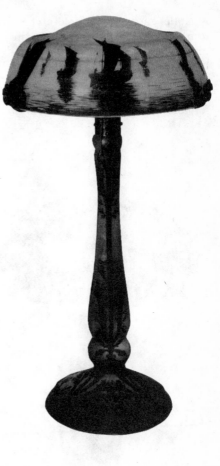

A Gallé cameo glass table lamp, with domed shade with undulating rim, the grayish body tinted blue and overlaid with transparent orange glass acid-etched with dragonflies, resting on sinuous bronze supports above a slender baluster base decorated in relief and similar colors with a pond, 62cm. high.
(Phillips) **$43,000**

A Gallé carved and acid-etched,
double-overlay table lamp, the
mushroom cap shade on the three-
branch mount, above waisted trumpet-
form pedestal base, the base and shade
with carved signatures *Galle*.
(Christie's) **$75,000**

A Gallé carved and acid-etched triple-
overlay table lamp, with three-branch
mounts, elongated baluster base, the
mushroom-cap shade with bun finial,
the white and yellow glass overlaid in
purple, blue and green, with pendent
flowers and a butterfly, each with
carved signature *Gallé*, 58.5cm. high.
(Christie's) **$47,190**

Arthur Lazenby Liberty was the archetypical Victorian entrepreneur. Starting life as an assistant in a London emporium, he rose to be the manager of a firm called Farmer and Rogers which sold Oriental imports to the rapidly increasing clientele of customers in search of beautiful things for their homes. Recognising the magnitude of the new market, Liberty took a chance and opened his own shop in Regent Street in 1875. Within five years it had proved to be a huge success and it is still thriving on its original site. His success was due to the fact that he had a discriminating taste and knew exactly what his customers wanted to buy.

A Liberty & Co. hammered pewter rose bowl, the design attributed to Oliver Baker, globular form with inverted rim, cast and applied decoration, set with five green glass studs, on five curved legs and trefoil feet, stamped *English Pewter made by Liberty & Co.*, 15.8cm. high.
(Christie's) **$750**

A Liberty & Co. Cymric silver and copper bowl, the shallow conical silver bowl with everted rim set with band of cabochon nephrites, mounted on elaborate copper scrolling feet, stamped *L&Co.*, *Cymric* with Birmingham hallmarks for 1901, 20.7cm. diameter, 680 grams gross.
(Christie's) **$2,150**

A Liberty & Co. pewter and enamel clock designed by Archibald Knox, rectangular, the body decorated in relief with stylized Honesty, the circular blue and green enameled clock face with Arabic chapters and red enamel details, stamped *English Pewter, Made by Liberty & Co.*, 19.8cm. high.
(Christie's) **$4,750**

An important Limehouse model of a cat, modeled and seated upright with its tail curled round its back legs, its eyes, whiskers and paws picked out in underglaze blue and with a solid wash of blue between the paws, 16.3cm. high.

This model is very similar to Staffordshire saltglaze cats of the same period. It is known that Staffordshire workmen were at Limehouse and other shapes made at the factory were strongly influenced by saltglaze. Although a small number of dog models are known from Limehouse they are of a much smaller scale.

(Phillips) **$8,160**

A very rare Limehouse dish of canted rectangular shape, painted in blue with two Oriental figures at a table, 17cm. x 22cm.
(Phillips)   **$6,175**

There were seven porcelain factories in Liverpool in the 18th century, of which three, Chaffers, Christians and Penningtons are generally regarded as forming the mainstream tradition from 1754-99.

The Chaffers' factory (1754-65) made a bone ash and a soapstone porcelain which are often difficult to tell apart as most of the standard shapes were identically produced in both.

Blue and white made up the bulk of production and showed a strong Worcester influence in terms of both shape and decoration, being painted in a free and pleasant style. Distinctive characteristics are the upturned lips of jugs and the fact that cream and sauceboats are often molded.

Liverpool creamware pitcher, England, 19th century, black transfer-printed with a three-masted ship flying an American flag enhanced with polychrome enamels, the reverse black transfer-printed with a spread wing American eagle encircled by a chain of 16 state names, 8¼in. high.
(Skinner) **$3,575**

Liverpool transfer decorated and handpainted creamware pitcher, England, early 19th century, handpainted in polychrome with Caleb Bates's ship, 'Venilia'; the other side transfer-decorated in magenta with 'Parting Wishes' and underspout with magenta spread-wing eagle with shield at breast over crossed flags, cannon, drum and presentation inscription *Caleb Bates*, 10½in. high.

The Venilia was built in Haverhill, Massachusetts in 1796 and was registered in Boston (Charlestown) in 1805. It was owned by Amos Greene, William Coleman Lee, Samuel Topliss and Key Walsh of Portsmouth, New Hampshire. The vessel was condemned at Barbados.
(Skinner) **$39,600**

The Loetz glass factory was established at Klostermühle in Bohemia in 1836, and was bought by Johann Loetz in 1840. During the 1880s it produced glass imitating onyx, jasper and other hardstones and cameo glass with simplified plant forms in blue and black.

It was in the following decade however, that it sprang to fame, when it started to produce glass in the Jugendstil (literally youth style) which was the German speaking world's equivalent of Art Nouveau.

Under the direction of Max Ritter von Spaun, Loetz's grandson, who was director from 1879–1908, this took the form of an iridescent glass which fell into two types. The first, Papillon, consisted of pearly spots covering a vessel, and the second, Phenomenon, consisted of glass threads undulating across a pearly surface.

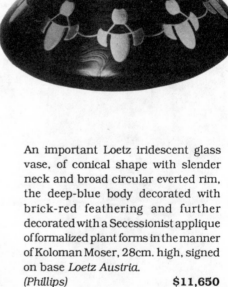

A Loetz oviform vase, the body with four dimples, 25.4cm. high.
(Christie's) **$1,350**

An important Loetz iridescent glass vase, of conical shape with slender neck and broad circular everted rim, the deep-blue body decorated with brick-red feathering and further decorated with a Secessionist applique of formalized plant forms in the manner of Koloman Moser, 28cm. high, signed on base Loetz Austria.
(Phillips) **$11,650**

Longton Hall was one of the first porcelain factories in the entire United Kingdom, and production commenced around 1750. Unsurprisingly, in these circumstances, initial output was somewhat primitive in quality, but the standard of both potting and decoration rapidly improved. Early pieces consisted mainly of the so-called 'Snowman' figures and mugs, plates, dishes etc. decorated in 'Littler's' blue. The underglaze was often runny and uneven, but has a brightness which was no doubt in imitation of Vincennes. The reserves were often left unfilled, giving the pieces a somewhat unfinished appearance.

William Littler had joined the venture in 1751 and by 1753-4 there was an improvement in the standard of potting, though decoration was still quite primitive. At this time the scarce Longton Hall powder blue vases, teapots and bottles were made.

A Longton Hall two-handled vase of rococo scroll-molded outline, painted with exotic birds in landscape vignettes within molded shaped cartouches reserved on a fluted ground applied with colored flowers and foliage, the scroll-molded handles similarly applied and enriched in puce, circa 1755, 21.5cm. high.
(Christie's) **$2,000**

A pair of Longton Hall pigeon-tureens and covers, the naturally modeled birds to left and right with purple feather markings sitting on oval twig-molded nests enriched in purple, green and yellow, the interior to one painted with scattered flowers and foliage, circa 1755, 22cm. long.
(Christie's) **$13,000**

In 1758 Johann Jakob Ringler established a porcelain factory for Duke Carl Eugen of Württemberg. Ringler had arrived there via Vienna, Höchst and various other centers, but it was at Ludwigsburg that he remained until his death in 1802.

The factory produced a distinctive smoky brown body, which, if the exquisite detail on some of the figures is anything to go by, was nevertheless excellent for modeling.

A pair of Ludwigsburg figures of a gallant and companion modeled by Franz Anton Pustelli, masquerading as peasants, elegantly dressed on one side and shabbily dressed as peasants on the other, half dressed in gilt-patterned and brightly colored clothes and the other half in tattered and traditional clothes, she with incised *Z.N.S.*, circa 1760, 13cm. high.
(Christie's) **$5,700**

A Ludwigsburg group of Bacchus and a Bacchante modeled by Johann Christian Wilhelm Beyer, the naked figures embracing and she squeezing a bunch of grapes into his bowl and her hair entwined with vine, she seated on a green and puce striped drape and he on an orange drape, on a high rocky base entwined with vine, a gadrooned ewer beside them and a satyr fondling a goat at their feet, circa 1765, 24cm. high.
(Christie's) **$5,350**

Charles Rennie Mackintosh (1868–1928) was one of the seminal figures of the Art Nouveau/Deco period. He was apprenticed as an architect in Glasgow, during which time he also studied at the Glasgow School of Art, winning a scholarship to visit France and Italy in 1890. After this, he also began to design furniture. In 1897 he won the competition to design and furnish the new Glasgow School of Art.

Mackintosh became the leading figure in what came to be known as the Glasgow School. Other members of the group were Francis Newbery, the headmaster of the School of Art, and his wife, Mackintosh's own wife Margaret MacDonald and her sister Frances who married the remaining member, the architect Herbert MacNair.

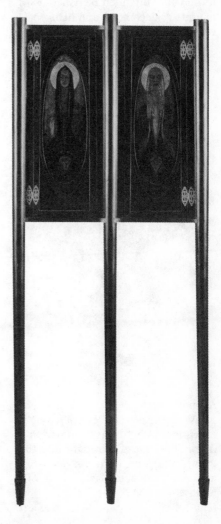

An ebonized and painted corner cabinet, designed by Charles Rennie Mackintosh, with painted panels by Margaret Macdonald Mackintosh, the two cupboard doors with pierced hinge plates, inset with oval painted and gilded panels depicting symbolic figures, circa 1897, 183cm. high.

Although associated with Queen's Cross Church, Glasgow, 1896–1899, where it was photographed at the back of the chancel, the cabinet was not part of the original contents of the church. Its early history is unknown, except that it was owned at one time by William Davidson, one of Mackintosh's early patrons.

(Christie's) **$23,000**

Louis Majorelle was born in France in 1859. He trained as a painter in Paris, but at the age of twenty took over his father's cabinet making business in Nancy, which had made 18th century reproduction furniture.

Majorelle however came under the influence of Emile Gallé, and began to produce Art Nouveau furniture in the Ecole de Nancy style, characterized by fluid, sculptural forms and often embellished with marquetry decoration and using local woods.

A Daum & Majorelle glass and wrought iron vase, the footed geometric wrought iron gridwork acting as a support and frame for the glass, blown through the frame, of tapering form, the glass with an inner translucent layer cased with pink, 35cm. high.

(Phillips) **$1,200**

A Louis Majorelle inlaid and carved kingwood, mahogany and amaranth cabinet, the shaped overhanging top with three-quarter gallery above a single curved cupboard door, 59cm. wide.

(Christie's) **$39,160**

A fine English white marble figure of Eve, by John Warrington Wood, the graceful Eve shown naked and seated with her legs folded beside her on a grassy mound, her delicate head turned to sinister, her long locks falling down her back, 19th century, 41in. high.

John Warrington Wood (1839–86) was born and studied in England, but spent much of his working life in Rome. Wood began exhibiting his sculpture at the Royal Academy in 1868 with four works which he sent from Rome. He was particularly interested in biblical figures, and often used such characters as vehicles for studies of the ideal female form.

(Christie's) **$58,432**

A George III statuary marble and Siena chimneypiece, the rectangular breakfront shelf above a plain Siena frieze with central tablet carved with an oval medallion depicting a classical female figure, flanked at either side by floral wreaths with ribbon tie crestings, late 18th century, 72in. wide.
(Christie's) **$36,520**

A white marble bust of Napoleon, as a
young man portrayed looking straight
ahead in deep contemplation, the front
inscribed *Napoleon*, the reverse *63*,
23³/₄in. high.
(Tennants) **$3,255**

A large white marble group of two
children on a swing, by Alessandro
Lazzarini, the boy wearing a hat and
with his trousers rolled up, his young
sister holding on to him, the simple
swing tied to a branch of an ivy-covered
tree trunk, late 19th century, 40¹/₈in.
high.
Alessandro Lazzarini (1869–1942) was
born in Carrara and studied at the
Carrara Academy. He was a pupil of
Carusi and Pelliccia and worked with
his half-brother Guiseppe Lazzarini.
Alessandro specialized in genre and
allegorical subjects and won medals
at both the 1889 and 1900 Expositions
Universelles.
(Christie's) **$94,000**

A fine Italian white marble figure of Juno, from the workshop of Lorenzo Bartolini, the naked goddess reclining against an embroidered cushion, first half 19th century, 32in. long.
(Christie's)   **$13,000**

A large pair of English white marble lionesses, after the Antique, reclining, their tails curled about their haunches, with stylized manes, on rectangular bases, 19th century, 42¹/₂ x 25 x 14³/₈in.

The present lionesses derive from the pair of Egyptian lionesses in basalt brought to Rome in antiquity, and now at the base of the Scalinata on the Campidoglio in Rome. These Egyptian lionesses inspired a generation of English 18th century connoisseurs, of whom the most prominent was Thomas Hope.
(Christie's)   **$90,024**

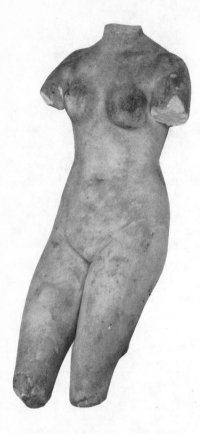

A Roman marble life size naked female torso from the 2nd century A.D., 38in. high.
(Dreweatt-Neate) **$13,650**

A pair of Napoleon III ormolu-mounted gray and white marble torchères inscribed *Thiébaut. Frères Fondeurs*, third quarter, 19th century.

Each urn crested with a foliate bouquet issuing four candlearms in the form of roses, above an ormolu band issuing twelve foliate scrolling candlearms ending in leaf-tip cast drip pans and cups, 88in. high.
(Christie's) **$104,500**

Italian baroque Verona marble lion fountain, late 17th century, in three sections, the recumbent lion on a plinth base supporting a turned and waisted vasiform standard below a circular basin, 36¹/₂in. high.
(Butterfield & Butterfield)

$6,600

A magnificent Italian marble group of Galatea riding a dophin, by Leopoldo Ansiglioni, the alluring naked nymph reclining against her dolphin, her arms reaching back and entwined about his tail as he bears her through the waves, her long tresses streaming behind her, signed on rim of the base *Ansiglioni 1880 Roma. Studio. O. Andreoni*, circa 1880, 54¹/₂in. high overall.
(Christie's) **$174,000**

The Martin Brothers cooperative, which set up in 1873, consisted of Robert Wallace Martin, who had worked for the Fulham pottery, and his brothers Walter and Edwin, who had previously been employed by Doulton. Walter was thrower, and Edwin decorator, while a further brother, Charles, became the business manager and ran a shop in Brownlow Street, London.

Martinware comes in a wide variety of shapes. The decoration is mainly incised, with the colors reminiscent of Doulton stoneware. The most common motifs are plants, birds, animals and grotesques, of which perhaps the most notable are R W Martin's 'wally birds'. These are often found as tobacco jars, with the heads forming the lids, and generally have a somewhat menacing air.

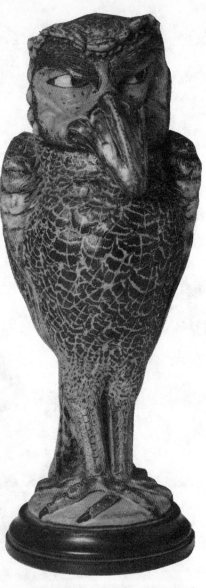

An unusual Martin Brothers spoon warmer, modeled as a grotesque, grinning, previously unknown species of mudfish, having lop ears, warts and a wide grin, incised *Martin London & Southall 5.9.1882* to base, 18cm. long.
(Phillips) **$5,250**

A good Martin Brothers 'barrister' bird, tall with a hooked beak and wig, wearing a somewhat sceptical frown, glazed green, brown with some blue, having a removable head, 46.5cm. high.
(Phillips) **$15,551**

An amusing Martin Brothers stoneware model of a baby owl, the creature has a pale brown rotund body resting on a circular base above ebonized stand, with large talons, its removable head having long ears and its beak open wide expecting a tasty morsel, 27.5cm. high, signed on the neck and base *Martin Bros. London & Southall* and dated *10–1895*.
(Phillips)   **$5,835**

A Martin Brothers vase, the writhen globular body with four handles modeled as snakes biting the rim of the vase, the vase glazed in buff and brown with incised details, the snakes green and pale, incised *12–1899*, 27.5cm. high.
(Christie's)   **$4,695**

A 'Grand Format' musical box by Nicole Frères, playing four overtures, with lever-wind, engraved silver tune sheet in rosewood veneered case, 27^1/$_2$in. wide. Accompanying this musical box is a letter (written in French) from Nicole Frères to their London Agents, dated April 1860.
(Christie's) **$54,780**

An Edison Gem phonograph, Model C No. 303891C, with patent combination gear attachment, Walshaw-type turnover stylus in C reproducer and black 18-inch octagonal horn with crane, circa 1908.
(Christie's) **$7,300**

A Polyphon 15⁵/₈in. table disc musical box with comb and a third movement, in quarter veneered walnut case with inlaid lid and interior print.
(Phillips) **$4,200**

Unnamed and hitherto unknown music automat, with 5 tunes, 15cm. metal cylinders with complete 57 tooth tone comb, 2 part spring winding and two mechanical dolls, in wooden case with wall attachment, circa 1890.
(Auction Team Koln)

$30,000

A Regina Corona 27-inch disk musical box with self-changing disk mechanism, double combs, magazine for twelve disks and mahogany case with glazed and pierced and carved upper doors and figured panel below, 67in. high.
(Christie's) **$21,000**

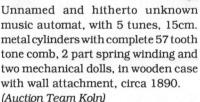

An HMV Model 202 gramophone cabinet with quadruple-spring motor, 'antique silver' 5a soundbox and tone-arm and oak case with fret and doors, 49^1/$_2$in. high.
(Christie's) **$4,250**

A Regina Sublima piano, No. 3040666, with 73-note roll-operated mechanism, electric motor drive, coin mechanism with mercury switch, printed instruction sheet and oak case with paneled lower half and glazed front to the roll compartment with transfers *Regina* and *Sublimo Piano*.
(Christie's) **$4,250**

A hand-turned Tinfoil phonograph with brass mandrel on steel threaded arbor with hand wheels at each end, with brass bearings on turned supports with screw release, 15in. wide.
(Christie's S. Ken)   **$6,500**

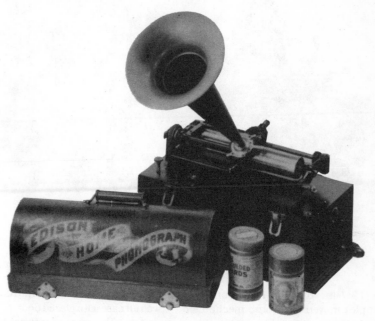

Edison Home Phonograph Model A, the first Edison cylinder player with decorative banner emblem, with 12 cylinders, 1898.
(Auction Team Koln)   **$1,600**

A 19⁵/₈in. upright polyphon in typical case, with coin mechanism and drawer, with four discs, 36in. high.
(Phillips) **$9,312**

A 19⁵/₈in. upright Polyphon with duplex movement, comb mechanism and drawer in typical walnut case with glazed door and pediment, 49¹/₂in. high.
(Christie's) **$10,250**

A 17¹/₄-inch Britannia upright disk musical box with duplex comb movement, coin mechanism and walnut case with glazed door, pediment and disk storage compartment at rear, on baluster supports over cupboard base, 93¹/₂in. high.
(Christie's) **$9,200**

Eternola Portablofon wind up gramophone with shaped octagonal wooden base, decorated cast iron arm and red metal horn.
(Auction Team Koln)
$1,889

An HMV Model 194 re-entrant tone chamber gramophone with gilt 5a soundbox in carton, quadruple-spring motor and mahogany case with doors and fret enclosing tone-chamber, 44in. high.
(Christie's) **$4,600**

A Triola mechanical zither with 25-note roll mechanism and twenty-four hand-played strings, on ebonized base.
(Christie's) **$4,000**

At the beginning of the 18th century the race was on in Europe to find the secret of the manufacture of Chinese-type porcelain. The winner was Augustus the Strong, Elector of Saxony, thanks to his sequestration of a young alchemist, J F Böttger, whom he originally employed to turn base metal to gold. When Böttger failed at this, Frederick set him the alternative task of porcelain manufacture under the eye of Ehrenfried Walther von Tschirnhaus, a Saxon physicist who was also fascinated by this challenge. Success finally came in 1710, and a new red and white porcelain manufactory was set up in the Albrechtsburg at Meissen.

Production problems persisted, however, and it was not until 1713 that the first pieces were offered for sale, the decoration of which was largely influenced by the court silversmith Johann Irminger.

The king wanted color, but Böttger was never really successful in finding enamels which would withstand the firing temperatures required to fuse them into the glaze, and much of his output remained white.

For 15 years painted decoration remained paramount, and was only superseded by J J Kaendler's relief molding and figurines in the late 1730s. From 1740 Kaendler's output was phenomenal. In addition to a constant supply of naturalistic figures, he designed new relief patterns for tablewares, and it is to him more than anyone that Meissen owes its long triumph, which started to wane only after the peace of 1763, when the victorious Frederick the Great of Prussia was successful in luring several fine modelers (though not Kaendler) to his new factory in Berlin.

A Meissen teapot formed as a crowing cockerel naturalistically modeled with black, gray and brown plumage, the exotic tail forming the handle and open beak the spout, circa 1740.
(Christie's) **$4,500**

A Meissen yellow-ground coffee-cup painted with a moustached chinoiserie figure bending towards and beckoning with his hand and standing on a terrace before a fence, a vase of flowers and a shrub with a bird above, circa 1730, 7cm. high.
(Christie's) **$23,000**

A Meissen chinoiserie cylindrical tankard painted in the manner of J.G. Höroldt with figures around a table playing mandolins and drinking tea before a palm tree, a man painting porcelain, figures watching clay being lowered in a basket from above and one using a wheel, all on a continuous terrace with flowering shrubs and birds and insects in flight, Belgian import marks for 1831–69, 18cm. high.
(Christie's)   **$21,350**

A Meissen figure of a seated Harlequin with a bird-cage after the model by J.J. Kändler and J.F. Eberlein, in a pink hat, checkered, scale and playing-card jacket over yellow trousers, seated beside an open bird-cage and holding up a bird to torment the cat below, circa 1745, 13.5cm. high.
(Christie's)   **$19,000**

A Meissen famille verte circular dish, the center painted in underglaze blue with a flowering plant within an overglaze enamel band of zig-zag panels and flowerheads and Oriental style peonies and chrysanthemums issuing from rockwork, circa 1730, 38cm. diameter.
(Christie's)   **$28,215**

A Meissen Fläschenhalter from the Swan Service modeled by J.J. Kändler and J.E. Eberlein for Count Brühl, of compressed oval shape with a gilt undulating rim and a band of pierced scrollwork above molded swans and herons flanking, on either side, a shell cartouche painted with the coat-of-arms of Heinrich Graf Brühl and Anna von Kolowrat-Krakowska, 1737–41. *(Christie's)* **$25,600**

A pair of Meissen Imari tureens and covers, each freely painted in the typical palette enriched with gilding, with two exotic cockerels among flowering peony and chrysanthemum flanking two black-lined lappets with peonies and foliage between borders of foliage and iron-red and blue-ground panels, circa 1735, 34cm. high.
(Christie's) **$60,000**

A pair of Meissen models of large pugs after the models by J.J. Kändler, naturalistically modeled with large eyes, black muzzles with long whiskers and brown markings, the female with her left paw raised to show her suckling puppy, circa 1740, about 24cm. high.
(Christie's) **$38,000**

A Meissen box and cover modeled as a tortoise, probably by Georg Fritzsche, with a yellow head and tail with black and iron-red markings and four yellow feet with black claws, the shell forming the cover and the body with purple Böttger luster and black, silver and gilt markings, circa 1725, 19.5cm. long.
(Christie's) **$38,000**

A Meissen Augustus Rex beaker-vase painted by J.E. Stadler, divided into three sections, the flaring top painted with two chinoiserie figures, one holding a large fan on a terrace flanked by shrubs of chrysanthemum and peony below exotic birds and insects, the bulging central part similarly decorated with a boy holding a sunshade over a dignitary carrying a basket of fruit, circa 1730, 39cm. high.
(Christie's) **$48,900**

A Meissen chinoiserie pear-shaped coffee-pot and cover painted in the manner of J.E. Stadler, one side with a man tending a plant and his companion blowing a pipe, the other with a woman offering fruit to a seated dignitary, both scenes within quatrefoil gilt line cartouches with panels of Böttger lustre and Laub-und-bandelwerk between sprays of indianische Blumen, circa 1728, 20cm. high.
(Christie's) **$30,000**

A large Meissen baluster vase and domed cover, the front and back painted with scenes after Watteau with quatrefoil cartouches with a man playing a mandolin and a lady singing and a man with a flute and his companion both in idyllic landscapes enclosed by extensive ombrierte gilt scrolls, the sides with smaller panels painted with Venetian scenes after Melchoir Küsel, circa 1740, 39cm. high. *(Christie's)* **$63,500**

An extremely large late Meissen group of Count Brühl's tailor riding on a goat, the tailor dressed as a courtier and wearing a flowered yellow coat over a flowered white waistcoat, high black boots and tricorn hat, the goat with scissors and iron hanging from his horns, and other tailoring impedimenta on both the goat and the tailor, 43cm. high. *(Christie's)* **$6,500**

A Meissen armorial circular dish from the Swan Service modeled by J.J. Kändler and J.F. Eberlein for Count Brühl, the shell-border painted with indianische Blumen flanking the coat-of-arms of Heinrich Graf Brühl and Anna von Kolowrat Krakowska, 1737–41, 42cm. diameter.

(Christie's) **$63,500**

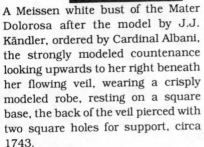

A Meissen white bust of the Mater Dolorosa after the model by J.J. Kändler, ordered by Cardinal Albani, the strongly modeled countenance looking upwards to her right beneath her flowing veil, wearing a crisply modeled robe, resting on a square base, the back of the veil pierced with two square holes for support, circa 1743.

There appear to be three extant examples of this model, one in a private collection, another in Dresden.

(Christie's) **$40,000**

A Meissen figure of a lady of the Mopsorden modeled by J.J. Kändler, in a puce dress with a crinoline skirt enriched with gilding and a turquoise flowered underskirt, carrying a pug dog and another at her feet peering from beneath her skirt, circa 1745, 28.5cm. high.

(Christie's) **$10,000**

Thomas Minton was born in 1765 and apprenticed at the Caughley Works where he was trained in the art of engraving copper plates for underglaze-blue painted designs. In 1793 he established his own works at Stoke on Trent, where it traded as Minton & Co from 1845 and Mintons Ltd from 1873. It was noted from the first for the high quality and diversity of its output, which at first consisted mainly of blue printed earthenware, though porcelain was added to the range in 1797. The original pattern book of that period survives today.

From 1847 large quantities of parian ware were produced, and figures were made by a number of eminent modelers. Various partners took responsibility for various branches of the firm, and by 1868 these separated. Minton, Collins & Co specialised in tile manufacturing, while C H Campbell became responsible for earthenware.

Minton had a strong presence at the Great Exhibition of 1851 where they displayed Sèvres style porcelain vases, terracotta and majolica garden ornaments, parian figures and tiles, all of which attracted much favorable comment. Pâte-sur-pâte decoration was introduced by the Sèvres-trained decorator and modeler Marc Louis or Miles Solon, who worked for Minton between 1870 and 1904.

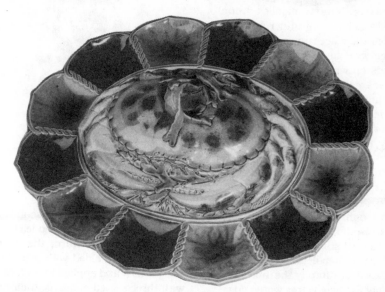

A Minton majolica oval seafood dish, the cover modeled as a large crab resting on a bed of green seaweed, the fronds curling up its back to form a loop handle, the dish glazed in turquoise on the interior and with a border of twelve dark-blue and mottled-ocher-glazed receptacles divided by bands of entwined ropetwist separating around the edge of the dish to form a scalloped rim, date code for 1859, 15³/₄in. wide.
(Christie's)   **$6,600**

A massive Minton majolica group of two frogs courting under a bunch of leaves, their faces turned towards each other with fond devotion and their hands entwined around the stem of the leaves, the male frog on the left placing his right hand on his heart, the female frog on the right, clasping in her left hand a fan placed across her belly, the white leaf of the fan reserved with a brown vermiculé pattern enriched in pink and turquoise, impressed mark and date code for 1876, 48in. high.

Although this large and humorous group would appear to be unknown, various artists such as John Henk and Paul Comolera created animal models for Minton; the hole in the back of the female frog would suggest that this group was intended as part of a larger composition, in the manner of the fountain made up of rocks, palm trees, storks and figures, modeled by Paul Comolera and exhibited at the 1878 Exposition Universelle in Paris. *(Christie's)* **$31,042**

A Minton majolica turquoise-ground vase and cover, the finial modeled as a putto blowing the horn, the drum-shaped body molded with a band of fret-pattern and applied in high relief with three seated maidens, their hair wreathed with vine-leaves, wearing fur-lined drapery and holding garlands of flower-entwined twigs and berried laurel falling in swags beneath their feet and below three goat-masks, date code for 1863, 22in. high. *(Christie's)* **$5,750**

A Mintons majolica teapot modeled as a tortoise with brown shell, green body and with shell knop, the interior pink, impressed marks and ref. diamond for 1878, 5in. high.
(William H Brown) **$6,650**

A Minton majolica-ware game pie dish and cover of oval shape, with double tied-twig handles, supported on four paw feet, the cover surmounted by a hound and hunting trophies, the sides molded with a pheasant and hare, 36cm., datecode for 1882.
(Phillips) **$1,870**

A large Minton majolica flower vase in the form of a fawn after a model by Paul Comolera, the young animal with a matt gray-brown body and white spotted markings, modeled standing to the left against a truncated hollow tree-trunk, nibbling an acorn, the brown-glazed trunk molded in relief with ivy and with fern-leaves in high relief, circa 1875, 32³/₄in. high.

Paul Comolera (1818–1897), was born in Paris and studied under the sculptor Francois Rude; working primarily as an animalier modeler, he followed in the footsteps of his compatriots Louis Solon, Albert Carrier de Belleuse and Hughes Protàt, among others, by joining the Minton factory.
(Christie's)   **$13,695**

A Minton majolica monkey teapot and cover, the smiling creature's head forming the detachable cover and its curling tail forming the handle, wearing a blue waistcoat reserved with pink fans and green leaves, its body and limbs curved around a large yellow nut and its right hand clutching a green leaf issuing from the bamboo-molded spout, date code for 1874, 6in. high.
(Christie's) $2,000

A Minton majolica jardinière in the form of a nautilus shell resting on coral and rocks, the shell with a whitish glaze on the exterior splashed with manganese beads, the striations enriched with stripes of ocher and manganese on the reverse, the interior glazed in turquoise within an ocher rim, the shell resting on a stem of rocks enclosed by a dark-pink coral formation, its multitude of interlaced branches meandering around the sides of the shell, date code for 1873, 26in. high.
(Christie's) $6,600

A Minton majolica circular pigeon-pie tureen and cover molded to simulate yellow wicker-work and with a turquoise-glazed interior, the tureen supported on the tails of three fan-tailed pigeons with shaded cream, gray and lilac plumage and colored heads, the birds perched on oak-branches with leafy interlaced twigs providing further support for the tureen, circa 1864.
(Christie's) $8,000

Mid 14th century Paris School, rare and unusual carved ivory mirrorback of circular form, carved in high relief with fighting knights on horseback before a twin towered portal with raised portcullis, figures on the ramparts and at the windows below a stepped gable, 12cm. diameter.

(Spencer's) **$49,000**

Flemish School, early 18th century, 'A Bacchanalian scene', oil on shaped canvas, incorporated in a carved gilt wood overmantel mirror with three beveled plates, carved with flowers and trailing leaves and surmounted by a pierced foliate cresting, 56in. x 58in. overall.

(Tennants) **$9,300**

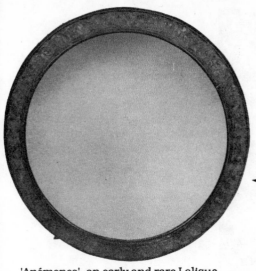

'Anémones', an early and rare Lalique frosted glass mirror, of circular shape molded with anemone blooms and leaves, heightened with pink foil backing, 39cm. diameter.
(Phillips) **$6,875**

A Regency mahogany and ebonized cheval mirror with rectangular beveled plate and swing mirror with simulated bamboo supports headed by flaming-urn finials, the supports each with adjustable ormolu candlesticks, on downswept legs with brass caps, repair to one leg, 35in.
(Christie's) **$7,600**

Country Queen Anne painted and decorated mirror, 18th century, painted black and white sprigs and flourishes, 17³/₈in. high.
(Skinner) **$10,450**

A early George III green-painted and gilded mirror with rectangular plate and frame pierced and carved with long and short C-scrolls entwined with foliage and with flower-swag cresting, the base centered by a gilt mask, 36³/₄ x 24in.

(Christie's) **$52,500**

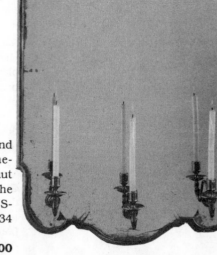

A Queen Anne silvered-wood and walnut girandole with cartouche-shaped beveled plate in narrow walnut and molded silvered-wood frame, the base mounted with three later S-shaped gilt-brass candle-branches, 34 x 23¹/₄in.

(Christie's) **$33,000**

A George III giltwood pier mirror, mid-18th century, 84in. high.

These mirrors were designed in the fashionable arcadian style of the mid 18th century, with rustic pilasters, flower-festooned and serpentined herms with Chinese busts and Ho-Ho birds beneath a pagoda-sweep crest. *(Christie's)* **$231,000**

A George II giltwood mirror with rounded rectangular divided plate, the frame carved with pilasters headed by acanthus capitals, C-scrolls, acanthus scrolls and flowerheads, the cresting carved with confronting C-scrolls headed by a ho-ho bird, 71in. x 36in. *(Christie's)* **$36,750**

A George II mahogany toilet-mirror with arched rectangular beveled plate in narrow frame carved with scrolling foliage and rocaille between fluted and rusticated supports carved with blind-fretwork with volutes at the bases on cancave-centered rectangular base edged with key-pattern on short cabriole legs and claw-and-ball feet, 18³/₄in. wide.
(Christie's) **$29,200**

A continental baroque style stained pine mirror, 19th century, with an oval plate within a conforming frame intricately carved with trailing foliage and putti, 75in. high.
(Christie's East)

$10,000

A fine silver-mounted violin bow by François Tourte, unbranded; the round stick mounted with a silver and ebony frog with pearl eye, the ferrule engraved *LEB*, the silver and ebony adjuster possibly a replacement. weight 61 grams.
(Christie's) **$43,000**

A Japanese 'Mermaid', late 18th/early 19th century, the dried head, rib cage and front claws being of a monkey's body, attached to a fish tail with dorsal and tail fins, mounted in a rectangular glass case.

    These creatures were supposedly caught at sea, but were actually elaborate hoaxes, originating from E. Asia, especially Japan. Such 'mermaids' were made with the dried parts of monkeys with fish tails, probably on a wooden core.
(Bonhams) **$2,100**

Paint and gilt decorated sled, America, late 19th century, painted blue and gilt inscribed *Elaine* at sides, 23¹/₂in. long.
(Skinner) **$935**

A Charles II polychrome beadwork basket with rectangular top, loop-handles and pierced trelliswork sides around a scene of an elegant couple in a garden with two dogs and a lion in front of a house, on a silk ground and pierced, spreading trelliswork base, 21^1/$_4$in. wide.
(Christie's) **$10,364**

A rare gold zodiac figure, standing barefoot on a tripod base, wearing an armor-like studded suit with a long tunic and shoulder pads, the right arm raised to the hip, the other holding a ram, modeled with well-defined features including penetrating eyes and prominent lips below a headress with three tight knots, 12th/13th century, 13cm. high.
(Christie's) **$20,000**

A mahogany cheese coaster of dished outline, the scrolled division and frieze edged with chainlink above rockwork and acanthus-carved frieze centered by a scallop-shell, the sides decorated with pounced trellis-pattern and with brass carrying-handles, on naturalistic legs and claw-and-ball feet, 20^1/$_4$in. wide.
(Christie's) **$3,098**

A pair of Nuremberg-type nose spectacles, Continental, 17th century, 3¹/₂in. wide.
(Christie's) **$8,784**

'Egg laying hen', early stamped metal vending machine made by C.F. Schulze & Co., Berlin. The hen sits on an oval basket and on insertion of 10pfg in her comb and turning of the handle a 12 part container for 59 eggs is moved so that an 'egg' (containing confectionery) is laid. Fully operational, circa 1900.
(Auction Team Koln) **$4,300**

A late 16th century Persia work thimble set with rubies alternating with paste sapphires, the top with four rubies set in a cross, and complete with a shagreen case, three-quarters of an inch high. It is thought that the thimble would have been part of a gift to Queen Elizabeth I from the Mogul Court. Noted as having been a 'Needle-woman Royall', the Queen was known to have possessed such artefacts, her personal inventories mentioning 'a needle case of Persia work garnished with rubies' and 'a nedall case of crystall garnyshed with silver gilt with two thimble in it'.
(Phillips) **$31,500**

A fine Märklin tinplate Leipzig two storey station for gauge 1, circa 1930, with lithographed brickwork, roof tiles and cobbled courtyard, hand painted details including ticket hall, doors, water fountain and clock tower with paper clock face and metal hands, glazed windows with electric interior lighting. *(Sotheby's)* **$17,800**

A magnificent Marklin hand-painted 'Gare Centrale' major railway station, gauge one, circa 1910, finished in varying shades of tan as simulated stone, with a green base and roof, the two story building features an outside workable clock, twin arched passageways, ticket, baggage and waiting room areas inside, glass windows, telegraph transmitting roof wiring and two beige glass lamps hanging on the trackside, $18^1/_2$in. x 34in. x $20^1/_2$in. *(Christie's)* **$22,000**

A five live steam Marklin cast iron and tinplate hand painted 'King Edward' passenger train, gauge 3, comprising an engine and tender painted black with red and yellow piping, a dining car with removable top, complete with tables, seats and small kitchen area, together with a sleeping car, furnished with rooms, curtains and lavatory, with removable top, both painted maroon and white, 68in. long overall. *(Christie's)*   **$19,800**

An extremely fine mid-19th century 5^1/$_2$in. gauge spirit-fired model of the Sheffield to Rotherham Railway Stephenson 2–4–0 locomotive and tender No. 45 'Albert', signed *Alfred Chadburn Maker 1855*, 14^3/$_4$in. x 36in.

The chassis of fletched riveted lacquered brass and wood is fitted with wood buffer beam, working leaf springs, brass wheels, the motion with outside Stephenson's link gear with pierced eccentrics. Tender details include brass wheels, hand-operated brake gear with wood blocks in brass shoes, spirit tank and three-lamp burner, dummy water tank, hand irons, and brass buffers. *(Christie's)*   **$24,700**

A Marklin 'Priscilla' tinplate live steam passenger liner, professionally restored in colors of white, red and tan with blue and gold piping, twin stacks, cabin, wheelhouse, twin lifeboat and mast, 20$^{1}/_{2}$in. long.
(Christie's) **$16,500**

Fleischmann, tinplate model of the liner 'Kron Prinzessin Cecile', made for a travel agency window display for the Norddeutscher Lloyd line, finished in fine quality detail, 156cm. long, circa 1907.
(Phillips) **$8,400.**

The whaleship "Sunbeam", plank on beam construction using many fine hardwoods, mahogany hull, pearwood deck, and basswood masts, carries all appropriate equipment, the tryworks, workbench, oil casks, and tools, 67in. wide.
(Eldreds) **$3,850**

A detailed $^1/_4$in.:1ft. scale builder's model of the Train Ferry Steamer 'Drottning Victoria', Trelleborg, built by Swan Hunter & Wigham Richardson Ltd., Neptune Works, Newcastle-upon-Tyne, for Swedish State Railways, Stockholm, 30 x 91in.

'Drottning (Queen) Victoria' was a train ferry steamer ordered by Swedish State Railways in 1908 for their trans-Baltic service to Northern Germany. *(Christie's)*   **$15,600**

Cased French Prisoner of War bone and ivory model of the British Frigate 'Fisgard 1796', England, early 19th century, fully rigged and finely detailed with polychrome figures of gun crews and sailors at various tasks on deck, 35in. wide.

This warship was built as the French Frigate Resistance and was taken by the British in 1797 and renamed the Fisgard. *(Skinner)*   **$16,500**

A Bugatti child's car, by Westwood, gas powered by single cylinder.
(Christie's) **$9,350**

A Marklin hand painted and stamped station newspaper kiosk, with four-gable roof, pay windows, clocks and relief work, circa 1910, 5in. high.
(Christie's S. Ken) **$5,600**

A fine Ernst Plank painted tinplate and brass steam horse-drawn fire engine, having vertical copper boiler with sight glass, blown down valve, pressure gauge, safety valve, whistle, burner and twin hinged panniers, circa 1903, 13$^{1}/_{2}$in. long without shafts.
(Christie's)

$31,000

A red aluminium 1/10 scale model Lancia FI D50 by Michele Conti with leather upholstery, one of four made in 1955 specially for Gianni Lancia.
(Finarte) **$16,000**

A finely engineered and well presented 3in. scale model of a Burrell single-cylinder, two-speed, three-shaft general purpose traction engine built by R. Simmons, Stowmarket, 29in. x 44in.
(Christie's) **$15,500**

A mechanical bank, a horse race, with flanged base, by J. & E. Stevens, designed by John D. Hall, 8in. high. *(Christie's)* **$12,100**

A mechanical bank, girl skipping rope by J. & E. Stevens, designed by James H. Bowen, 8in. high. *(Christie's)* **$25,300**

Cast iron Old South Church still bank, America, late 19th/early 20th century, with original paint and paper label inscribed *Old South Church gathered 1669, first house built 1776 this house erected 1729 Desecrated by Br. Tr'ps 1775–6*, 13in. high. *(Skinner)* **$4,675**

Ettore Bugatti's personal attache case, the hinged lid opening to reveal the leather-lined fitted interior with manicure set, hair brushes and cologne bottles.
(Christie's) **$8,250**

Original typescript of Enzo Ferrari's book 'La mei gioie terribile' consisting of 167 sheets, with margin notes in violet ink, mostly by Enzo Ferrari.
(Finarte) **$18,000**

Large illuminated 'Ferrari Service' sign in double sided flexiglas complete with electrics, 1970s, 77 x 178 x 17cm.
(Finarte) **$5,500**

An original radiator grill for the Alfa Romeo 1750, complete with enamel badge.
(Finarte) **$1,600**

A complete 'fruit and smoking' service in yellow cut glass, personally commissioned in not more than 12 sets by Enzo Ferrari as Christmas gifts for his closest collaborators in the 1960's.
(Finarte) **$2,500**

1950 Alfa Romeo Alfetta Tipo 158, a diecast ashtray inscribed *Alfa Romeo Campione del Monde 1950, 11 Ciran Premi–11 Vittorie*, 7in. high.
(Christie's) **$1,000**

A poster designed by Paolo Cassa for the XXIV Mille Miglia Brescia, 11–12 May 1957, 70 x 100cm.
(Finarte) **$5,514**

Motoring Poster, 'Monaco, ler et 2 juin 1952', lithograph in colors by B. Minne, 48 x 31in.
(Christie's New York)
$8,250

A mid 18th century ivory netsuke of a snarling tiger, signed, 1³/₈in. high. *(Christie's)* **$33,000**

A finely patinated ivory netsuke of a magic fox dancing on its hind legs, the cord attachment formed by the tail, unsigned, 18th century, 11cm. *(Christie's)* **$11,165**

A pale boxwood netsuke of a long-haired mermaid with an infant at her breast, signed in an oval reserve *Kokei*, late 18th century, 4.6cm. *(Christie's)* **$4,235**

A finely lacquered group of seven netsuke formed as boy-dolls, four playing musical instruments, two holding lanterns, and one astride a hobby-horse, their kimono decorated in hiramakie, aogai and red, the head, hands and feet in shibuichi-ji, unsigned, 19th century, each approx. 5.4cm. high. *(Christie's)* **$18,420**

An ivory netsuke of a mermaid, the creature holding a shell, stained facial and scale detail, signed *Ren*, 19th century.
(Christie's) **$19,360**

An ebony netsuke depicting two South Sea Islanders struggling with a large piece of red coral, their eyes inlaid in ivory, the base with an inlaid red lacquer seal, probably Tomoe, 19th century, 5.7cm.
(Christie's) **$4,235**

Ivory netsuke of two skeletons wrestling, 19th century, signed *Gyokosai*, 2¹/₄in. high.
(Skinner) **$880**

An important wood netsuke of a foreigner standing with one hand on his head while holding a small dog in the other, his eyes inlaid in amber and the dog's in brass, his frock coat inlaid with silver buttons and with a large central decorative circular rivet passing through the body to a central ring attachment at the back, signed *Suzuki Katsusuke*, 18th century, 12.8cm.

The figure clearly represents a native servant from one of the Dutch Colonies, generally called Kurombo by the Japanese; his breeches and leggings appear to be Dutch 17th century but the frock-coat may be Chinese.
(Christie's) **$26,950**

Following the establishment of the porcelain factory at Meissen, the rulers of the other German states were anxious to set up their own ventures. One of the most successful was at Nymphenburg in Bavaria, where production began in 1753 and continues to the present.

The original factory was situated at Neudeck, under the patronage of the Bavarian Elector, who had married a granddaughter of Augustus the Strong, and it was transferred to Nymphenburg itself in 1761.

A Nymphenburg figure of a parrot modeled by Dominicus Auliczek, its plumage painted naturalistically in green, yellow, iron-red and blue, perched on a tree-stump with a rocky base applied with moss, impressed shield mark and ID to the plinth, circa 1765, 15.5cm. high.

(Christie's) **$8,000**

A Nymphenburg white figure of a beggar modeled by Franz Anton Bustelli, wearing tattered clothes, in a contra-posto pose holding out an empty tattered hat in his right hand, his bearded head turned to one side and his left arm resting on a staff, a sling about his shoulders containing a bowl and a spoon, circa 1760, 17cm. high.

(Christie's) **$40,000**

A George III ormolu perfume-burner by Matthew Boulton, the domed circular pierced lid with fruiting finial on an acanthus cap above bands of flowerheads and beading with spreading alternate anthemia and flowerheads, 10³/₄in. high.

The design of this perfume burner corresponds almost exactly with one illustrated in N. Goodison, Ormolu: The Work of Matthew Boulton. Goodison suggests that many perfume-burners were bought simply as ornaments in view of the lack of literary or pictorial evidence for the custom. They simply represented yet another element of the early 1770's passion for the Antique. However, Mrs. Montagu did write to Boulton asking for the return of a silver perfume-burner that she had lent him to examine 'for my friends reproach me that I do not regale their noses with fine odours after entertaining their palates with soup and ragouts. The cassolettes used to make their entry with the dessert and chase away the smell of dinner'.

(Christie's) **$19,470**

A Charles X ormolu surtout-de-table with circular mirrored plate, the pierced frieze cast with scrolling anthemia divided by three nozzles and three lyres above lion-masks on block feet cast with acanthus, the feet engraved on the underside *dun*, 28in. diameter.

(Christie's) **$15,850**

A pair of Empire mantel ornaments depicting Venus advised by Cupid, and Venus chastising Cupid, one with a robe, Venus sitting on a rock and a contrite Cupid, the other with a crouching Venus with Cupid with quiver, 13¹/₄in. high.

(Christie's) **$19,000**

325

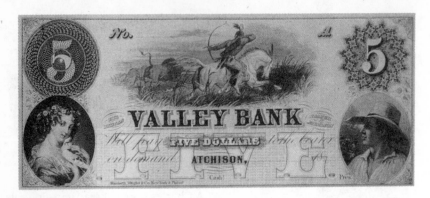

A Five-Dollar note from a unique uncut sheet of four banknotes printed for the Valley Bank of Atchison, Kansas, circa 1860.
(Christie's) **$34,100**

One of two surviving United Kingdom Treasury Notes, payable on demand for One Million Pounds, issued in London, 30 August 1948.

A few high denomination Treasury Notes, including a £10 million note, were issued in August 1948, for internal use as 'records of movement'. The large sums of money sent from the United States as part of the Marshall Aid Fund made these notes necessary, though they were in use for only six weeks. All but two of the notes were destroyed. It is believed that the two extant notes were officially canceled so that they could be given to the senior administrators of the fund as souvenirs.
(Christie's) **$45,322**

Bank of England Note, J.G.
Nairne: £5 21 February 1910
issued at Plymouth.
(Phillips)   **$7,750**

A Hawaiian Islands 500-Dollars banknote, undated (1879).
  One of three known examples.
(Christie's)

$22,000

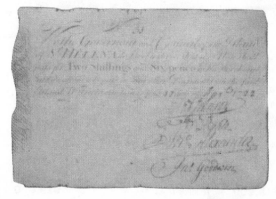

St Helena, 1722 2/6d issued
by The Governor and council
of the Island; the first paper
currency of St Helena was
produced in 1717 for a total
issue of £400. This note is
believed to be the only surviving
paper money of that period.
(Phillips London)

$8,855

A St. Louis cruciform millefiori carpet-ground weight, the central blue, green, white and red cogwheel with four radiating spokes of red-centered white canes edged with red and green twisted ribbon dividing the millefiori ground into triangular panels of colored canes, mid 19th century, 7.9cm. diameter.
(Christie's)　　　　　　　**$8,900**

'Grenouille', a Lalique amethyst-tinted glass paperweight modeled as a seated frog, 2³/₄in. high.
(Christie's)　　　　　　　**$8,600**

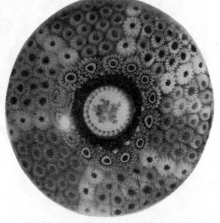

A Clichy spray-weight, the large purple flower with red and white center surrounded by yellow dots growing from a slender dark-green stalk with three green leaves, the pale pink bud with ribbed petals growing from a turquoise stalk with a single dark-green leaf, mid-19th century, 7cm. diameter.
(Christie's)　　　　　　　**$15,500**

A St. Louis dated paneled carpet-ground sulphide weight, the center with a circular sulphide medallion painted with a bouquet within a circle of green-centered pink and white canes, on a paneled ground of alternate pale-green and pink-centered white canes and including a cane inscribed *SL 1848*, 6.5cm. diameter.
(Christie's)　　　　　　　**$19,000**

Pearlware was the name given in 1780 by Josiah Wedgwood to a whitened version of his celebrated creamware which he had just developed successfully.

This was made by adding a touch of blue coloring to the body. It could be just as thin as porcelain, and formed an excellent background for blue printing, enabling it to compete favorably with Chinese wares. It was quickly adopted by many other potteries, and became extremely popular in the late 18th/19th centuries.

A pearlware toby-jug holding a frothing jug of ale, in blue, yellow and manganese jacket, circa 1790, 10in. high.

(Christie's S. Ken) **$2,150**

A Lakin & Poole pearlware group of the assassination of Marat, Charlotte Cordé standing holding a metal knife in her right hand, her high bonnet embellished with a green bow, her dress painted with scattered flower-sprays and dots and wearing a green underskirt and white apron tied at the waist with a gilt band and puce bow, the fallen figure of Marat with blood gushing from a wound to his left breast wearing turquoise-lined pale-lilac waistcoat and jacket, beige breeches and striped stockings, 35cm. high.
(Christie's) **$4,100**

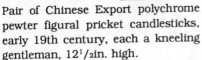

Pair of Chinese Export polychrome pewter figural pricket candlesticks, early 19th century, each a kneeling gentleman, 12¹/₂in. high.
(Skinner Inc) **$7,150**

A Liberty & Co. Tudric pewter clock designed by Archibald Knox, tapering rectangular form intersected with shaped rectangular panel, decorated with rectangular panels of abalone, circular dial with Roman chapters, stamped *Tudric*, circa 1902, 16.7cm. high.
(Christie's) **$2,700**

Pewter candlestick, England, circa 1675, octagonal bobeche over conforming ringed standard, medial drip pan and base, rubbed touch mark, 8¹/₂in. high.
(Skinner) **$7,700**

A pair of Liberty & Co. Tudric pewter twin-branched candelabra designed by Archibald Knox, each tapering square section central column with pierced decoration of leaves and berries on tendrils, similarly decorated curved arms and sconces with plain drip pans, 27.8cm. high.
(Christie's) **$3,250**

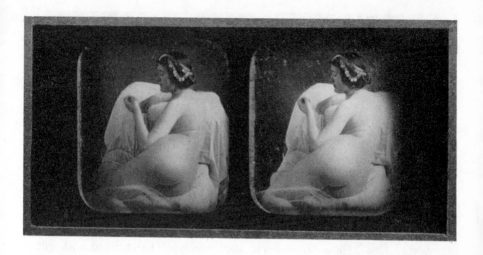

Reclining nude with gilt head-dress, 1850s, stereoscopic daguerreotype, hand-tinted, gilt highlights, paper-taped.
(Christie's) **$7,650**

Max Yavno, 'Muscle Beach Los Angeles', 1949, printed later, gelatin silver print, $7^7/8$ x $13^3/8$in., signed in pencil on the mount, titled in pencil on the reverse of the mount.
(Butterfield & Butterfield) **$4,400**

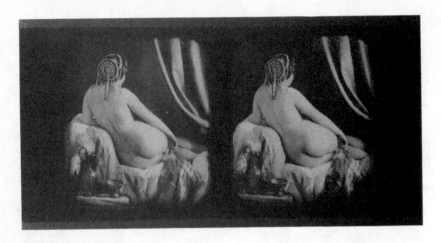

A very rare 1850's stereoscopic Daguerreotype, hand-tinted with gilt highlights, of a reclining nude, inspired by Ingres, by an anonymous photographer.
(Christie's) **$15,000**

Oscar Wilde, a head and shoulders portrait photograph, signed and inscribed *Bobbie, from his friend OW,* mounted on card, 9¹/₂ x 7¹/₄in.
(Christie's S. Ken) **$3,200**

El Lissitzky (Russian, 1890–1941), Pelikan Tinte, photomontage/photogram 1924, toned gelatin silver print, $8^3/8$ x $5^3/4$in.
(Christie's)

$132,000

Diane Arbus (American, 1923–1971), "A Jewish giant at home with his parents in the Bronx, N.Y.", 1970 gelatin silver print, $14^1/4$ x $12^7/8$in.
(Christie's)

$26,400

Reclining nude reading a book, 1850s, stereoscopic daguerreotype, hand-tinted, paper-taped.
(Christie's)   **$7,650**

Gustave Le Gray (1820–82), 'The Great Wave, Sète, 1856–59, albumen print from two negatives, 12³/₈ x 15¹/₂in., mounted on album leaf, titled *Rade de Cette* in ink on mount.

Le Gray exhibited his innovative seascapes to an ecstatic critical response in London at the Photograph Society in December 1856 and in Paris in 1857.
(Christie's)   **$31,000**

Lewis Carroll (The Reverend Charles Lutwidge Dodgson) (British, 1832–1898) Irene, 1863, oval albumen print, $8^3/_4$ x 7in.
(Christie's) **$19,305**

A cabinet card studio portrait of the young Winston Churchill in tropical uniform probably taken in Egypt prior to the Omdurman campaign, 1898, signed Winston, 8 x 5in.
(Christie's S. Ken) **$5,134**

An Art Deco Strohmenger baby grand piano and stool, in bleached burr walnut, the semi-circular body having three arches under solid supports meeting at the pedals, the double stool en suite.
(Phillips) **$13,400**

A Louis XV style parcel-gilt 'Vernis Martin' grand piano, by Erard, decorated by Lucien Simonnet, with a shaped top with a gadrooned edge above a conforming case carved with foliate scrolls on cabriole legs with foliate scrolling feet and casters, decorated overall with lovers in landscapes and putti, 56in. wide, 80in. long.
(Christie's, East)
$41,800

Pilkington's Tile and Pottery Co. was set up in 1892 at Clifton Junction Lancashire, to manufacture tiles, but from 1897 the production range was extended to include buttons, vases etc. Shortly afterwards the decoration of bought-in biscuit vases also began.

Opalescent glaze effects were discovered in 1903 and from then on the production of glazed earthenware known as Lancastrian pottery began. These wares, which consisted of vases, bowls, trays etc. were usually simple in shape, but decorated in a wide palette of colors often with a crystalline or opalescent effect.

The company was run by two brothers, William and Joseph Burton, who were both ceramic chemists and who were instrumental in developing the lustre decorated pottery which formed the bulk of the factory's 20th century production.

A Pilkington's Royal Lancastrian lustre vase decorated by Gordon Forsyth, painted in red and gold lustre with bands of tudor roses, 1915, 8¹/₂in. high.
(Christie's S. Ken)   **$665**

A large and important Pilkington Lancastrian lustre vase, painted by Gordon Forsyth to commemorate the Brussels International Exhibition of 1910 where the British and Belgian sections burned, depicting in vividly colored lustres, tangled metal amid flames, and two figures emblematic of Britannia and a muse of the Arts, 51cm. high.
(Phillips)   **$18,825**

A very rare French long wheel-lock holster pistol with slender two-stage barrel with a ribbed molding at the muzzle and stepped breech, the rear section fluted and struck with a mark, full-length border engraved tang, flat lock of French form with chamfered borders, walnut full stock engraved with birds, monsters, animals, fruit, flowers and foliage on a ground of brass wire scrolls and stars, circa 1600–10, probably Sedan, 32³/₄in. long. *(Christie's)* **$51,128**

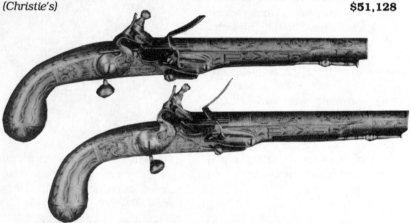

A pair of Scottish all steel flintlock belt pistols, 18.5cm. multi-stage barrels engraved with scrolls, scroll engraved locks signed *T. Murdoch*, steel stocks with lobe butts engraved with panels of scrolls, chevrons and waved decoration, and inlaid beneath with three bands of silver, the butts also inlaid with silver triangles and circles, complete with their turned and pierced steel ramrods, circa 1780. *(Phillips)* **$11,000**

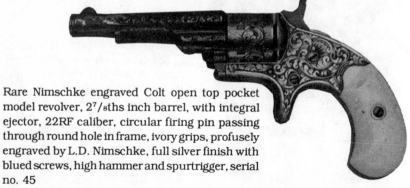

Rare Nimschke engraved Colt open top pocket model revolver, 2⁷/₈ths inch barrel, with integral ejector, 22RF caliber, circular firing pin passing through round hole in frame, ivory grips, profusely engraved by L.D. Nimschke, full silver finish with blued screws, high hammer and spurtrigger, serial no. 45

(Butterfield & Butterfield) **$7,700**

Rare factory cased and engraved Colt
new service D.A. revolver, caliber 45
Colt, 7^1/$_2$ inch barrel, nickel finish,
factory engraved with mother-of-pearl
grips bearing sunken Colt medallions,
lanyard ring on butt, left side of frame
inscribed *W.M.E. MARTIN/Malay
States/Forest Service*, serial no.
318072, made in 1923. Fitted in a
French style Colt factory leather case
lined in blue satin and velvet.
(Butterfield & Butterfield)

$12,100

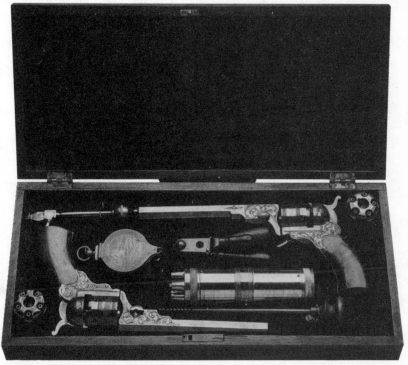

Pair of cased belt model Paterson revolvers (No. 2), Patent Arms Manufacturing
Company, circa 1837–40, serial no. 626 and 678, in untouched condition,
original fitted case with brass presentation plaque engraved *Abraham
Bininger*, barrel 5^1/$_2$in. long.

These revolvers were probably made for Abraham Bininger of New York
City.
(Skinner)   **$242,000**

Rare Colt model 1905 automatic pistol with combination holster/stock, caliber 45, seven shot magazine, 5 inch barrel, blued finish with case hardened rounded hammer, checkered walnut grips, serial no. 1892, shipped in 1908.

(Butterfield & Butterfield) **$17,600**

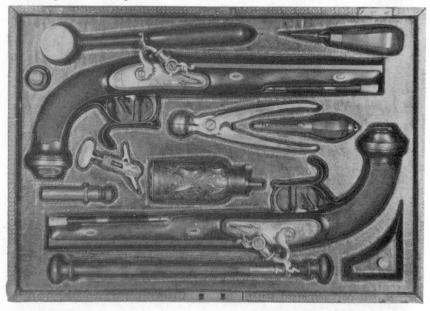

A rare pair of fulminate primed target or dueling pistols with probable royal connections, 24cm. sighted octagonal damascus barrels with micro-groove rifling, foliate engraved locks signed *Lehanne a Herve*, with tubular vents for the fulminate detonated by plungers in pivoted housings, double set triggers, full stocked, the checkered butts with gold shield shaped escutcheons.

(Phillips) **$9,900**

A fine and rare seven-barrel flintlock box-lock pepperbox revolver with hand-rotated turn-off barrels, engraved action signed within trophies of arms, engraved thumbpiece safety-catch retaining traces of original blued finish, rollers, engraved trigger-guard, and plain flat-sided figured walnut butt with chamfered sides, by John Twigg, London, circa 1781–87.
(Christie's) **$20,999**

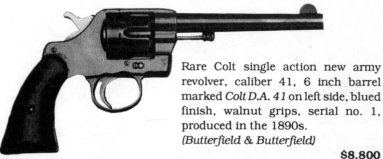

Rare Colt single action new army revolver, caliber 41, 6 inch barrel marked *Colt D.A. 41* on left side, blued finish, walnut grips, serial no. 1, produced in the 1890s.
(Butterfield & Butterfield)

$8,800

Cased Colt new police 'Cop and Thug' model revolver British proofed, 4 1/2 inch barrel with two line Pall Mall address, 38 CF caliber, rare nickel finish with blued hammer, checkered 'Cop and Thug' style hard rubber grips, serial no. 17879. Complete with original English oak casing with Colt label in lid, accessories include cleaning rod, screw driver, and cartridge block.
(Butterfield & Butterfield)
$6,050

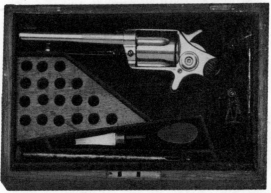

A pair of polychrome-painted plaster figures of Chinamen in court dress with nodding heads, both holding ceremonial staffs, one leaning forward, on integral simulated marble square bases, early 19th century, 15³/₄in. high.

In Johann Zoffany's portrait of Queen Charlotte of England, painted circa 1765, a pair of such chinoiserie figures appear in the background.

(Christie's) **$8,900**

A painted plaster-of-Paris bust of Thomas Edison, head and shoulders, signed *G. Tinworth 1888 and Doulton & Co., Lambeth*, the front inscribed *EDISON with Colonel Gouraud's compliments*, 22¹/₂in. high.

George Tinworth (1843–1913) was a wheelwright's son from Walworth who developed a natural talent for sculpture and whose first entry at the Royal Academy in 1866 was a plaster-of-Paris group.

Two other examples of the bust are known, one in the possession of the City of London Phonograph & Gramophone Society. Colonel Gouraud was Edison's British agent in the 1888–93 period, and the busts were presumably given to favored clients or sales representatives.

(Christie's) **$2,000**

'Butterfly dancers', a bronze and ivory group cast and carved from a model by Prof. Otto Poertzel, of two ballerinas dancing in formation, each poised on tip-toe, their costumes of gold patinated bronze and cold-painted red and green decoration, on octagonal green onyx plinth, signed in the bronze *Prof. Poertzel*, 41.5cm. high.
(Christie's) **$18,000**

Prince Charles Edward Stuart, the Young Pretender, 1736 enamel on copper by Jean-Etienne Liotard (1702–1789) oval, 2¹/₄in. high.
(Christie's)   **$125,000**

A portrait miniature by William Grimaldi (1751–1830), of Prince William of Gloucester, in gold figured blue coat with red collar and cuffs, the background with red curtain and pillar, oval, 4¹/₈in. high, in a chased gilt metal frame with ribbon cresting.
(Christie's)   **$10,000**

John Hoskins (fl. circa 1645), Lady Mary Glamham, in low-cut black dress trimmed with white lace and brooch at corsage, wearing pearl necklace and earrings, signed with initials and dated *1648*, oval, 2⁷/₈in. high.
(Christie's)

$35,838

Charles Henard (French, b.c.1757), 'The Comtesse de Valence with her elder daughter, Félicie', signed and dated 1790, circular, 31³/₄in. diameter.
(Christie's) **$15,500**

John Smart (British, 1742–1811), 'A Lady', signed with initials and dated 1788 and I for India, oval, 2³/₄in. high, in a gold hinged locket.
(Christie's) **$19,457**

A miniature portrait by Richard Cosway, R.A. (1742–1821) of a lady, possibly Lady Elizabeth Lindsay, facing right, in decolleté white and gold dress with frilled border, cloudy background, in the base of a gold locket, 2in. high.
(Christie's) **$26,000**

Art Deco found one of its most vivid expressions in the bronze and ivory, or chryselephantine, figures of F Preiss. Virtually nothing is known about Preiss, save that he was probably born in Vienna. Even his forename is in doubt, though an Ideal Home Exhibition Catalogue of the time refers to him as Frederick, which is probably simply an anglicisation of Friedrich. His work, which appeared in the 20s and 30s, was closely copied by one Professor Otto Poerzl of Coburg, so closely in fact that there has been speculation that they may be one and the same.

'The Archer', a bronze and ivory figure cast from a model by Ferdinand Preiss of a girl with drawn bow, in a gold-patinated tunic with train, with polychrome enameled sword and headdress, on a green onyx base with ivory bun feet, 22.3cm. high.
(Christie's)   **$10,500**

'Balancing', a cold-painted bronze and ivory figure, cast and carved from a model by Ferdinand Preiss, as a young woman wearing a green tinted bathing costume and silvered tights, she poses with arched back balancing an amber colored ball on an upraised hand, 38cm. high.
(Phillips)   **$12,800**

'Lighter than Air', a bronze and ivory figure, cast and carved from a model by Ferdinand Preiss, of a female figure poised holding a glass sphere above her head, wearing a silver patinated gown, mounted on a green and brown shaped onyx base, 33.5cm. high.
(Christie's) **$7,800**

'Cabaret girl', a bronze and ivory figure, cast and carved from a model by Ferdinand Preiss, of a dancing girl poised on tip-toe, with arms outstretched, wearing a green and silver-patinated costume and skull cap, on a green onyx plinth with faceted base, 38cm. high.
(Christie's) **$18,000**

'Torch Dancer' a bronze and ivory figure, cast and carved from a model by Ferdinand Preiss, of a dancing girl poised standing on one leg, her head thrown back and arms outstretched holding two flaming torches, wearing green and red patinated pantaloons with floral decoration, 41.5cm. high.
(Christie's) **$12,750**

'Autumn Dancer', a bronze and ivory figure, cast and carved from a model by Ferdinand Preiss, of a dancing girl poised on tip-toe with one leg raised before her, one hand above her head, wearing a bronze cold painted turban and a gold-pink short dress, 36cm. high.
(Christie's) **$14,000**

'Sonny Boy' a bronze figure, cast from a model by Ferdinand Preiss, of a boy standing with his hands in pockets, dressed in shorts, the underside of the feet with stamped founder's marks, mounted on an onyx and black and white marble striated base, 30.5cm. high.
(Christie's) **$2,750**

Deed for a parcel of land in West Brewster in the vicinity of Wing's Island. The deed is between the Sachem of Satucket and Governor Thomas Prence. Dated 1674. Signed by Prence and the Sachem. It has an assignment below from Prence to John Freeman, his son-in-law. The deed lists both Prence and William Bradford as purchasers. The signatures of Mark Snow, Jeremiah Howes, Jas. Noomaonk, Nen Manumut, John Freeman and Thomas Hinckley also are present either as witnesses or attestors. Hinckley and Prence both served as Governor. The Sachem and the other two Indians were all students of the Reverend Samuel Treat of Eastham. Mark Snow and John Freeman were both officers of the Plymouth Militia. Documents of this age, rarity and Cape Cod origin rarely, if ever, appear for public auction.
(Eldreds) **$3,520**

This collage is derived from the original watercolor of the Mozart family by Carmontelle in the Musée Carnavalet. The picture was painted during Wolfgang's first stay in Paris from November 1763 to April 1764 and depicts the seven-year-old prodigy at the harpsichord with his father playing the violin and his sister Marianne ('Nannerl') singing. Delafosse engraved the composition in 1764 and Leopold Mozart in a letter of 1st April 1764 wrote that he thought the painting was very well done.
(Christie's) **$6,750**

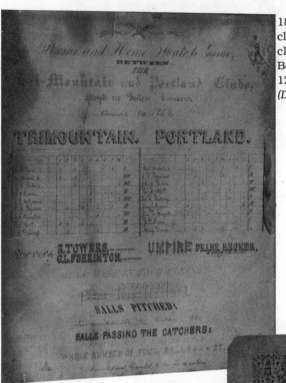

1859 Tri-mountain & Portland clubs very early professional club scorecard, played on Boston: commons, 15^1/$_4$in. x 12^1/$_4$in.
(Du Mouchelles)

$26,000

Large Mughal inlaid illustrated manuscript page, 17th/18th century, depicting a raja mounted on a prancing dappled steel and gesturing upwards to a maiden holding a golden vessel and seated in an ornate howdah on a richly caparisoned elephant guided by a female attendant perched on the top of its head, 24^3/$_4$ x 14^7/$_8$in.
(Butterfield & Butterfield)

$6,600

An unpublished original comic postcard by Donald McGill captioned *Everybody's Loved by Someone.*
(Henry Spencer)   **$1,400**

The first twelve amendments to the Constitution of the United States, printed by Bennett Wheeler (1754–1806), 15⅝ x 12¼in.

The two year political struggle to ratify the Constitution was particularly protracted in Rhode Island. By August of 1789, eleven states had ratified the Constitution and Rhode Island had refused to even call a convention. Following the adoption of the Constitution by North Carolina, Rhode Island alone remained intransigent and was in effect an independent republic. Pressure on the state's Anti-Federalists increased when Congress set January 15, 1790 as the date when economic sanctions against Rhode Island would begin. In an effort to appease the Anti-Federalists, Congress recommended twelve amendments to the Constitution for consideration by the state legislatures. A special session of the Rhode Island legislature ordered that 150 copies of the amendments, the future U.S. Bill of Rights, be printed and distributed to the towns for consideration. Of the 150 copies printed, this is the sixth known copy.
(Skinner)   **$7,700**

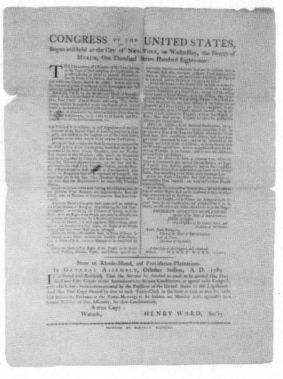

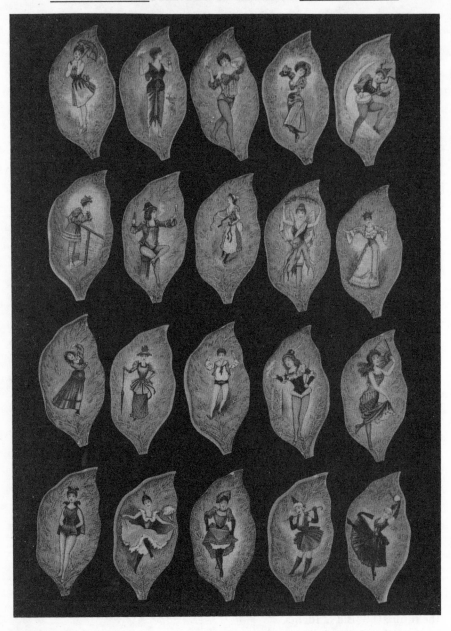

Wm. Clarke and Son, cigarette cards 'Tobacco leaf girls', the complete set of twenty cards, circa 1898.
(Phillips)   **$6,840**

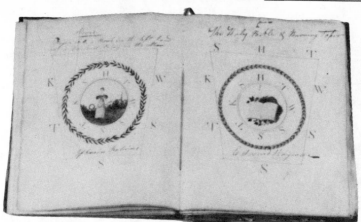

Masonic mark book, King Hiram Chapter of Greenwich Village and King Solomon's Chapter of Warren, Massachusetts, circa 1825, leather-bound with marbleized paper cover bearing fifty-three pages of Freemason names and marks, 8 x 6⁵/₈in.

A note accompanying the book inscribes 'From the names and marks in this book I believe it to be the books of Marks of King Hiram Chapter R.A.M. of Greenwich Village, Mass., which existed from about 1815 until about 1836. Some of the marks contained herein are also those of some of the Charter members of King Solomon's Chapter R.A.M. this book was a part of the properties of King Solomon's R.A. Chapter of Warren, Mass., John T. Jordan was a member of King Hiram Chapter and a charter member of King Solomon's Chapter. Jordan was born in 1799 and died their in 1879. He now rests in Quabbin Park Cemetery, Ware, Mass.'*(Skinner)* **$3,300**

An illustrated booklet by Phinehas Post, Connecticut, late 18th century, depicting several illustrations including a bird, Eve, a mermaid, a man, and a skeleton, all accompanied by poetic verse; two pages are folded to reveal another hidden drawing, watercolor and ink on paper, 4⁵/₈ x 3¹/₂in.

Phinehas Post was a resident of the Colony of Connecticut in the County of Wendham. There are deeds dating from, 1770, 1771 and 1772 documenting that Post was of age to buy land.
(Christie's) **$3,300**

Across the Continent. "Westward the Course of Empire Takes Its Way", by F.F. Palmer, lithograph with hand-coloring, 1868, on wove paper, the colors fresh, with wide margins, laid down on Japan, 17³/₄ x 27¹/₄in.
(Christie's) **$14,300**

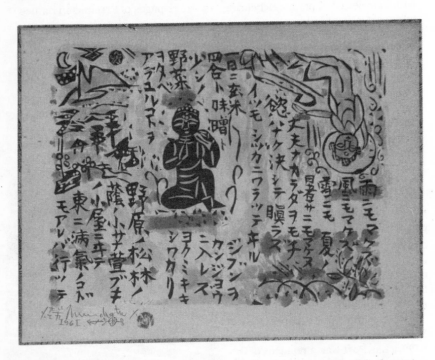

Munakata Shiko (1903–1975): One hand-colored Japanese woodblock print entitled 'Ame ni mo makezu', featuring a pair of bodhisattva figures in an abbreviated landscape setting superimposed with a long poetic passage, the bottom left margin dated 1961 and signed Shiko, dimensions of print 14¹/₂in. x 19in.
(Butterfield & Butterfield) **$17,600**

Life in the Woods. "Returning to Camp", by L. Maurer, lithograph with hand-coloring and touches of gum arabic, 1860, on wove paper, with margins, $18^{13}/_{16}$ x $27^3/_4$in.
(Christie's) **$3,300**

Andy Warhol-Marilyn-silkscreen, printed in colors, 1967, signed in pencil and stamp numbered 75/250 on reverse, published by Factory Addition, New York, the full sheet printed to the edges, the colors bright; in good condition apart from four spots at each corner being rubbed, 36in. x $35^7/_8$in.
(Christie's) **$46,000**

'Semaine d'Aviation du Lyon, du 7 au 15 Mai 1910', lithograph poster in colors, by Charles Tichon, printed by Emile Pecaud, Paris, some soiling, backed on linen, 61¹/₂ x 46in.
(Christie's) **$5,291**

'The American National Game of Base Ball. Grand Match for the Championship at the Elysian Fields, Hoboken, N.J.', lithograph with hand-coloring, 1866, on wove paper, with margins, 19³/₄ x 29³/₄in.
(Christie's) **$16,500**

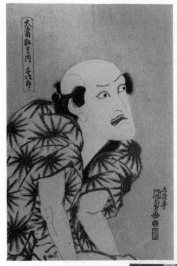

An okubi-e portrait of the actor
Nakamura Utaemon III in the role of
the monkey trainer Yojiro, woodblock
print, 15³/₈ x 10¹/₂in.
(Christie's) **$143,000**

Henri de Toulouse-
Lautrec, Le Divan
Japonais, lithograph
printed in colors,
1892–3, on buff wove
paper, a fine
impression, the colors
good and strong, with
margins or printed to
the edge of the sheet as
published, generally in
very good condition
and without the
backing or creases that
one usually associates
with impressions of
this print, 800 x
622mm.
(Christie's)
$56,750

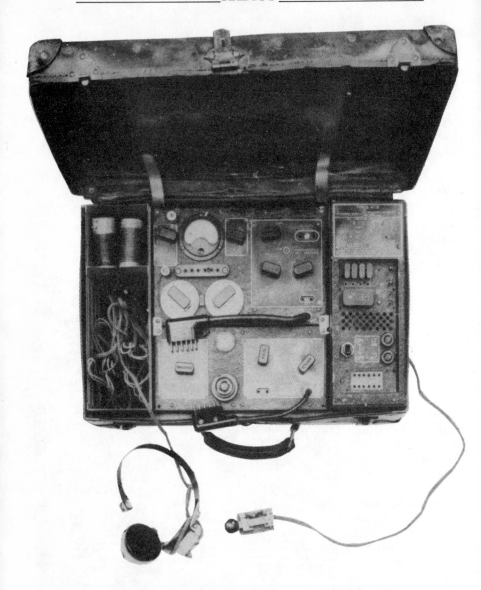

An S.O.E. agent's suitcase wireless receiver/transmitter with earphones and tap key, the millboard suitcase (into which it is built) measuring $16^1/2$in. x $12^1/2$in.

This model (in use from 1943 onwards) had the advantage of almost instantaneous conversion from mains to battery power to avoid a tell-tale break in transmission if the mains were cut by security forces.

(Christie's) **$2,167**

A Marconiphone Multivalve Type RB7 receiver in smoker's cabinet style mahogany case with BBC transfer and doors enclosing three control panels marked *M.W.T. Co.*, 20¹/₂in. high, circa 1923.
(Christie's)   **$6,500**

A radiogram television incorporating Baird Televisor with disk and valve in upper two tiers, the base containing speaker, electric turntable and pick-up in drawer and Alba radio receiver, in mahogany cabinet, 54in. high.
(Christie's)   **$3,500**

Lucie Rie (b.1902) is an Austrian artist potter who trained under Powolny in Vienna. In 1938 she came to the UK as a refugee from Nazism and opened a button factory in a London mews, where she was joined by fellow refugee Hans Coper.

Her early pre-war work had consisted of simple, thinly potted stoneware, sometimes polished or covered with rough textured glazes, her style influenced both by functionalist ideals and by Roman pottery. Her mark at this time was a painted *LRG* over *Wien*.

An exceptionally fine bronze porcelain vase by Lucie Rie, with reddish brown shoulder and inner rim, LR seal, circa 1972, 9¹/₂in. high.
(Bonhams)   **$4,900**

A superb porcelain bowl by Lucie Rie, uranium yellow with deep bronze running band at rim, impressed seal, circa 1975, 7in. diameter.
(Bonhams)   **$12,120**

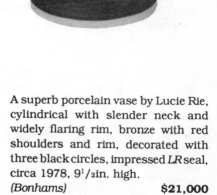

A porcelain inlaid sgraffito bowl by Lucie Rie, covered in a pink glaze between two bands of turquoise, the rim and foot covered in a lustrous bronze glaze, circa 1980, 18.2cm. diameter.

(Christie's) **$5,000**

A rare porcelain bowl by Lucie Rie, the white glazed exterior inlaid with small brown circles each with a dot, circa 1968, 5in. diameter.

(Bonhams) **$6,650**

A superb porcelain vase by Lucie Rie, cylindrical with slender neck and widely flaring rim, bronze with red shoulders and rim, decorated with three black circles, impressed *LR* seal, circa 1978, 9¹/₂in. high.

(Bonhams) **$21,000**

Rare iron frame Henry rifle, caliber 44 RF, 24 inch barrel with fifteen shot tubular magazine, cleaning rod in butt, blued finish, walnut stock, serial no. 192.

Only about 300 Henrys were produced with iron frames.

(Butterfield & Butterfield) **$34,100**

Volcanic carbine, manufactured by New Haven Arms Company, caliber 38, 16$^1/_2$ inch octagonal barrel, blued finish, unengraved brass frame and butt plate, walnut stock, case hardened hammer, blued lever, serial no. 86.

(Butterfield & Butterfield) **$23,100**

Rare Winchester 'One of One Hundred' model 1873 rifle, caliber 44–40, 24$^1/_2$ inch octagon barrel, first type with mortised dust cover, engraved and banded on breech and muzzle, top of barrel engraved *One of One Hundred*, deluxe checkered stock and forearm, crescent butt plate, nickeled frame with blue barrel and case hardened lever, hammer, and butt plate, serial no. 19,001, made in 1876.

With factory letters and documents pertaining to the early history of the gun. Only eight manufactured.

(Butterfield & Butterfield) **$60,500**

Winchester model 1876 rifle, second model, caliber 50 express (50–95), 26 inch round barrel with half magazine, blued finish, case hardened frame, forecap and lever, checkered deluxe stock and forearm, shot gun butt, standard address, serial no. 9901, made in 1880.
(Butterfield & Butterfield)   **$16,500**

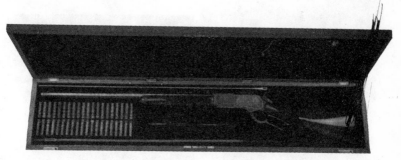

Gzowski Presentation Model 1876 Winchester from the John R. Woods Collection.
(Butterfield & Butterfield)   **$517,000**

Rare Colt double rifle, caliber 45–70, 28 inch round side by side barrels, double trigger and double hammer, case hardened frame, hammers and butt plate with brown damascus finish on barrels, oil stained checkered walnut stock and forearm, blued trigger guard, lever and rear and front sight, special hinged rear sight and typical front sight, engraved on frame, trigger guard and hammers, shot gun type butt plate, serial no. 24.
(Butterfield & Butterfield)   ₤·   **$20,900**

A Netherlandish large roemer of light-green tint, the convex bowl supported on a hollow cylindrical stem applied with four rows of raspberry-prunts, on a high trailed conical foot with a kick-in base, mid-17th century, 26cm. high.
(Christie's) **$11,000**

A Netherlandish green-tinted large roemer, the ovoid bowl merging into a hollow cylindrical stem applied with raspberry prunts beneath a milled band, with high kick-in base and on a narrow spun foot, 17th century, 26cm. high.
(Christie's) **$10,700**

The foundation of the Rookwood pottery in 1880 received enormous publicity because it was established by a Cincinnati society lady, Maria Longworth Nichols. Its initial aim was to produce a better art pottery rather than commercial success, but in 1883 William Taylor, a friend of Mrs Nichols, was appointed manager, and he both extended the range of designs and organised a distribution network on sound commercial lines.

Two Rookwood Pottery tiger eye vases, Kataro Shirayamadani, Cincinnati, Ohio, exhibited at the Universal Exposition in Paris, 1900, elongated baluster form with incised underglaze decoration of cranes in flight, shades of brown and gold, with an original paper label incorporating a kiln logo and the *Rookwood Pottery*, 14^1/2in. high.
(Skinner) **$3,000**

Rookwood Pottery scenic vellum plaque, Cincinnati, Ohio, 1914, executed by Edward George Diers, (1896–1931), rectangular with scene of a forest clearing in shades of blue, brown, sea green and cream, 10^3/4in. high
(Skinner) **$1,600**

A Rookwood standard glaze pottery Indian portrait vase, decorated by Grace Young, date cypher for 1905, 30.5cm. high.
(Skinners) **$5,250**

Konya area prayer rug, Central Anatolia, mid 19th century, (small areas of restoration), 5ft. 2in. x 3ft. 8in.
(Skinner Inc.) **$14,000**

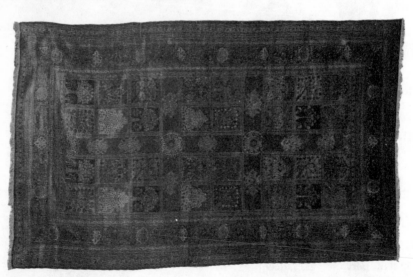

An antique silk Tabriz garden carpet, 196 x 118in.
(Christie's) **$55,440**

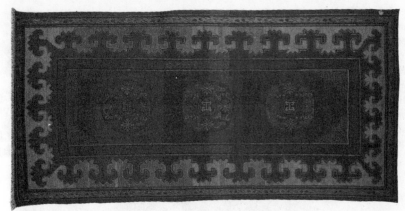

A Yarkand corridor carpet, circa 1800, 148 x 71in.
(Christie's East)   **$143,000**

'The Kinsale', a Liberty hand-knotted woollen Donegal carpet, the turquoise
field of checkered design with stylized pink and yellow rose flowerheads and
leaves, alternated with green thorned stems, in a mauve border with similar
running rose and stem design between plain and scolloped strips, (circa
1903), 455cm. x 346cm. *(Christie's)*   **$32,010**

Grenfell hooked rug, Grenfell Labrador Industries, Labrador, circa 1925, worked in shades of coral, green, red, yellow, lavender and gray on black ground, bears fabric label and string tag printed *Made in Labrador International Grenfell Association*, 25³/₄ x 39¹/₂in. (Skinner) **$3,400**

An antique Saryk bridal Asmalyk, 19th century, the background piled with a mixture of two shades of ivory wool is decorated with rows of stylized lilies depicted in indigo-blue and madder-red, 2ft. 9in. x 4ft. 8in.

Only three examples of this rare type of Turkoman artefact have been published to date. (Phillips) **$35,600**

Inscribed pictorial hooked rug, America, 20th century, worked in shades of beige and gray on a polychrome ground, inscribed *The sands of time are running low soon to my maker I must go – I have no fear tho worried be what I will say to my husbands*, 35 x 48in. (Skinner) **$2,750**

Sir Sydney Gordon Russell (b. 1892) was a famous English furniture designer and master craftsman, who established the Russell Workshops in Broadway, Worcs. making machine made versions of such traditional English designs as rush-seated, ladder backed chairs.

He specialized in the use of English woods such as oak and yew with the wood grain emphasising the linear design. From c 1930 onwards his work had a major influence on the styles of the 50s and 60s.

A good Gordon Russell English walnut yew and ebony bureau bookcase, the paneled doors inlaid with yew banding and ebony stringing and enclosing shelves, the drop front enclosing compartments and drawers with two half drawers and three full drawers below similarly inlaid, with ebony pulls, 1.9m. high.
(Phillips) **$10,750**

An oak blanket chest designed by Gordon Russell, slim rectangular shape, the lid with three wrought-iron strap hinges terminating in 'fleur-de-lys', with carved borders top and bottom, supported on six flat rectangular section legs, with original paper label, dated *20.6.27*, 70cm. high, 166.5cm. wide. *(Christie's)* **$8,000**

A saltglaze effect is achieved by glazing during the firing with salt thrown into the kiln at a temperature above 2,000°F, where it combines chemically with the silicate in the clays to form a durable sodium silicate glaze which has the orange-peel appearance associated with Chinese porcelain.

Most early saltglaze ware is coarse and brown, but after the 1740s, when Staffordshire potters had achieved a light white stoneware body comparable in delicacy and durability with Chinese porcelain, the process was also used very successfully with this.

Later it was also colored with enamels.

A Staffordshire saltglaze white figure of Zhongli Quan, the bearded Immortal holding a fan and a peach, wearing an open long-sleeved coat revealing his grotesque paunch, the lower part of his tunic tied with a girdle elaborately knotted and tasseled, circa 1750, 18.5cm. high.
(Christie's)   **$13,000**

A Staffordshire saltglaze polychrome baluster jug with strap handle, painted with a figure and buildings in a landscape vignette within a lobed puce feuilles-de-choux and foliate cartouche below the spout inscribed with the initials *REC* and with scattered insects, circa 1760, 22cm. high.
(Christie's)   **$12,400**

A Staffordshire saltglaze Admiral Lord Vernon commemorative mug, the cylindrical body with slightly spreading foot molded in relief with the Royal Arms of England with the initials *GR* above and a winged cherub's head below, the reverse with a standing figure of Admiral Vernon and a townscape with battle-ships in the foreground, circa 1740, 19cm. high. *(Christie's)*   **$17,350**

A Staffordshire saltglaze scratch-blue dated two-handled cup of flared form with strap handles, each side incised with trailing flowering branches and with the initials *H:W.* above the date *1756*, 30.5cm. wide.
(Christie's)   **$22,750**

A Staffordshire saltglaze polychrome globular punch pot, with green crabstock handle and foliage molded spout, circa 1760, 19cm. high overall. *(Christie's)* **$8,000**

A Staffordshire saltglaze bear-jug and cover, its head forming the cover and with pierced snout suspending linked chain, a young bear suspended between its forepaws, its collar, eyes, forepaws and the young bear enriched in dark-brown spots, circa 1750, 21cm. long.
(Christie's) **$2,950**

A rare Staffordshire white saltglaze camel teapot and cover, the seated animal with a buckled saddlecloth and a howdah molded in relief with a standing figure of a camel and a tree, the handle in the form of a scaly fish, the fluted cover with flammiform finial, 14.5cm. high.
(Christie's) **$4,300**

Needlework sampler, "Anna Brynbèrgs work done in the Eleventh Year of Her Age 1795", Philadelphia, Pennsylvania, worked with silk threads in shades of blue, green, yellow, peach, cream and black on a gauze ground, 15¹/₄ x 17¹/₂in.
(Skinner) **$5,500**

Rare needlework sampler, worked by Sally Johnson Age 12, Newburyport, Massachusetts, 1799, one of a small and important group of samplers worked in Newburyport from 1799–1806, this needlwork is the most complex of the known examples with central panel of alphabets, verse and signature cartouche enclosed by vignettes of gentry in various pursuits, some attended by black servants, and servants tending fields of sugar cane, 19 x 27in.

Sarah (Sally) Johnson was born March 25, 1787, the second child of Nicholas and Mary Perkins Johnson in the family's large brick home at the corner of Federal and Mill Streets. Sally's father, Nicholas Johnson (b. 1752), was a very prosperous merchant, as well as a ship master in partnership with John Newmarch Cushing. Mr. Johnson traded with Russia, India, the Far East and the West Indies, his travels possibly inspiring some of the tropical motifs in his daughter's sampler. Sally Johnson married John Chickering on January 30, 1812 and died December 14, 1868.
(Skinner) **$33,000**

From the 16th century pottery was made at Kagoshima (formerly Satsuma) prefecture in Japan. Korean potters provided the early inspiration - the main kilns at Naeshirogawa and Ryumonji were developed under them, and early pieces are notably Korean or Chinese in style.

From the 18th century however, Satsuma ware is essentially a hard, gray-white or vellum colored earthenware with a crackle glaze, which is embellished with extravagant gilding and enameling. It was introduced to the West at the Universal Exhibition in Paris in 1867.

A very large Satsuma vase decorated in various colored enamels and gilt, with two elegantly decorated carts in formal garlands of chrysanthemums, wild pinks and bamboo fences, the shoulders with a continuous brocade design interspersed with mon and dragons, the neck and base with floral lappets, late 19th century, 61.5cm. high.
(Christie's) **$38,500**

A Satsuma figure of Kannon decorated in various colored enamels and gilt, the seated divinity wearing an elaborate necklace and robes decorated with swirling cloud, mon and lozenge design, in her left hand a lotus, her elaborate headdress with a central Buddha, signed *Yasukyo saku*, late 19th century, 61.5cm. high.
(Christie's) **$8,700**

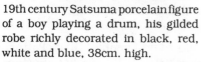

19th century Satsuma porcelain figure of a boy playing a drum, his gilded robe richly decorated in black, red, white and blue, 38cm. high.
(Finarte)   **$5,726**

Fine Kinkozan Satsuma vase, 19th century, signed *Dai Nihon Kinkozan*, tapering globular form, reserves of eight immortals and samurai, diaper and medallion borders, 15in. high.
(Skinner)   **$9,500**

A fine and large Satsuma oviform jar and cover decorated in various colored enamels and gilt with three shaped panels depicting flowering shoots of peony and chrysanthemum, the panels bordered by boldly sweeping harp-shaped patterns accommodating birds, flowers and foliage, the foot with a band of lappets, signed *Nihon Satsuma, Kinran Toki, Tokozan zo*, late 19th century, 52.5cm. high.
(Christie's)   **$69,350**

This intriguing title (*SEG* is the usual mark) is found on the products of the Paul Revere Pottery, which was set up at the beginning of the 20th century for the purpose of training girls from poor immigrant families in Boston. The profits from the pottery were used to fund the girls' education in other subjects. The output mainly consisted of earthenware, nursery and breakfast bowls and dishes and these were decorated with birds, flowers or mottoes, often around the borders. The name Saturday Evening Girls Club is something of a misnomer, since the potters worked eight hours a day.

Saturday Evening Girls Pottery bowl, green glazed half-round with sgraffito interior border of yellow nasturtium blossoms outlined in black below, 8¹/₂in. diameter.
(Skinner)   **$935**

Saturday Evening Girls Pottery decorated motto pitcher, Boston, Massachusetts, early 20th century, with incised and painted band of rooster decoration above the words *Oh. Up. In. The. Morning. Early. That. Is The Way. Quite. Clearly*, black and white on turquoise ground, 9³/₄in. high.
(Skinner)   **$2,200**

Saturday Evening Girls pottery decorated bowl, Boston, Massachusetts, 1913, executed by Sara Galner, exterior with incised and painted band of daffodils in shades of yellow, green, brown, and blue on green ground.
(Skinner)   **$9,250**

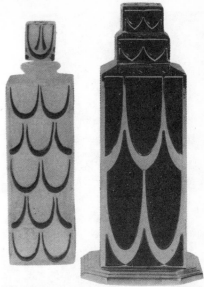

'Pluie D'Or, a Baccarat enameled clear bottle for A. Gravier, of triangular section, enameled in black, orange, green and yellow with flower sprays, with triangular domed stopper, 5³/₄in.
(Bonhams) **$7,250**

'Le Nouveau Gardenia', a Lalique clear glass perfume bottle and stopper, for Coty, of tapering hexagonal form, intaglio molded to each facet with a fairy clutching at a long stemmed flower, her gossamer wings extending to the base, heightened with green staining, 13.6cm. high.
(Phillips) **$4,500**

'Parfum A', a black enameled frosted bottle for Lucien Lelong, of square section, each side molded with black enameled swags, 4¹/₈in. high.
(Bonhams) **$8,000**

'Fougères', a Lalique clear glass scent bottle and stopper, of rectangular outline molded in relief to the one side with an oval green stained panel centered with the head and shoulders of a woman in floral gown, to the reverse with a maiden inhaling the scent of a flower, enclosed by fern leaves heightened with green staining, 9.2cm. high.
(Phillips) **$9,400**

'La Joie D'Aimer', a Baccarat enameled clear bottle for A. Gravier, of octagonal form, with swollen neck, enameled in black and orange with an abstract pattern, the angular gray-stained stopper molded with foliage, 5^1/$_8$in.
(Bonhams) **$2,400**

A Chelsea gold-mounted scent-bottle and stopper modeled as a cat with brown fur-markings, seated erect with a mouse in its mouth, its head forming the stopper, the oval domed base painted with flowers, circa 1755, 6.5cm. high.
(Christie's) **$3,950**

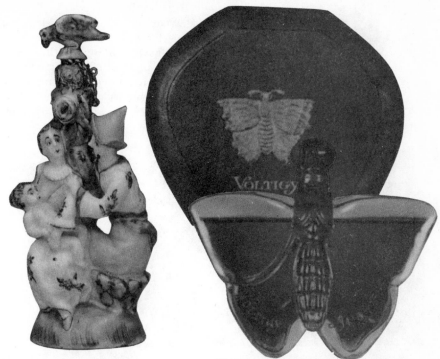

A gold-mounted scent-bottle and stopper of 'Girl in a Swing' type modeled as a Chinese family with a Chinaman embracing a Chinese lady holding an infant, their clothes painted with flowers and he wearing a yellow conical hat and trousers, seated to either side of a tree-stump applied with a pink rose and foliage, circa 1755, 9cm. high.
(Christie's) **$5,500**

'Voltigy', a Baccarat clear bottle for A. Gravier, modeled as a butterfly with outstretched wings, the body stained in pink and black, molded with *Voltigy A. Gravier*, 3⅝in.
(Bonhams) **$30,000**

A gold-mounted pug scent-bottle and stopper of 'Girl in a Swing' type, naturally modeled as a seated pug bitch with black fur-markings, on a domed oval base painted with pink roses, stamped gold mounts, circa 1755, 6.5cm. high.
(Christie's) **$5,900**

'Me Voici', a Baccarat enameled clear bottle for A. Gravier, of shoe form, with faceted stopper, the bottle enameled in green, blue, orange and yellow with Egyptianesque floral patterns, 4in. wide.
(Bonhams) **$10,500**

'Quatre Soleils', a Lalique amber-tinted scent bottle and stopper, the angular bulbous body molded with four chrysanthemum flowerheads each with gold foil backing, 7.2cm. high.
(Christie's) **$28,000**

A Chelsea gold-mounted peach scent-bottle and stopper naturally modeled and colored, the neck and stopper formed as a branch with leaves, stamped gold mounts, circa 1755, 7cm. high.
(Christie's) **$8,250**

'Malice', a Baccarat enameled clear bottle for A. Gravier, of squared baluster form, the grooved edges enameled in blue, the front enameled in black, the blue-edged square stopper molded with red ladybird on grasses, 4³/₈in.

(Bonhams) **$3,000**

'Hantise', a Baccarat black enameled pink opaque bottle for A. Gravier, of multi-faceted ovoid form, with gilt metal bullet-shaped stopper and circular foot, the body enameled with a scales design and flower sprays, 4⁵/₈in.

(Bonhams) **$6,000**

A George II mahogany and needlework cheval fire-screen with rectangular rising panel inset with a petit point needlework scene depicting The Rape of Proserpine in a chariot, framed by flowering foliage and strapwork backed by pale green watered silk, 32in. wide. *(Christie's)* **$107,000**

A painted four-leaf screen decorated with a scene in the manner of Francis Barlow of a spaniel and a goose arguing in an idyllic pastoral landscape with other birds, a cottage and a ruin surmounted by a cockerel, in a molded grained surround, the reverse green-painted, each leaf $86^{1}/_{4}$in. x $26^{1}/_{2}$in. *(Christie's)* **$13,550**

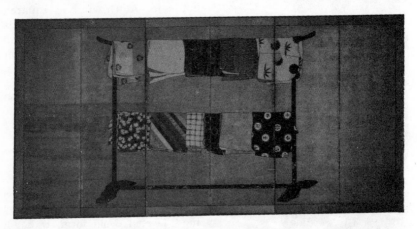

One of a superb pair of Chinese six-leaf screens, painted in sumi, color and gofun on gold painted silk, with Ta ga sode 'Whose sleeves?' motif, one with folded robes on a rack and the other with three robes hung on a rack, unsigned, each leaf 174.3cm. x approx. 60cm. *(Christie's)* **$100,000**

A Regency mahogany and parcel-gilt hall-seat, the scrolled back carved with acanthus and centered by a heart-shaped cartouche with the arms of the Langham family with the motto Nec Sinit Esse Fero, flanked by boars' heads above a bed of acanthus scrolls and anthemia, 94in. wide.
(Christie's) **$33,000**

An Italian gray-painted settle, the arched back painted with putti and a winged angel with a horn supporting an armorial cartouche, with a sun above a tower headed by a coronet, flanked by acanthus scrolls, with solid molded seat and shaped apron painted with putti flanking a flower-filled urn flanked by drapery swags and acanthus scrolls, late 17th century, 84in. wide.
(Christie's) **$25,750**

A walnut and burr walnut double chair-back settee with waved toprail and vase-shaped splats headed by scallop shells, the out-scrolled arms with eagle's-head terminals, with bowed padded seat covered in pale blue florally-patterned damask, on cabriole legs headed by lion's-masks, and claw feet, early 18th century, 57¹/₂in. wide.

(Christie's) **$8,150**

A George III beechwood sofa in the style of Thomas Chippendale, the hump-back, sides and double bowed seat covered in faded chintz, the channeled frame carved with husks and with ribbon-tied cresting, the fluted seat-rail with patera, on six stop-fluted turned tapering legs carved with long leaves and headed by paterae, 53in. wide.

The overall shape, particularly the arm-supports and the use of cramp cuts, are all features that can be found on the documented work of Thomas Chippendale. *(Christie's)* **$14,500**

Porcelain production began at Sèvres in 1756 when the Vincennes factory was moved there, and the first 14 years of its output are considered by many to be unsurpassed.

At first, a soft paste porcelain was made, with silky glazes and richly ornate decoration. It was hugely expensive to make, however, and had the further disadvantage that it could not be molded into complex shapes, which tended to fracture in the kiln. Nevertheless, it was dear to the heart of Louis XV, who was wholly responsible for funding the operation, and his mistress Mme de Pompadour. He assisted it further by issuing several decrees granting virtual monopolies in favor of Sèvres, and even acted as salesman in chief, holding annual exhibitions at Versailles and selling off the pieces to his court.

Sèvres products are remarkable for their brilliant ground colors and chemists were constantly at work developing new tones.

A Sèvres oval plaque painted by Pauline Laurent after F.X. Winterhalter with a three-quarter length portrait of Queen Victoria in ceremonial regalia standing in an interior before a window and an orange curtain trimmed with yellow tassels, circa 1858, 7^1/2in. high.
(Christie's) **$7,600**

A pair of Louis XV ormolu-mounted Sèvres bleu nouveau pots-pourri en forme de limaçon, each in the shape of a snail shell with circular slightly domed lid with spiral molding surmounted by seashells, with pierced key-pattern collar, circa 1763–68, 6^1/2in. wide.
(Christie's) **$17,500**

A pair of gilt-metal-mounted Sèvres-pattern two-handled vases and covers of tapering oviform, painted by Desprez with battle scenes, one showing armies confronting each other across a plain, the other with a battle skirmish, the scenes continuing to show châteaux on the reverses, the covers enriched with crowns, mounted with pine-cone finials, one cover with imitation gilt interlaced L and Sèvres mark, late 19th century.

(Christie's) **$40,172**

A gilt-metal-mounted Sèvres-pattern tapering oviform vase and cover painted by J. Pascault with a continuous bacchanalian scene of a maiden seated before a distant forest, squeezing grapes into a goblet, wearing a white robe and a lilac drape, with a cherub beside her and three cherubs overhead holding grapes and pink drapery, late 19th century, $58^{1}/_{4}$in. high.

(Christie's) **$13,695**

A pair of Sèvres gilt-metal-mounted green-ground tapering-oviform vases and covers with white and gilt solid strap handles, the bodies painted in the style of Boucher with young girls in extensive gardens, one dancing as she plays a tambourine, the other standing barefoot and holding a basket of flowers, iron-red printed marks and date codes for 1862, $14^{1}/_{2}$in. high.

(Christie's) **$3,650**

A large Sèvres porcelain vase, designed by Emile Decoeur, decorated by P. Gaucher, with a narrative frieze of mermaids, nereids and sea creatures in tones of blue and green, 50cm. high.

(Christie's) **$11,000**

A composite garniture of three large gilt-metal mounted Sèvres-pattern vases and covers of slender tapering oviform, the white grounds painted by J. Pascault in a pale palette with maidens seated attended by cherubs in shaded wooded landscapes, one vase with the figures studying musical scores, she leaning against a vase of flowers on a stone table and wearing a diaphanous white fichu, a turquoise skirt and with roses tumbling over her lap, the rims cast with bands of leaves and on beaded shaped-square feet, late 19th century, 60³/₄in. high.

(Christie's) **$58,432**

Shaker turned bowl with mustard wash, probably Harvard, Massachusetts, late 19th century. 9 in. diameter.
(Skinner) **$8,250**

Painted Shaker armed rocker, New Lebanon, New York, circa 1830.
(Skinner) **$12,100**

Yellow painted oval Shaker carrier, probably Harvard, Massachusetts, late 19th century, three fingered box with carved handle.
(Skinner) **$6,600**

Shaker cherry ministry dining table, probably Enfield, New Hampshire or Harvard, Massachusetts, first half 19th century, the cherry two-board scrubbed top above an arched maple base with original red wash, and carved maple feet, 84 in. long.
(Skinner) **$82,500**

Shaker iron stove, probably Harvard, Massachusetts, circa 1800, the lift lid above a base with canted corners on cabriole legs ending in wrought penny feet.
(Skinner) **$4,675**

Shaker maple armed rocker, New Lebanon, New York, circa 1850, old splint seat over-upholstered, 44³/₄ in. high.
(Skinner) **$10,450**

Shaker painted pine washstand, Harvard, Massachusetts, 19th century, the hinged lid opens to a storage compartment above a cupboard with two half-shelves; all over original red wash, 36in. wide.
(Skinner) **$11,000**

A George III mahogany extending serving-table with rectangular breakfront top, the frieze carved with a rosette edged with fluting flanked by flowerhead swags and fluttering ribbons with foliate lower border, on tapering legs headed by urns and interrupted with roundels, 108³/₄in. wide.
(Christie's) **$87,600**

A George III mahogany sideboard banded overall in tulipwood and inlaid with ebonized and boxwood stringing, the bowed top centered by an oval and enclosing a shelf, above a concave-fronted section simulated as two doors between concave-fronted pilasters flanked by a bowed door to each side inlaid with an oval, 51in. wide.
(Christie's) **$17,500**

A Shapland and Petter oak sideboard, the rectangular cornice overhanging a central reserve decorated with a copper relief panel of stylized flowers above shelf, 228cm. wide.
(Christie's) **$9,000**

A George III mahogany bowfronted sideboard with a mahogany-lined drawer in the arched center flanked by oval-inlaid cupboard door on the left and a cellarette drawer on the right, with a secret compartment at the back, banded with rosewood on square tapering legs, 60^{1}/₄in. wide.
(Christie's) **$25,000**

Carved and painted mermaid tavern sign, America, 19th century, 22in. long.
(Skinner) **$3,190**

A carved and painted cigar store Indian, American, late 19th century, carved in the form of an Indian princess with a gold feather headdress above long groove-carved black hair and carved gold earrings over a polychrome carved dress and cape, the figure grasping a knife and bundle of cigars, standing on a tapering box base, 72¹/₂in. high.
(Christie's) **$13,200**

Carved and painted tavern figure of King Gambrinis, America, 19th century, 26¹/₂in. high.
(Skinner) **$2,860**

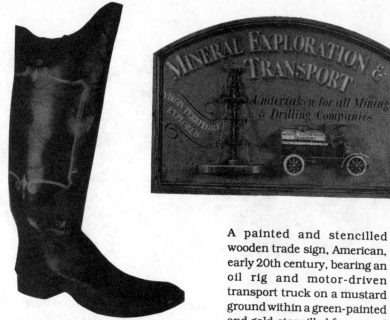

Painted and decorated rubber trade sign, Ales Goodtear Shoe Co., Nagatuck, Connecticut, late 19th century, painted red and enhanced with white and blue pinstriping, 35^1/$_4$in. high.
(Skinner) **$935**

A painted and stencilled wooden trade sign, American, early 20th century, bearing an oil rig and motor-driven transport truck on a mustard ground within a green-painted and gold-stencilled frame and inscribed *Mineral Exploration and Transport undertaken for all Mining and Drilling Companies/Virgin Territory Explored/Mineral Exploration Transport*, 24in. high.
(Christie's) **$3,520**

French carved and polychromed wood tailor's trade sign, circa 1900, the tailor depicted in shirtsleeves, waistcoat and trousers and wearing gold spectacles beneath bushy brows, in profile bending over a counter cutting a sheet of white fabric with oversize scissors, 26^1/$_2$in. wide.
(Butterfield & Butterfield)
$660

Pair of paint decorated tin shields, possibly Pennsylvania, late 19th century, each with a patriotic emblem, polychrome painted, 19¹/₂ x 15in.
(Skinner) **$3,850**

A good ammunition display board, the center with Eley trade mark encompassed by a circle of cartridges and a further circle of brass cased ammunition, the corners with tins of caps, on a gray card background, labeled *J. Odell, Newport Pagnell,* 80.5cm. x 65cm.
(Phillips) **$2,489**

'Special Retailers of Rolls-Royce Cars', a metal showroom advertizing sign used outside one of the twenty-five showrooms in London during the 1920s, 28¹/₄in. wide. *(Christie's)* **$1,870**

Painted and decorated painter's sign, America, late 19th century, painted red and embellished with white, yellow and blue flourishes and inscription *The Huested Studio Open Thursday.* *(Skinner)* **$1,320**

A painted wooden snuff or tobacco figure of a Scotsman, standing wearing a red tunic, tartan sash and kilt, his right hand aloft holding a pinch of snuff, his left hand with a snuff mull, 37¹/₂in. high, 19th century. *(Bonhams)* **$3,300**

Silver chafing dish, Jacob Hurd, Boston, circa 1745, pierced bowl with everted rim and removable pierced grate raised on three molded scrolled supports ending in hoofed feet, with handle 16³/₄in. long, 16³/₄ troy oz. *(Skinner)* **$22,000**

An Elizabeth I silver-mounted tigerware jug, chased with foliage and bead ornament, the cylindrical neck mount engraved with strapwork and foliage, by John Jones, Exeter, circa 1575, 8in. high. *(Christie's)* **$9,000**

George III sterling mounted ostrich egg cup and cover by Allen Dominy, London 1798, the cup set on trumpet form pedestal base with reeded edge and bright cut decoration, the shell with silver gilt liner and bright cut rim, 12¹/₂in. high. *(Butterfield)* **$1,100**

A George III silver fox head stirrup cup with naturalistic chasing, gilt interior, 1773. Makers: Louisa Courtauld and Geo. Cowles, $4^1/4$oz.
(Graves Son & Pilcher)

$6,300

One of a pair of important George II three-light candelabra, each on spreading circular base and four shell and foliage feet, chased above with panels of basketwork, the stems formed as male and female satyrs seated on a scroll pedestal and supporting a festooned and fluted socket, by John Le Sage, 1744, $16^3/4$in. high, 278ozs. The design for the candelabra was first used by Thomas Germain the great Paris goldsmith in 1734–35, and a pair of that date is in the Espirito Santo collection, Portugal. Indeed so proud of this design was Germain that he is shown pointing to a single example in the portrait of the goldsmith and his wife by Nicolas de Largilliere in 1736, now in the Gulbenkian Foundation, Lisbon.
(Christie's)

$382,000

A Russian silver-gilt tankard, realistically cast and chased in the form of a tree-trunk with flowering branches, the spreading foot with applied figures of two bears, the scroll handle as a branch with foliate twigs forming the hinged cover, by Robert Kokhun, St. Petersburg, 1868, 10^1/₈in. high, 3,315 grs.
(Christie's) **$10,560**

Silver mug, George Hanners, Boston, circa 1740, tapering cylindrical form with molded mid-band and base band, scroll handle, engraved with foliate monogram, marked below rim and at base, 10 troy oz.
(Skinner) **$5,500**

American Aesthetic Movement sterling tea caddy by Kennard & Jenks, Boston, Massachusetts, circa 1880, engraved in the Japanese taste on the four sides and lid, the lift off lid set with cast figures of a watchful owl and a rodent at diagonal corners, 5in. high.
(Butterfield & Butterfield)
$5,500

A model leopard, realistically chased with fur and engraved with spots and with detachable head revealing a gilt-lined well, engraved with the crest of the Skinners' Company and with hinged back flap, the interior of the head engraved with a presentation inscription, 1928, 10¹/₂in. long overall, 33ozs. *(Christie's)* **$3,200**

A set of three William III cylindrical casters, each on low-domed foot, the bodies with central molded rib, the covers with bayonet fittings, pierced and engraved with stylized foliage, by Joseph Ward, 1698, 6¹/₄in. and 7³/₄in. high, 23ozs.
(Christie's) **$17,500**

A fine tureen and cover, designed by Georg Jensen, the bombé bowl with curved leaf and bud handles on four scroll feet with stem and flower head decoration, the oval stepped and domed cover with elaborate rose and bell flower finial, 31.5cm. long, 1980 grams.
(Christie's) **$23,500**

A Victorian shaped rectangular silver-gilt vinaigrette, the lid chased in high relief with a view of St. Pauls, Nathaniel Mills, Birmingham 1852, 1⁴/₈in.
(Christie's S. Ken) **$4,850**

A pair of silver scissors, the tapering blades joined through a figure-of-eight-shaped spring-handle and decorated on each side with a bird in flight and scrolling foliate patterns on a stippled ground, Tang Dynasty, 14.7cm. long.
(Christie's) **$14,750**

A fine early Victorian silver-gilt circular shield, the central boss cast and chased with Britannia, attendants and hippocamps amidst waves, the flat border chased and applied with cutters, sloops and a frigate and with a shaped plaque with Royal Arms above, the plaque engraved "Royal Yacht Squadron, 1838. The Gift Of Her Most Gracious Majesty Queen Victoria", by Benjamin Preston, 1837, 17¹/₂in. diameter, 102ozs.
(Christie's) **$24,500**

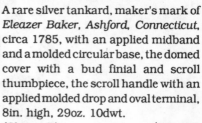

An Italian parcel gilt circular wine taster, the center chased with a recumbent sleeping dog within a border of stylized foliage, the upcurved rim chased with lobes, floral swags and a band of beading, Turin, probably mid 17th century, 5¹/₄in. diameter, 117 grams.
(Christie's) **$22,600**

A rare silver tankard, maker's mark of *Eleazer Baker, Ashford, Connecticut,* circa 1785, with an applied midband and a molded circular base, the domed cover with a bud finial and scroll thumbpiece, the scroll handle with an applied molded drop and oval terminal, 8in. high, 29oz. 10dwt.
(Christie's) **$37,400**

A Belgian altar cruet, comprizing shaped oval tray and two ewers and covers, the tray with chased foliage border, the center engraved with a Saint within a laurel wreath, the fluted ewers each on domed octofoil foot, by Johannes Moermans, Antwerp, circa 1660, the tray 15¹/₂in. wide.
(Christie's) **$35,000**

A George II Irish silver gilt charger, the raised matt center chased with putti and goat in a landscape within a wide border chased with masks, fruit and putti, and with reeded rim cast at intervals with shells, 21in. diameter, Dublin, circa 1741, by John Laughlin, 108ozs. *(Greenslades)*

$5,250

An important Christofle seven-piece sculptural tea service, designed by Albert-Ernest Carrier-Belleuse, 1880, cast in the silver workshops of Messrs. Broeck and Heintze, chased by Messrs. Trotet and Roze, with stamped French hallmarks and *Christofle.*

The service was praised for being exceptionally innovative, and in inspiration, may be said to be a herald of the Art Nouveau style, the main body of which it pre-empted by over a decade.
(Christie's)

$82,250

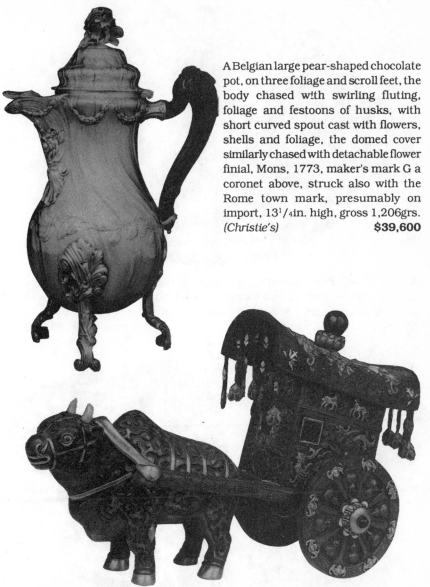

A Belgian large pear-shaped chocolate pot, on three foliage and scroll feet, the body chased with swirling fluting, foliage and festoons of husks, with short curved spout cast with flowers, shells and foliage, the domed cover similarly chased with detachable flower finial, Mons, 1773, maker's mark G a coronet above, struck also with the Rome town mark, presumably on import, 13¹/₄in. high, gross 1,206grs. *(Christie's)* **$39,600**

An inlaid silver ox and ceremonial cart, the ox standing foursquare with head raised, chased with foliate scrolls in relief, the hooves and harness gilt, the cart with cast chased dragons in relief, the detachable arched roof with pairs of deer and beasts at the sides, the top with bats and pomegranates below a lapis lazuli finial and suspending butterflies, late Qing Dynasty, 47cm. long.
(Christie's) **$8,500**

BASKETS

A fine George II two-handled bread basket, by Paul de Lamerie, the sloping sides of simple pierced trellis-work with interlaced flat-chased grooved strands, 8.5cm. high, 33cm. long, circa 1731, 40.5ozs.
(Phillips) **$175,000**

A George III silver-gilt oval basket, on spreading foot pierced and chased with palmettes and anthemion ornament, the wirework sides with applied vine tendrils, grapes and leaves, with ribbon and foliage border, by Thomas Arden, 1805, 13¹/₄in. long, 54ozs.
(Christie's) **$12,850**

BOWLS

A rare James II monteith bowl, the body plain apart from simple lobing in panels, by George Garthorne, 1685, 31cm., 42oz.
(Lawrence Fine Art) **$80,000**

A large Walker & Tolhurst hammered silver bowl designed by Gilbert Marks, bulbous cylindrical form with inverted rim, with chased decoration of fruiting apple branches, with parcel gilt interior, mounted on four scrolled feet, stamped with maker's marks *WW BT* and London hallmarks for 1902, 24cm. high; 26.5cm. diameter, 2248.3 grams.
(Christie's) **$9,495**

BOWLS

A Gorham Sterling and mixed metal punchbowl and ladle.
(Skinner) $18,700

A silver rose bowl by Bernard Cuzner, the rounded bowl with rolled rim
decorated with a repoussé rose briar frieze with five applied stylized rose
heads, the petals of each set with mother-of-pearl with centers of five
garnets, the bowl on a convex ring supported on five twisted pilaster legs,
with Birmingham hall marks for *1911*, 18.5cm. high.
(Christie's) $25,600

COFFEE POTS

A George I plain tapering octagonal coffee pot, with curved octagonal spout, molded borders and domed cover with bell-shaped finial, by Edward Vincent, 1723, 9¹/₂in. high, gross 25ozs. *(Christie's)* **$32,000**

A George III coffee pot of baluster circular form, the hinged cover, spout and spreading base with banded edging with acorn finial and scroll wood handle, 10³/₄in. high, Daniel Smith and Robert Sharp, London 1780, 813gms, 26.1oz. *(Bearne's)* **$6,000**

FLATWARE

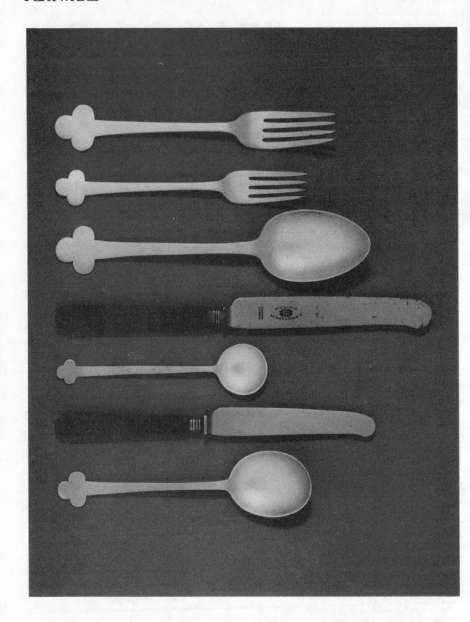

An E. Bingham & Co. 42-piece electroplated table service, designed by
Charles Rennie Mackintosh, with flat trefoil finials, the knives with black
bakelite handles and steel blades.
(Christie's) **$15,000**

FLATWARE

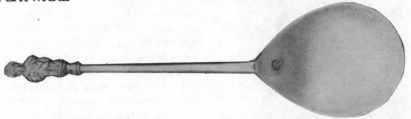

A very rare Henry VII Apostle spoon, St. James the Greater carrying a pilgrim's staff, length 18cm., punched in the bowl with an early variation of the crowned leopard's head, and on the stem with the obscure maker's mark representing a Gothic L (?) and the date letter for London, 1490. *(Phillips)* **$40,000**

A Liberty & Co. silver and enamel ceremonial spoon, designed by Archibald Knox, the shaped handle with elaborate entrelac design and blue-green and red enamel, the bowl repeating this motif and with blue and green enamel, stamped *L & Co, Cymric* with Birmingham hallmark for 1900, 20.5cm. long, 95 grams. gross. *(Christie's)* **$6,400**

A rare pair of large silver ragout spoons made for Moses Michael Hays, maker's mark of Paul Revere, Boston, 1786, each with oval bowl and downturned rounded-end handle bright-cut engraved with pendant flowers and a roulettework oval cartouche enclosing script initials *MRH*, each marked *REVERE*, 12in. long, 8oz.

Moses Michael Hays, merchant of New York, Newport, and Boston, is known among American silver scholars for his association with two famous silversmiths, Paul Revere and Myer Myers. Between 1783 and 1792, Hay's name appears twenty-five times in Revere's Daybooks, the two-volume daily account book from Revere's silversmithing business.
(Christie's) **$46,200**

Sunburst celebration, attributed to John Scholl (1827–1916), Germania, Pennsylvania, 1907–1916, painted in red, white and blue with a carved and turned spoked and honeycomb-shaped wheel turning upon a carved support and over a carved horizontal brace bearing a pair of spoked honeycomb-shaped wheels above four ogee legs on an X-stretcher, 62¹/₄in. high.
(Christie's) **$7,150**

Snowflake stand, attributed to John Scholl (1827–1916), Germania, Pennsylvania, 1907–1916, painted in white and gold with a spoked snowflake-shaped wheel spinning upon a turned and carved fluted plinth with four spoked and demi-shield shaped ornaments over four downswept legs above ball and spindle spokes on an X-stretcher, 68in. high.

The 1870 U.S. Census for Potter County describes Scholl as a house carpenter. Born in Germany, Scholl emigrated to Pennsylvania with his wife in 1853. He began carving his sculptures in 1907 upon his retirement and created at least forty-five pieces. The snowflake stand and the sunburst celebration are examples of his more developed work and probably date towards the end of his career.
(Christie's) **$8,800**

A quartz crystal snuff bottle, early 19th century, the front and reverse carved in relief as a Spanish dollar coin with the value of eight reales, minted for the Mexican territories, with the bust of King Charles III and date 1781 on one side, and the Spanish royal coat-of-arms on the other.
(Christie's) **$6,250**

A fine enameled glass snuff bottle, Ye Family workshop, circa 1930, finely painted in famille rose enamels to one side with a rooster standing on ornamental rockwork, above three chicks feeding beside a flowering tree peony, the reverse with its mate and two more chicks below hibiscus and orchids, iron-red Gu Yuexuan mark on base.
(Christie's) **$9,000**

An extremely rare Imperial porcelain snuff bottle, molded in relief and decorated in famille rose enamels with a continuous landscape scene, on one side the poet Su Dongbo in a pleasure boat on a turbulent river beneath overhanging cliffs, a lady steers the boat for the party and a boat-boy sleeps on the prow; the reverse with scholar inscribing a rockface with a calligraphy.

This group of Imperial porcelain-molded snuff bottles were made at Jingdezhen from the latter part of the Qianlong period until the early years of the Daoguang reign. Thereafter their production continued, but as non-Imperial copies of the originals. They were clearly inspired by Imperial ivory and lacquer snuff bottles, carved in the Palace Workshops, and sent South as models, as the earlier examples are monochrome and copy lacquer and ivory. Gradually other monochrome colors were introduced and then polychrome enameled examples evolved as the type became independent of its original models.
(Christie's) **$17,750**

A Meissen gold-mounted yellow-ground cartouche-shaped snuff-box, painted after engravings by Melchior Küsel, each side with a quatrefoil panel painted with a Venetian cappricio, including figures beside canals, palaces and ships within brown and double gilt lines, between four molded bands with gilt trellis, the contemporary gold mount with scroll thumbpiece and later French warranty mark, circa 1740, 6.5cm. wide.
(Christie's) $85,000

A Swiss rectangular gold snuff-box set with a Roman micro-mosaic, showing Rinaldo and Armida, in a wooded landscape setting, signed *F. Depoletti*, the box with engine-turned panels, by S. Chaligny, Geneva, circa 1820, 3³/₄in. long.

Francesco De Poletti, one of the most important of the Roman mosaicists, had his workshop at 32, via Condotti. He was active during the first half of the 19th century.
(Christie's) $41,000

An important Frederick Augustus III oval gold and hardstone snuff-box, set on all sides with a Zellenmosaik of rural landscapes with architectural capriccios and rustic figures bordered in gold, engraved with husks, swags and a guilloche, signed *Neuber a Dresde* on the bezel, by Johann Christian Neuber, Dresden, circa 1770, 3³/₈in. long.

Born in Neuwunsdorf on 7th April 1736, Johann Christian Neuber was apprenticed at the age of seventeen to Johann Friedrich Trechaon. On 13th July 1762 he became a master of the goldsmith's guild in Dresden, and in 1769 he succeeded his father-in-law Heinrich Tadell as director of the Green Vaults. By 1775 he had been appointed Hofjuwelier to the court of Friedrich Augustus III.

(Christie's) **$82,250**

A Meissen chinoiserie silver-gilt mounted oval snuff-box probably painted by J.G. Heroldt molded with purple Böttger lustre gadroons outlined with gilding, the cover painted with merchants at discussion on a quayside beneath palm trees, junks in the distance, one with a sail bearing Chinese characters, the base with two figures catching birds and the interior of the cover similarly decorated with figures sitting on packages and smoking pipes beside an estuary, circa 1723, 7cm. wide.

(Christie's) **$100,000**

A gold and silver-mounted opaque blue enamel snuff-box by Fabergé, (Workmaster Henrik Wigström [1862–1923]), 1⁷/₈in. square.

(Christie's) **$94,600**

A Meissen Royal presentation gold-mounted armorial snuff-box of oval bombé form, painted by J.G. Herold with a portrait of Augustus the Strong, the front with the Arms of Saxony and Poland surmounted by a crown and supported by two chinoiserie figures, the reverse with two figures holding The Star of The Order of The White Eagle of Poland, circa 1730.

Augustus the Strong (1670–1733), Elector of Saxony and King of Poland, revived The Order of The White Eagle of Poland in 1705 and The Star on the reverse of this box undoubtedly represents this event.

Johann Gregor Herold had been Court Painter (Hofmaler) since 1723 and would have almost certainly painted this exceptional commission himself.

A fine George II cartouche-shaped gold snuff-box, the interior of the lid set with an enamel portrait of Mary, Countess of Bute by Christian Friedrich Zincke, circa 1750, 2³/₄in. wide.

(Christie's) **$71,500**

(Christie's) **$379,000**

A remarkable Staffordshire slipware owl jug and cover, the head lifting off to form a drinking cup, the body molded in buff colored clay and 'juggled' in brown and cream slip to simulate feathers, 23cm.
(Phillips) **$33,500**

A rare black man ordinary toby jug with a black face and gray wig, seated in a chair and holding a pink lustered frothing jug of ale, he wears a bright green tricorn hat, bright blue coat with yellow buttons, spotted yellow waistcoat, ocher breeches and raspberry boots, on a sponged green canted square base.
(Phillips) **$1,360**

A large Staffordshire model of a lion with a fierce expression and pale brown coat and mane, standing on a rectangular base with one paw upon a ball, the acanthus molded base colored in green, yellow and black, 29cm.
(Phillips) **$2,380**

Luxembourg, 1852, 10c. black strip of five and a pair on an envelope.
(Christie's) **$15,000**

China, 1941, Sun Yat-Sen $2 in a
vertical pair with inverted center.
(Christie's) **$42,800**

Canada, 1898, 2c Christmas Proof, part of the entire production file.
(Christie's) **$60,500**

Bermuda, 1854, W.B. Perot postmaster's stamp 1d., red on bluish wove paper on original envelope from Hamilton to St. Georges.

This stamp is generally considered to be the finest of the eleven recorded examples of the first type Perot issue. It is one of the two recorded examples dated 1854 on bluish wove.
(Christie's)

$337,810

United States, 1847, First issue 10c. black marginal pair.

The envelope is dated 2 July 1847: this is the earliest known usage of a United States postage stamp. *(Christie's)* **$132,000**

Great Britain, 1840, 2d. blue mint marginal block of six.
(Christie's) **$27,170**

A large French ceramic jardinière and stand, the bowl decorated in relief with roses and on the rim with three large butterflies painted in naturalistic colors, the stand decorated in mottled browns and pinks flanked by bulrushes and foliage and a large naturalistic heron, total height 1.28m., signed 'Jerome Massier fils, Vallauris A.M.'
(Phillips) **$5,252**

A Gothic painted wood pedestal, probably designed by the office of William Burges, the square overhanging molded entablature supported on a column with cushion capital, the contoured circular foot mounted on square section plinth, with red, turquoise, cream and gilt painted floral decoration, 79cm. high.
(Christie's) **$4,250**

A mid-Georgian mahogany bottle-stand with arched carrying-handle and four divisions with canted sides on ogee bracket feet, 17¹/₄in. wide.
(Christie's)

$11,682

A pair of mahogany octagonal waste paper baskets each with molded top above pierced gothic fretwork, 13¹/₄in. high.
(Christie's) **$6,776**

A George III satinwood whatnot with four canted rectangular tiers, the top tier with a mahogany and cedar-lined frieze drawer, on molded supports, 16³/₄in. wide.
(Christie's) **$20,000**

A Louis XVI ebonized and parcel-gilt
pedestal with stepped canted square
top with flower-filled guilloche-pattern
frieze, the fluted shaft hung with
drapery swags on a stepped base
carved with laurel leaves, 48in. high.

This pedestal, festooned with nailed
draperies, recalls the neo-classical
designs of the architect Jean Francois
Neufforge (1714–91), whose Recueil
élémentaire d'Architecture (1757–80)
aimed to emulate the 'majestic manner
of the ancient architects of Greece'.
(Christie's)   **$32,500**

A pair of George II giltwood
torchères with part ebonized
circular tops and pierced
shaped shafts carved with
foliate scrolls, drapery and
strapwork upon scrolling
tripod bases carved with
acanthus and shaped feet,
42^1/$_2$in. high.
(Christie's)

$25,000

A rare Regency carved giltwood and gesso half round three-tier jardinière of undulating outline, with guilloche, lyre and husk ornament, the tiers with removable troughs and inset with verre églomisé panels depicting musical trophies and figures, 2ft. 2in. wide. *(Phillips)* **$8,850**

A George IV mahogany folio stand on shaped legs, 45^1/2in. wide overall. *(Dreweatt-Neate)* **$5,000**

A Federal inlaid mahogany and birch-veneered wash-stand, Portsmouth, New Hampshire, 1790–1810, the rectangular top pierced with three circular openings and edged with a three-quarter gallery over a geometric-banded apron inlaid with rectangular frame birch reserves edged with checkered banding over a medial shelf and frieze drawer decorated with similar birch reserves, 16^1/2in. wide. *(Christie's)* **$22,000**

A Regency mahogany metamorphic library step chair, after a patent by Morgan & Saunders, the overscrolled and carved top rail above a horizontal bar 'S'-splat, the padded seat folding out to form four steps on saber legs with brass cappings and castors.
(Phillips) **$5,000**

A set of George III mahogany library steps with two flights of steps with molded rail and baluster banisters divided by stop-fluted columns above pierced risers carved with C-scrolls and pierced on the landings with lozenges and quatrefoils on cluster-column supports headed by blind fretwork and joined by waved pierced stretchers on casters, 123in. high.
(Christie's)

$97,350

A set of George IV metamorphic mahogany library steps, with four rectangular red leather-lined treads on turned and baluster supports, above a rectangular well with turned edge, on turned legs and brass caps, 36in. wide.
(Christie's) **$8,250**

A set of Regency rosewood library steps with six fluted treads, brass hand-supports and turned supports with scrolling acanthus sides and ribbed tapering front feet, the back feet with bronze lotus leaf casters, 51in. wide. *(Christie's)*
$44,500

The Arts and Crafts movement found one of its greatest exponents in the U.S.A. in Gustav Stickley (1857–1942). He was the eldest of six brothers and although he trained as a stone mason he became a famous furniture designer. In his youth he designed mainly chairs in the American Colonial style, but in 1898 he founded the firm of Gustav Stickley of Syracuse, New York, which specialized in the Arts & Crafts or Mission style of furniture (from the furniture supposedly housed in the old Franciscan missions of California). He also published a magazine 'The Craftsman', which popularized this new style.

Rare Gustav Stickley sideboard, circa 1902, the top shelf galleried on three sides, the cabinet with two drawers with metal square faceted pulls and lozenge shaped back-plate with lag screws above two paneled doors with butterfly keys and metal key plates and pulls, light finish, unsigned, 48in. wide.
(Skinner) **$3,500**

Gustav Stickley double bed, circa 1907, no. 923, tapering vertical posts, centering five wide slats, signed, 57$^{1}/_{2}$in. wide.
(Skinner) **$3,300**

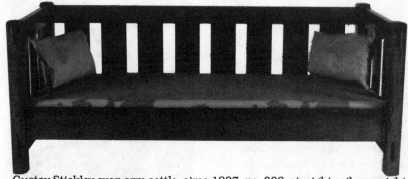

Gustav Stickley even arm settle, circa 1907, no. 208, straight rail over eight vertical slats on back, three on each end, cushion seat upholstered in reversible vinyl with Southwestern designs in colors of straw and vanilla, 76in. long.
(Skinner)   **$8,500**

Gustav Stickley Morris chair, circa 1910, no. 332, adjustable back, four horizontal slats, flat arm over five vertical slats, straight seat rail, unsigned.
(Skinner)   **$3,800**

Gustav Stickley hall settle, circa 1907, recessed panel back, plank sides with cut-outs at top through tenons, hinged seat compartment over straight skirt, medium brown finish, signed with red decal, 47⁵/₈in. wide.
(Skinner)   **$4,750**

Leopold and J. George were younger brothers of the famous Gustav, with whom they obviously enjoyed a somewhat complicated relationship. They were at first employed by him in his firm at Syracuse, New York, but left to found L. & J.G. Stickley at Fayetteville, in 1900. Like Gustav, they based their designs on Craftsman furniture, sometimes using veneers and laminated members, and their pieces are identifiable by the name L. & J.G Stickley in red.

Unlike Gustav, however, they were also open to other influences, and were perhaps more realistic in seeing that their products also had to find a market. They were certainly readier to compromise in terms of putting some embellishments on the basic style. They later made furniture designed by Frank Lloyd Wright and by 1914 were turning out reproduction pieces as well.

They bought out their elder brother 1916, when the firm, still in existence today, became the Stickley Manufacturing Co.

L&JG Stickley armchair, No. 420, circa 1910, four horizontal back slats, flat arms with front corbels, arched seat apron, leather upholstery spring cushion seat, 31^1/4in. wide.
(Skinner)   **$550**

L. & J.G. Stickley prairie settle, Fayetteville, New York, circa 1912, no. 220, wide flat arms and crest rail supported by corbels over inset panels, two per side and six across back, spring cushion seat, 84^1/2in. wide.
(Skinner)   **$19,000**

An ash-glazed stoneware face-jug, attributed to Evan Javan Brown, Georgia, 20th century, with front in the form of a grinning face, an incised goatee, the handle pulled from the back and ceramic chards for eyes and teeth, 6¹/₄in. high.
(Christie's) **$2,420**

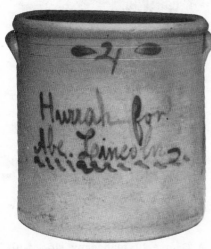

Cobalt decorated stoneware crock, probably Ohio or Pennsylvania, circa 1860, the four-gallon crock inscribed *Hurrah for Abe Lincoln*, in cobalt, 11¹/₂in. high.
(Skinner) **$4,400**

An incised and cobalt-decorated stoneware harvest jug, New York, 1805, the squat drum-form body with applied handle and cylindrical neck and spout, decorated on the obverse with incised floral vine below a fish, the reverse with a Masonic apron, inscribed and dated *J. Romer, 1805*, 7in. high.

Captain John Romer (1764–1855) was the son of Jacob, one of the captors of the British agent Major Andre in 1780. John Romer served in the militia during the Revolution and was a captain in the War of 1812. He was a member of Solomon's Lodge of Free and Accepted Masons in Mount Pleasant, New York, and remained an active member during his lifetime. His gravestone is decorated with fraternal emblems.
(Christie's) **$6,050**

A George IV ormolu-mounted mahogany and parcel-gilt X-frame stool attributed to Morel and Hughes, the padded rectangular top covered in pink velvet, the supports headed by stylized lion-masks and carved with stiff leaves, centered by a flowerhead mount and joined by a double-baluster stretcher, and on paw feet, 22in. wide. *(Christie's)* **$52,500**

A Napoleon III giltwood stool attributed to A.M.E. Fournier, the circular top covered in buttoned green silk with waved rope-twist apron and conforming legs and stretchers, 21in. diameter.

Fournier was a tapissier established from 1850 at 109, Boulevard Beaumarchais and subsequently at 12, Boulevard des Capucines. He exhibited tapestry and bedroom and drawing-room furniture at the 1867 Universal Exhibition.
(Christie's) **$6,500**

A George III mahogany stool with rectangular upholstered seat covered in associated polychrome gros point floral needlwork on a blue ground on cabriole legs carved with acanthus sprays and pendant bellflowers ending in scrolled toes, 24in. wide.
(Christie's) **$31,150**

An Italian walnut stool with serpentine padded seat with tassels, a foliate scroll bar to each end on bearded satyr supports with later turned feet, late 19th century, 40in. wide.
(Christie's) **$2,303**

A Tudor oak stool with later canted rectangular plank seat and waved arcaded apron, on faceted legs joined by arcaded stretchers, legs shortened, mid-16th century, 17¹/₂in. wide.
(Christie's) **$9,650**

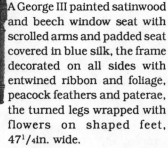

A George III painted satinwood and beech window seat with scrolled arms and padded seat covered in blue silk, the frame decorated on all sides with entwined ribbon and foliage, peacock feathers and paterae, the turned legs wrapped with flowers on shaped feet, 47¹/₄in. wide.
(Christie's) **$11,600**

A George III mahogany stool, now lacking seat, with stop-fluted frieze and paneled tapering legs carved with pendant bellflowers and spreading feet, 32¹/₂in. wide.
(Christie's) **$17,500**

A pair of early George III mahogany stools, each with serpentine upholstered rectangular seat covered in eau-de-nil damask, the frieze with solid serpentine front and back edged with foliage and carved with flower-sprays centered by shell clasps framed by trellis-and-rosette, the straight sides of waved outline applied on beech, centered by scallop-shells, on cabriole legs headed by scallop-shells, 26¹/₄in. wide.
(Christie's) **$165,500**

A George III mahogany stool with upholstered seat covered in turquoise floral cut-velvet, the frieze with solid serpentine front and back edged with foliage sprays and centered by foliate cabochons surrounded by trellis ornament, on cabriole legs carved with clasped acanthus sprays ending in scrolled feet, 25in. wide.
(Christie's) **$14,600**

Gerald Summers (1899–1968) trained originally in London as an engineer. He first ventured into furniture design when he made some pieces for his wife's bedroom, and then, in the early 1930s, in partnership with her, formed the company known as The Makers of Simple furniture.

A Makers of Simple Furniture beechwood towel horse, designed by Gerald Summers, the shaped form divided at the base, white painted, 77cm. high.
(Christie's)   **$615**

A Makers of Simple Furniture laminated birch armchair designed by Gerald Summers, cut and shaped to form a curved top rail with central splat and curved arms extending into plank legs.
(Christie's)   **$10,230**

A rare Makers of Simple Furniture laminated birchwood display stand by Gerald Summers, consisting of two circular shelves joined by 2-shaped support, 61cm. high.
(Christie's)   **$2,000**

A Roman circular micro-mosaic table-top inlaid with a wicker basket with flowers including roses, a tulip, violet, a narcissus and lily-of-the-valley and a butterfly, on a ledge, within a Greek-key border, mid-19th century, 26¹/₂in. diameter.
(Christie's) **$23,750**

A glass table top by Giovanni Rossignani of circular form, constructed from approximately twelve hundred pieces of Greek and Roman glass inlaid on white marble, centered by a sun-burst and a radiating triangle-pattern within a border of octagonal reserves filled with stars, repaired and rebacked, assembled in the 2nd quarter of the 19th century, 30in. diameter. The glass fragments used in such tables come from mosaic glass vessels, mostly bowls, dating from the late 1st century B.C. to the early 1st century A.D. These include fragments of millefiori, ribbon glass, reticelli and glass imitating marbles such as giallo antico and verde antico.
(Christie's) **$67,500**

An Italian specimen marble table top composed of a central panel of malachite framed by seventy-two squares of various marbles and hardstones including bluejohn, lapis lazuli, jaspers, brocatelles, Siena and onyx marbles within a Siena border, 91cm. square, possibly late 18th/early 19th century. *(Phillips)* **$17,500**

A Florentine pietra dura plaque with a parrot on its perch on a table with an Etruscan krater vase, a vase of flowers and ewers on a black slate ground, circa 1870, 16in. x 23¹/₂in.

Popular in the second half, 19th century, these are generally described as influenced by the designs of Antonio Cioci (active 1722–92). *(Christie's)* **$32,500**

An empire bronze and ormolu gueridon with circular specimen marble top inlaid in a star pattern with various marbles including brocatelle, Siena, porphyry, onyx and lapis lazuli within a serpentine border edged with an egg-and-dart molding, on a tapering tiered triangular shaft mounted with Egyptian caryatids above winged female figures and an urn, 31in. high. *(Christie's)* **$41,000**

A French ormolu-mounted rosewood, mahogany and burr walnut writing table inlaid overall with boxwood and harewood, the rounded rectangular leather-lined top with edge molded with stiff leaves, the frieze with two drawers and two false drawers, on toupie feet, mid-19th century, 55in. wide. *(Christie's)* **$9,200**

A Regency green and gilt japanned tripod table with rounded rectangular top decorated with chinoiserie figures fishing by a pagoda within a foliate border on a grained and gilt turned shaft with downswept legs and spade feet, 28^1/$_2$in. high.
(Christie's) **$7,000**

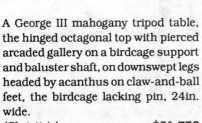

A George III mahogany tripod table, the hinged octagonal top with pierced arcaded gallery on a birdcage support and baluster shaft, on downswept legs headed by acanthus on claw-and-ball feet, the birdcage lacking pin, 24in. wide.
(Christie's) **$21,750**

Italian micro-mosaic occasional table in the rococo taste, third quarter 19th century, the black circular top centered by a spray of flowers in a circular red marble banded border, a further spray of flowers and a butterfly hovering enclosed by a similar outer border, the surround carved as leafing branches, 30in. high. *(Butterfield & Butterfield)* **$2,200**

An attractive Regency period rosewood combined teapoy and table with parquetry decoration. *(Henry Spencer)* **$3,500**

Queen Anne cherry dressing table, Connecticut, 1750–80, 33in. wide. *(Skinner)* **$17,600**

A good early Victorian circular inlaid marble chess-top table bordered with bands of colored geometric and leaf motifs, on burr walnut triform stem with carved base and scroll feet, 36in. diameter.
(Graves Son & Pilcher)
$7,350

An ormolu-mounted ebony, boulle and pietra dura center table, the rectangular Florentine pietra dura top inset with fifteen rectangular tablets, decorated with birds, fruit and flowers around a central flower vase, on a black marble ground within a griotte and pietra paesina marble border, third quarter 19th century, the frieze panels possibly late 18th/early 19th century, 51$^{1}/_{2}$in. wide.
(Christie's)
$216,000

A Queen Anne cherrywood tea-table, probably Northampton or Hatfield, Massachusetts, 1740–1760, the deeply scalloped molded top above a rectangular frame with flat arched apron on cabriole legs and pad feet, 35in. wide.

Scalloped-top furniture was produced along the Connecticut River valley in the second half of the 18th century. The form is believed first to have developed in Wethersfield, Connecticut, and subsequently to have been made in the Northampton and Deerfield areas as cabinetmakers trained in the Wethersfield tradition migrated North.

(Christie's)

$38,500

A Regency ebony Pembroke table inlaid with brass lines, the rectangular twin-flap top edged with milled brass border, the frieze fitted with a mahogany-lined drawer on spirally-turned tapering legs joined by an H-shaped stretcher, 38in. wide.

This Pembroke table combines the 'French' taste for brass inlay with English 'antiquarian' taste for exotic Goanese ebony furniture, turned in the 'Elizabethan manner'.

(Christie's)

$52,250

A Chippendale carved mahogany dressing-table, Philadelphia, 1760–1780, the molded rounded rectangular top above a case fitted with a thumbmolded long drawer over a thumbmolded short drawer centered by a pair of short drawers and fluted canted corners above a shaped scrolling apron centering a pendant scallop shell, on cabriole legs, 34in. wide. *(Christie's)*

$22,000

A George III mahogany miniature tripod table with circular tip-up top on turned stem and cabriole base, 14in. diameter.
(Christie's)   **$7,400**

A Victorian slate pedestal table, the circular top with pietra dura floral band, the baluster shaped support on incarving triangular platform base, 22in. diameter.
(Greenslades)   **$5,930**

439

A George II ebonized and giltwood console table in the manner of William Kent with rectangular verde antico marble top above a Greek key-pattern frieze alternating with flowerheads supported by an eagle on a rockwork base and stepped plinth carved with flowerheads and egg-and-dart moldings, 36in. wide.

This baroque style of table is associated with the name of William Kent (d. 1748), who illustrated a console table accompanied by an eagle in Alexander Pope's translation of Homer's Odyssey, 1726, the year in which he was appointed Master Carpenter to George I's Board of Works. *(Christie's)*

$73,500

A Regency parcel-gilt rosewood and burr-elm center table, the banded circular tilt top edged with foliage, on a canted concave-sided spreading triangular support with ropetwist and scroll angles, on scroll feet, 53in. diameter.

(Christie's) **$20,650**

An early Victorian mahogany, ebony and marquetry center table attributed to E H Baldock, the octagonal tilt-top with simulated rosewood leather-lined rim within a band inlaid with trophies of music, war and astronomy, and ribbon-tied floral bouquets with scrolled frieze, on spreading quadripartite base inlaid with floral bouquets and downward scrolling legs, 56in. wide.
(Christie's) **$17,000**

A Louis XV giltwood console table with molded eared serpentine brèche violette top, the waved apron carved with interlocking chain pattern and centered by a pair of ribbon-tied bagpipes within confronting C-scrolls and rockwork on cabriole legs headed by reeds and birds and entwined with vine leaves, 34in. wide.

The serpentined 'rococo' frame, with festooned ribbon-guilloche and ivy-wreathed reeds incorporating musical and sporting trophies comprized of rustic bagpipes and clastinettes and a putto with hounds and birds, reflects the ornamental patterns published by Jacques-François Blondel in his Decoration of 'Maisons de Plaisance', vol. II, 1738.
(Christie's) **$39,000**

A late Victorian brass-mounted rosewood bureau plat, of Louis XV style, the shaped rectangular red leather-lined top above a waved frieze with three drawers, on cabriole legs headed by rockwork clasps and foliate sabots, with brass label of Druce & Co, 54in. wide.
(Christie's) **$6,000**

A Regency brass-mounted and inlaid mahogany serving-table inlaid with boxwood and ebonized stringing, the break-fronted bowed top with brass-railed back with vase-shaped finials and two plate tracks, the edge inlaid with a ribbon pattern, on turned tapering reeded legs headed by anthemia and brass paw feet on shaped blocks, 87^1/2in. wide.
(Christie's) **$52,250**

A George III ormolu-mounted mahogany bonheur-du-jour possibly by John Okeley in the style of David Roentgen, the stepped top lifting to reveal a mirror and well flanked by two platforms with solid galleries with checkered inlay above three tambours, the central one enclosing pigeon-holes and a step-fronted drawer, on eight square tapering legs with block feet, 36^{1}/$_{2}$in. wide.

The cabinet's tripartite cartonnier design, and stepped 'Pantheon' forms, restrained 'Grecian' checker mille-raies inlay, combined with compartments ingeniously concealed behind hinged drawers, etc., are typical of the elegant furniture manufactured in the mid-1780s by David Roentgen (1743–1807) of Neuwied and exported to various European centers.

(Christie's)   **$116,000**

Winter: a Flemish tapestry probably Brussels, late 17th century, 116 x 129in.

(Christie's) **$82,500**

A rare Brussels Gothic allegorical tapestry woven in wools and silks depicting the path of a young nobleman through life, with God enthroned and surrounded by angels in the center, the young nobleman portrayed at three stages during his journey surrounded by richly clad allegorical figures and with the prophet Jonah on the left at the bottom, early 16th century, 137in. x 132in.

(Christie's) **$206,000**

A rare Brussels Gothic allegorical tapestry woven in silks and wools with well preserved and fresh colors depicting the winged figure of Fame surrounded by various allegorical and biblical figures in richly caparisoned robes and trampling the Fates underfoot with her distaff, the top with an angel flanked by two groups of courtly figures including a bride and bridegroom in bowers, early 16th century, 13ft. ¹/₂in. x 11ft. 8in.

In this panel courtiers witness Fame holding an orb and reading from a book of virtue and attended by various poets and historians triumphing over death. The Fates Atropos, Lachesis and Clotho, personifying Death, are trampled underfoot. The bride extends to the bridegroom a scroll exhorting that the liberal arts be supported, for Fame will be overthrown.

(Christie's) **$523,600**

This 'Flemish' landscape tapestry, woven at Louis XVI's Gobelins factory and inspired by Brussels tapestries of the 1530s, depicts peasants occupied in the activities of the month of November. It is one of a set of tapestries commissioned in 1767 from the master weaver Pierre-François Cozette (d. 1801), whose mark they bear. It is bordered with a flowered trellis embellished with flower-and-fruit festooned cartouches, displaying Louis XVI's arms and cypher, accompanied by Apollo, the sun god's mask, and the Zodiac sign for Sagittarius, 156 x 52in.

(Christie's)   **$209,000**

Winter: from Les Portières des Dieux: a silk Gobelins tapestry, late 18th century, 100 x 100in.

This golden tapestry with Saturn is from a series of the Seasons, portraying gods and goddesses, which were produced in 1699 to serve as door-curtains for the palaces of King Louis XIV.

(Christie's) **$88,000**

A thang-ka of Samvara and Vajravarahi, West Tibet, 15th century, 17 x 13^1/$_2$in. Tibetan thang-kas are temple paintings on canvas, originally mounted between cloth panels. Usually kept rolled up, they were unrolled on auspicious occasions. Samvara is one of the most important gods in the Tibetan Buddhist pantheon. He belongs to the ishtadevata group of gods, on whom acolytes were encouraged by priests to meditate in order to acquire some of their mental power. In this thang-ka he is shown embracing his female consort. *(Christie's)* **$52,800**

A George III amaranth, rosewood and marquetry tea-caddy of rectangular shape with stepped top surmounted by an ormolu classical urn within a spotted circle of friendship, flanked by two panels, one with a Greek lyre and Cupid's arrow, the other with a lute and triangle, with glass mixing-bowl engraved with oak leaves and acorns and two hobnail cut-glass caddies with silver tops, one inscribed *INDIA*, the other *CHINA*, 13^1/$_2$in. wide.

The 'Etruscan' type ornament combined with chinoiserie reflects fashionable taste of the late 1760s.
(Christie's) **$33,000**

A rare late Regency hardstone veneered tea caddy of rectangular form, the canted lid and tapering sides with geometric decoration in the form of mainly English hardstones inset in alabaster, on turned alabaster feet, 11^1/$_2$in. wide.
(Phillips) **$2,850**

Right-A George III fruitwood tea-caddy in the form of a Cantaloupe melon, 4^1/$_2$in. wide.
(Christie's) **$6,850**

A small late 18th century ivory tea caddy with silver hinges and fleur de lys mounts, 4in. high.
(Russell, Baldwin & Bright)

$8,400

Left-A George III fruitwood tea-caddy in the form of an apple, 4¹/₂in. wide.
(Christie's)

$5,150

A set of three oblong George III tea caddies, each on scrolling base, chased with Chinese figures and buildings, lions' masks and quatrefoils within scroll panels, by Frederick Vonham, 1763, with twelve teaspoons with leaf-shaped bowls and stems, 49oz.
(Christie's)

$17,500

A William Morris & Company embroidered wool portiere designed by Henry Dearle, circa 1910, the central rectangular reserve embroidered with a flowering tree and song birds, 244 x 180.5cm.
(Christie's) **$71,600**

A late 18th century needlework embroidery of a hare and three leverets, executed in fine long and short stitch, possibly by Mary Linwood (1755–1845), English, 51cm. x 70cm.
(Phillips) **$5,055**

An orphrey, of cruciform shape worked on linen, with Christ on the Cross attended by two Angels and with God the Father above, the Centurian draining the Precious Blood and Mary Magdalen at the foot of the Cross grieving with St. John the Divine, 48in. x 21in., perhaps South German, circa 1400.
(Christie's) **$30,000**

Knitted appeal to President Andrew Johnson, Washington Insane Asylum, February, 1868, worked in yarns in brown, red, gray, blue and natural wool. The long inscription asks President Johnson to influence the nation to pray and 'to releav (sic) the secret of President Lincoln's death and inspire the people with love towards John Wilks (sic) Booth', the closing with a plea to 'pity the people and insane – Dr. C. Nichols, Dr. W. Godding and M.P. Johnson to Justice', 20 x 28in. *(Skinner)* **$1,100**

An important Tiffany favrile iridescent glass vase, of shouldered baluster form supported on small circular foot, decorated below the shoulders with a band of café-au-lait/lemon swirls against pale peacock blue with shades of green and violet with waved bands of similar colors above and below, 29.5cm. high.
(Phillips) **$12,250**

A fine silver and mixed-metal pitcher, maker's mark of *Tiffany & Co., New York*, circa 1880, the spot-hammered sides and handle applied with a dragonfly and butterflies amid a trailing vine of gold and copper, 7³/₄in. high, gross weight 26oz. 10dwt.
(Christie's)

$28,600

A silver-applied copper inkwell, maker's mark of *Tiffany & Co., New York*, 1902, on four acanthus claw feet, the copper body applied with silver strapwork with applied flowerheads, the hinged domed cover with fitted liner and ball finial, 6³/₄in. high.
(Christie's) **$3,520**

Tiffany Cypriote vase, basic green body overlaid with blue-black metallic iridized glass and three lustrous gold leaf-form decorations, 6¹/₂in. high
(Skinner) **$10.000**

A fine silver, enamel and stone-set 'Viking' vase, maker's mark of *Tiffany & Co., New York*, circa 1901; designed by Paulding Farnham, with a pierced circular rim with grotesque masks above etched interlacing strapwork against polychrome enameling set with cabochon green tourmalines and orange garnets, the shoulder applied with stylized masks, 12in. high, 30oz.
(Christie's) **$22,000**

A Carette tinplate two-seat runabout, circa 1908, a handpainted white keywound Runabout with composition figure, stop and go lever, handbrake, headlights, lanterns, button-tufted seat, and rubber tires on spoke wheels, 10^1/$_2$in. long.
(Christie's) **$9,350**

A Marklin tinplate 'Aeropal' hand or steam operated lighthouse roundabout, circa 1909, hand painted in red, white, green and blue including simulated stone on the center lighthouse, six handsome sailboats with passengers which spin about, with stairways and many flags aloft, 19in. high.
(Christie's) **$22,000**

A fine early Doll and Cie ferris wheel ride, entirely hand-painted, consisting of six swinging gondolas, each with two passengers which rise and fall as the canopied amusement park ride swings them up and down by activating the side gear (lacking gear chain), 13^1/$_2$in. high.
(Christie's) **$4,180**

A large Bing tinplate keywind transitional open Phaeton, circa 1902, hand-painted in yellow with maroon piping, leather removable seats, steering, brake, springs, wire wheels, rubber tires and large cowl lamps, 13³/₄in. long. *(Christie's)* **$24,200**

A large hand-enameled tinplate Phaeton, circa 1885, attributed to Lutz, finished in dark blue, black and green cross-hatching, white and red seats, floral decorated foot-panel, cast red wheels, candle-powered front lantern, complete with store label from Paris, 20in. long. *(Christie's)* **$22,000**

Victorian house diorama, America, late 19th century, mixed media including wood, printed paper cut-outs and straw flowers in a glass vitrine; seashells on lawn arranged to read *E. Waters*.
(Skinner) **$990**

A Lincoln pedal car, circa 1935, finished in lime green with forest green fenders/running boards, features include chrome plate steering wheel, split window windshield with side panes and electric lights, 45in. long.
(Christie's) **$8,800**

A Carette tinplate keywind open Phaeton, circa 1914, lithographed in yellow and black, with red piping, brake, large front windshield, cowl and headlamps, driver and rear passenger, 12¹/₂in. high.
(Christie's) **$5,060**

A flock-covered barking Boston terrier, with chain pull growl, moving lower jaw and glass eyes, 18in. long, French.
(Christie's) **$653**

A fine Steiff black mohair plush teddy bear with wide apart rounded ears, black boot button eyes, hump back and elongated felt pads, 19in. button in ear marked *Steiff*, 1912.
(Phillips) **$16,000**

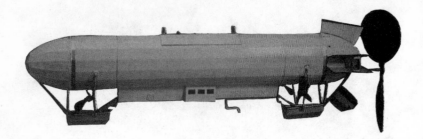

An early Marklin tinplate keywind Zeppelin, circa 1908, hand-painted in a light cream, with twin silvered open gondolas, having passenger cabin in between, and four motors, with large working propellor at rear, 18in. long. (Christie's)   **$9,900**

The famous George Brown tinplate 'Charles' hose reel, circa 1875, finished in royal blue and white with beautiful hand-painted decorative scroll work, twin brass bells and large cast wheels, probably the rarest early American tin toy known to exist, 23in. long. (Christie's)   **$231,000**

A rare Marklin refreshment trolley, painted tinplate white trolley cart with blue rim, gold-turned posts, red wheels and undercarriage, the cart is complete with painted composition food products, tin and glass tableware, 9in. long.
(Christie's) **$3,740**

A rare Marklin rabbit automaton with carriage, circa 1910, featuring a fur covered rabbit fitted with an on/off clockwork mechanism which when activated causes the rabbit to stroll forward pushing the tinplate embossed wicker and scroll decorated carriage containing a baby rabbit with glass milk bottle, 11in. tall.
(Christie's) **$9,350**

A good Märklin tinplate fairground carousel toy, circa 1910, beautifully hand-painted, original paint and transfers, original hand-cranked musical movement, six sided center column finished in white lined gold, and with painted floral decoration to alternate faces, plaster figures riding contemporary hide covered pigs, and white and gold painted shell-form chairs, diameter of base 41cm.
(Sotheby's) **$85,000**

A large tinplate Marklin child's kitchen stove, with six burners and utensils including a kettle, fish kettle with tap and side shelves, 21^1/$_2$in. wide, circa 1900. *(Christie's)* **$1,305**

An extraordinary Marklin tinplate fire set, circa 1919, consisting of three keywind matched fire trucks, each hand painted in red, black and yellow with rubber tires, all three bear the Marklin metal embossed shield on the front panel. The fire pumper has working gears that pump water and a chain drive; the fire patrol wagon consists of an overhead ladder and hose, with seating for six fireman; the ladder truck has chain gears that extend the ladders. All three vehicles are housed in their own hand-painted tinplate curved-roof firehouse of simulated stone, firehouse 21 x 17 x 14in. *(Christie's)* **$79,200**

A fine oversized early Marklin tinplate horsedrawn hansom cab, the cast lead white and black horse on wheels pulls a beautiful hand-painted two-wheel hansom cab, with opening front doors and high cabby seat at the rear, 28in. long overall.
(Christie's)   **$18,700**

A magnificent early French tinplate horse-drawn open double decker tram, circa 1890, hand painted in dark green and back with yellow and red piping, destination side boards reading 'Ville de Marseille' – 'Longchamp Joliette', by the Compagnie Generale de Omnibus, with double open ended stairways, top and interior seating, railings, cast yellow wheels, five open windows on each side, and fretwork decorations, pulled by a pair of brown metal horses in livery, trotting with small wheels for easy movement, 42in. long overall.
(Christie's)   **$71,500**

A Regency black and gilt tole tray with raised pierced rim, later painted with Napoleon observing the field of battle, within a border of anthemia, 30in. x 22in. *(Christie's)* **$2,775**

An inlaid waiter with an everted brim, on four cast feet, by Tiffany & Co., 1878–91, 9¹/₂in. diameter, gross weight 10oz. *(Christie's)* **$19,800**

A mid-Georgian brass-inlaid padoukwood tray in the style of John Channon with rectangular top, the gallery pierced with ovals, the re-entrant angles mounted with brass above a shallow frieze fitted with a drawer, on shaped feet, 18³/₄in. wide. *(Christie's)* **$8,750**

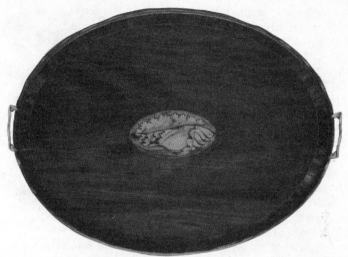

A George III inlaid mahogany serving-tray, probably English, 1780–1800, with a scalloped gallery and two brass carrying handles over a crossbanded border centering an oval reserve engraved and shaded with a shell on a green ground, 28¹/₄in. wide.
(Christie's) $1,500

Good Regency papier mâché painted tray, circa 1815, painted with the Battle of Trafalgar, with five warships, including Admiral Nelson's VICTORY, exchanging fire in fierce combat, in predominant tones of blue-green, brown, orange-red, and white, within a narrow gilt and red line border, 22 x 29¹/₂in.
(Butterfield & Butterfield) $3,300

Urbino, the capital of the Duchy of the same name, became a maiolica centre only in 1520, when "Guido da Castello Durante" established a workshop there. Guido was the son of Nicola Pellipario, who had worked at Castel Durante, and his father joined him at Urbino in 1527. It was Nicola Pellipario who popularized the istoriato style, with which Urbino came to be especially associated.

Their Fontana workshop produced many pieces, including large wine coolers, salvers, pilgrim bottles and stands, with a characteristic decoration of arabesques and grotesques painted in color on a white ground edged in yellow and picked out in orange.

An Urbino istoriato large dish of cardinal's hat form, painted in the Fontana workshop with God appearing to the people of Israel before a fortified town in a rocky landscape with mountains in the distance, the reverse inscribed *Esod, II./L'inhuman, empio, crudèl Farone*, circa 1550, 44cm. diameter.

(Christie's) **$45,000**

An Urbino Istoriato dish of shallow cardinal's hat form, painted with The Contest between the Pierides and the Muses, the naked or scantily attired figures at discussion and playing musical instruments, flanking a watery grotto beneath trees issuing from rockwork and with a fortified hill town in the distance, circa 1540, 40cm. diameter.

(Christie's) **$55,000**

A documentary Urbino dish, painted in the workshop of Guido di Merlino, showing Coriolanus exiled from Rome, circa 1540, 16$^{1}/_{4}$in. diameter.

(Christie's) **$316,030**

An Urbino Istoriato large dish painted in the Fontana workshop with the legend of Deucalion and Pyrrha after the flood, throwing rocks over their heads in order to create the new race seen emerging from the stones, the temple of the prophet on a rocky outcrop to the left, circa 1550, 40.5cm. diameter.
(Christie's) **$75,240**

A very spirited Urbino Istoriato plate painted by Francesco Durantino, showing the victorious Scipio, with a number of soldiers surrendering their arms, and with brightly colored tents in the background, one of which has a Roman flag inscribed *SPQR*, in bright shades of blue, brown, ocher, yellow, green and black, 29cm.
(Phillips) **$25,000**

An Urbino Istoriato dish painted in the workshop of Orazio Fontana with Christ appearing to Mary Magdalene beside a ruined pillar in an extensive rocky landscape with bushes and grasses, three figures by the open tomb on the left and three shepherds with their flock to the right, circa 1540, 42.5cm. diameter.
(Christie's) **$109,000**

A Venetian mold-blown vase, the oviform body with flared neck molded with a frieze of cherub's heads alternating with escutcheon and with stylized foliage between, the lower part with radial gadroons, supported on a lightly ribbed compressed knop above a spreading foot with folded rim, 16th century, 22.5cm. high.
(Christie's) **$21,250**

A Venetian latticinio tazza in vetro a retorti, decorated with vertical bands of lattimo thread and gauze, the shallow circular bowl supported on a clear merese above a knopped baluster section and thick clear merese, on a conical foot, 17th century, 16.5cm. diameter.
(Christie's) **$23,350**

A Venini bottle vase, designed by Fulvio Bianconi, compressed cylindrical form with short cylindrical neck, the amber-tinted glass inlaid with deep amber and white abstract forms, acid-stamped *Venini Murano, Italia*, 23cm. high. *(Christie's)* **$13,000**

A Venini 'Vetro Pezzato Arlecchino' vase, designed by Fulvio Bianconi, cigar form, the patchwork design made up of red, green, blue and clear cased glass, acid-stamped *Venini Murano Italia* and paper label *Venini Murano*, 28cm. high.
(Christie's) **$14,000**

A Venini 'Vetro Pezzato Artecchino', designed by Fulvio Bianconi, of circular section with straight sides tapering towards the base, composed of irregular squares of clear, blue, turquoise and red glass, 17cm. high.
(Phillips) **$4,911**

The first hard-paste porcelain factory was established in Venice in 1720 by Francesco Vezzi (1651-1740), a wealthy goldsmith. In this he enlisted the assistance of the dubious Christoph Konrad Hunger, who had already deserted Meissen in 1717, claiming to be able to help duPaquier in Vienna. He had at least learned enough there to enable him to help Vezzi produce true porcelain, but he then reverted to type and quit Venice for Meissen again in 1727. He promptly disclosed that Vezzi was reliant on Saxon clays, whereupon their export was promptly banned, forcing the factory to close.

A Venice (Vezzi) blue and white teabowl painted in a gray-blue with two birds in flight among plants and flowering shrubs flanked by buildings between blue line rims, the interior with a flower and the underside marked *Venezia*, circa 1725, 7.3cm. diameter. *(Christie's)* **$11,750**

A Venice (Vezzi) octagonal teapot of tapering form, the shoulders and base molded with stiff leaves, with a straight spout and strap handle, naively painted perhaps by Duramano with chinoiserie figures, one side with a figure shooting duck with a bow and arrow before a figure hiding behind a mound and a lady with a parasol, circa 1725, 9cm. high. *(Christie's)* **$26,800**

The porcelain factory of Claude Innocent Du Paquier was established in Vienna during the early years of the 18th century. Though it received no state patronage, the Emperor granted it many privileges and it became the second factory in Europe to commence hard paste porcelain manufacture, following the defection of the Meissen arcanist Stölzel in 1719 and Böttger's half-brother, Tiemann who brought the kiln designs from that factory.

Early Vienna porcelain can be distinguished from Meissen by the flatness of the glaze, which becomes greenish when thickly applied, and footrims tend to be rough and unglazed. Like Meissen, the early designs owe much to silver shapes.

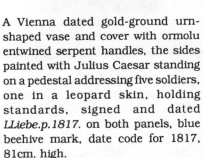

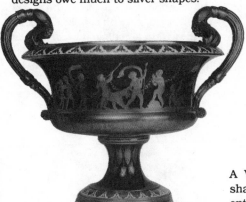

A Vienna two-handled circular green and gold-ground vase, the reeded handles terminating in five branches before pendant bunches of fruit, the green-ground with a continuous band of chased gilt putti linked by trails of ivy, playing musical instruments, with a goat and a leopard and dancing above a gilt band chased with vines and palmettes, date code for 1813, 61cm. wide.

(Christie's) **$52,650**

A Vienna dated gold-ground urn-shaped vase and cover with ormolu entwined serpent handles, the sides painted with Julius Caesar standing on a pedestal addressing five soldiers, one in a leopard skin, holding standards, signed and dated *LLiebe.p.1817.* on both panels, blue beehive mark, date code for 1817, 81cm. high.

Leopold Lieb, working at Vienna 1812–36, was famous for his depiction of historical subjects and in 1815 was awarded a prize by the factory for his work.

(Christie's) **$28,200**

Vincennes may be said to be the birthplace of the famous Sèvres factory, whither it was removed in 1756 on the orders of King Louis XV.

The entire operation began however at Vincennes between 1738-40, when two financiers, Orry de Vignory and Orry de Fulvy were granted a permit by Louis to use the chateau there for experiments in porcelain manufacture. Their first managers, the brothers Dubois, proved unreliable and were sacked in 1741. Their assistant, François Gravant, took over and his efforts were more successful.

In 1745, with the king increasingly interested, a group of prominent figures was brought together to run the factory with the Orrys and Gravant, its capital was greatly increased, it received a 'privilege' from the king, and the period of its true greatness really began.

A Vincennes tureen, cover and stand of oval form, gilt with panels of birds in flight within scrolling gilt cartouches on a bleu lapis ground, 25.5cm. wide. *(Phillips)* **$7,820**

A Vincennes large pot-pourri vase and a cover, the shoulders with puce and gilt foliage scrolls with harebells suspending sprays of flowers including wood anemones, cornflowers and grasses between seven pierced holes molded with gilt cartouches, palm fronds and flowerheads above shaded puce, blue and gilt tapering pilasters the centers with a ribbon threaded with flowerheads, circa 1752, 32cm. high.

This shape was produced in four sizes of which this is the largest, only this size has molded gilt flowerheads below the pierced holes, a drawing for the model is preserved in the archives at Sèvres.
(Christie's) **$34,500**

Charles F Annesley Voysey (1857–1941) was an architect and prolific designer of furniture, textiles, carpets, tapestries, wallpapers, ceramics and metalwork. He set up his own practice in 1882 and the following year designed his first wallpapers and textiles. He was much influenced at this time by Arthur Mackmurdo of the Arts & Crafts Exhibition Society and the Century Guild. Voysey also exhibited at the former in 1893.

Voysey's furniture was much in the spirit of the Arts & Crafts Movement, rectilinear in form, with little embellishment, and executed mainly in oak.

An oak side chair designed by C.F.A. Voysey, the back with arched back rail and square section finials, the central back plat pierced with heart-shaped motif, the seat with drop-in rushed panels, on square-section legs with plain stretchers.
(Christie's) **$6,000**

A German oak green stained writing desk in the style of C.A. Voysey, 110.5cm. wide.
(Christie's) **$3,520**

An oak desk top stationery cabinet designed by C.F.A. Voysey, rectangular section, with single paneled cupboard door, applied with shaped panel with pierced heart-shaped motif, 38.7cm. high
(Christie's) **$1,750**

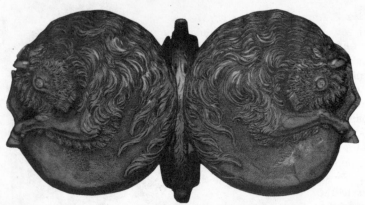

A gold hunter cased chronograph, cast and chased in the form of a buffalo, the case and movement by Nicole, Nielsen & Co., London, for Edward and Sons, London and Glasgow, the gilt three-quarter plate lever movement with Nicole's patent keyless work on the backplate, chronograph work under dial engaged by button on band, 18K gold cuvette, white enamel dial with tachymeter scale enclosing roman chapters and subsidiary dials for seconds and 60-minute register.

This watch was made in anticipation of the Pan-American Exposition, held in Buffalo, New York, May 1 – November 1, 1901. The event inspired the creation of the 'Order of the Buffaloes' society, as well as a fad for jewelry with buffalo motifs. Made at a cost of $700, this watch was meant to be exhibited as the greatest achievement of the jeweler's craft. The Pan-American Exposition was delayed, due to the Spanish-American war. During this time, the watch was kept in a safe-deposit vault.

(Christie's)   **$26,400**

Robert & Courvoisier: fine and rare gold Bras En L'Air Verge pocket watch in engine-turned case, the signed white enamel dial with sectors in Roman numerals for the hours and in Arabic numerals for the minutes, a gilt automaton indicating the time with its arms by depressing the pendant, the head turning left and right with the action of the watch, the dial further decorated with black and white checkered pattern and gilt foliate design, the signed frosted gilt fusée movement with pierced bridge cock, 56mm. diameter.

(Christie's)   **$22,000**

An 18 carat white gold perpetual caldendar wristwatch with moonphases and chronograph, signed *Patek Philippe & Co., Geneve*, with circular nickel-finished lever movement, gyromax balance, free sprung regulator, 24 jewels, the silvered matt dial applied with baton numerals, windows for day and month, three subsidiary dials indicating constant seconds combined with 12 hour register, register for 30 minutes combined with leap-year indication, fitted box and setting pin, 36mm. diameter.

(Christie's)   **$78,210**

An enameled gold center seconds watch, the movement signed *Ilbery, London*, the engraved gilt and partly skeletonized duplex movement with going barrel, steel five-arm balance, gilt curvette, white enamel dial with roman chapters, circa 1810, 57.5mm. diameter.

(Christie's)   **$26,400**

A fine enameled gold verge watch, the case signed *Huaud le Puisné fecit*, the purpose made movement signed *Hoendshker, Dresden*, finely painted with 'Roman Charity' after Simon Vouet, the paneled band enhanced with four fanciful landscapes and signature cartouche, the interior with further allegorical picture, the loose ring pendant now altered to stirrup, 40mm. diameter.

Jean-Pierre Huaud (1655–1723) called 'le pusiné' (second-born) was a member of the prolific and highly regarded Geneva family of enamel painters. 'Roman Charity', one of their most popular subjects, depicts the story of Cimon, an aged condemned prisoner, kept alive by his daughter Peto who suckles him at her breast.
(Christie's)   **$38,500**

A rare tonneau-shaped single button chronograph wristwatch, signed *Cartier, European Watch & Co.*, circa 1935, with circular nickel-finished lever movement, bi-metalic compensation balance, 25 jewels, the silvered matt dial with Roman numerals, two subsidiary dials indicating constant seconds and register for 30 minutes, blued-steel Breguet-style hands, the tonneau-shaped case with inscription on the back, 35mm. long.
(Christie's)   **$104,280**

A fine and rare 18ct. gold keyless open-face split-second chronograph carousel by J.W. Benson, in plain case, the white enamel dial with Willis to the back, with chain fusée, London 1906, 59mm. diameter.
(Christie's S. Ken)   **$50,000**

A rare 18 carat gold single button chronograph wristwatch with enamel dial, signed *Vacheron & Constantin, Geneve*, with gilt-finished jeweled lever movement, bi-metalic compensation balance, gold cuvette, the white enamel dial with Arabic numerals, two subsidiary dials indicating constant seconds and register for 30 minutes, 35mm. diameter.

According to Vacheron & Constantin only ten watches like this have been produced.

(Christie's) **$115,830**

A finely enameled gold center seconds watch, Ilbery, London, the engraved gilt skeletonized duplex movement with going barrel, steel five-arm balance, white enamel dial with roman chapters, gold hands, the bezels of the gold case set with split pearls, the band champlevé enameled, the back with finely painted full length portrait of Chinese nobleman in garden landscape, circa 1820, 57.5mm. diameter.

(Christie's) **$33,000**

An 18 carat gold perpetual calendar wristwatch with moonphases and chronograph, signed *Patek Philippe & Co., Geneve*, with circular nickel-finished lever movement, mono-metalic compensation balance, precision regulator, 17 jewels, the silvered matt dial applied with Arabic numerals, windows for day and month, three subsidiary dials indicating constant seconds, register for 30 minutes and date combined with phases of the moon, 35mm. diameter.

(Christie's) **$108,625**

An Art Deco Egyptian revival pocket watch, circa 1925 by Cartier. *(Christie's)* **$6,179**

Gold Lemania wristwatch, the round face with Ferrari inscription 1950s. *(Finarte)* **$4,000**

An 18 carat pink gold perpetual calendar chronograph wristwatch with moon phases, signed *Patek Philippe & Co., Geneve*, circa 1950, with circular nickel-finished lever movement, bimetalic compensation balance, wishbone regulator, 23 jewels, the silvered matt dial applied with Arabic numerals, three subsidiary dials indicating constant seconds, register for 30 minutes and date combined with phases of the moon, windows for day and month, outer ring calibrated for pulsation, with 18 carat pink gold Patek Philippe buckle. *(Christie's)* **$213,840**

Robert & Courvoisier: fine and rare gold Bras en l'air verge pocket watch in engine-turned case, the signed white enamel dial with sectors in Roman numerals for the hours and in Arabic numerals for the minutes, a gilt automaton indicating the time with its arms by depressing the pendant, the head turning left and right with the action of the watch, 56mm. diameter. *(Christie's)* **$21,250**

476

An Indian khanjar with finely watered recurved double-edged blade with three gold-damascened lines over nearly its entire length on both sides, the forte chiseled in low relief on each side with arabesques and flowering foliage picked out in gold, mutton-fat jade hilt of scrolled form with inverted lotus-shaped quillon-block, 18th/19th century, 15³/₄in. long.
(Christie's) **$8,250**

A fine Javanese kris with five-wave pattern-welded blade, the gandja and forte with greneng and encrusted with engraved gold foliage and flower-heads on each side, the latter with gold-encrusted antelope and pierced and chiseled dragon's head, in original wooden scabbard with characteristic highly figured sarongan and gold kendelan embossed and chased with scrolling foliage on the outer side, 20¹/₂in. long.
(Christie's) **$5,300**

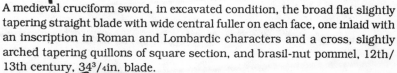

A medieval cruciform sword, in excavated condition, the broad flat slightly tapering straight blade with wide central fuller on each face, one inlaid with an inscription in Roman and Lombardic characters and a cross, slightly arched tapering quillons of square section, and brasil-nut pommel, 12th/13th century, 34³/₄in. blade.
(Christie's) **$20,000**

An Indian dagger with watered slightly curved double-edged blade cut with lines forming ridges along its entire lengths on both sides, mutton-fat jade hilt with fish-tail pommel and swelling grip widening into a pair of short quillons and decorated overall with a design of linked gold tear-drops set with green foiled gems, 19th century, 16¹/₂in. long. **$6,400**

A good 18th century executioner's axe, the steel head with crescentic blade and convex cutting edge, attached to ash handle, 40^{1}/$_{4}$in. high.
(Bonhams)   **$560**

A very rare German combined four-barreled matchlock gun, mace and spear with wooden cylindrical head stained black and containing four iron barrels, bound on the outside with three iron bands, the upper two set with iron spikes, and hinged lid with leaf-shaped spear with reinforced tip, circa 1600, 34in. long.
(Christie's)   **$9,130**

A fine Italian medieval sword with flat tapering double-edged blade of flattened hexagonal section with a wide shallow central fuller on each face of the forte inlaid in copper with a triangle surmounted by a cross, and inscribed on one face in Nashki script, early 14th century, 333/4in. blade.

The inscription reads in translation: 'Deposited in the Arsenal in the frontier city of Alexandria in the name of al-Malik Abu Nasr Shaikh al-Mu'ayyad in the year 818 AH (1415 AD)'.

This is one of a group of swords which are thought to have been presented under treaty by the Lusignan King of Cyprus to the Egyptian ruler.
(Christie's)   **$51,128**

A rare Saxon left-hand dagger, the stout leaf-shaped blade of flattened hexagonal section changing to flattened diamond section at the point, with central fuller on each face and fluted ricasso, the hilt of blackened iron, fig-shaped pommel of polygonal section capped with a silver plate engraved with triangular panels framing foliated scrolls, one involving an owl, silver button, and tapering wooden grip bound with silver wire, circa 1570, 16¹/₄in.

(Christie's S. Ken) **$22,000**

A German sporting crossbow with robust steel bow struck with a mark and retained by its original cords, original string of twisted cord, wooden tiller swelling towards the middle and veneered with panels of natural staghorn engraved with scrolling foliage beneath, early 17th century, 24³/₄in. and 13in.

(Christie's) **$9,600**

Carved and painted trumpeting angel weathervane, America, 19th century, the figure of a woman with trumpet painted white, black, pink and blue-green, 33¼in. long.

(Skinner) **$2,200**

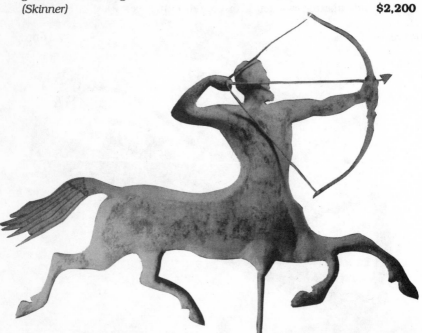

A fine and rare molded and gilt copper weathervane attributed to A.L. Jewell & Co., Waltham, Massachusetts, circa 1870, the galloping swell-bodied centaur, with drawn bow and arrow and shaped head and beard, the flowing tail embellished with molded grooves, 39in. long.

The mythical centaur is an inspired choice for an American weathervane; the centaur is represented in the night sky by Sagittarius, the archer. Having a centaur atop one's roof reflected a melding of classical traditions and emerging American folk art, and may well have symbolized a striving toward the lofty and the majestic.

(Christie's) **$33,000**

Wemyss Ware is the most distinctive product of the Scottish potteries. Its trademarks are free flowing designs on white of roses, cherries and apples.

The pottery of Robert Heron & Sons was based at Kirkcaldy in Fife and its fame really began when a young Bohemian decorator called Karl Nekola joined the staff in 1883. He became Art Director and by the time he died in 1915 he had made Wemyss Ware famous. The name was taken from nearby Wemyss Castle, the home of the Grosvenor family who did much to popularize the pottery with their upper class friends in London.

A Wemyss ware button, painted with a thistle head, stamped, $1^3/4$in. diameter.
(Christie's)   **$1,842**

A late 19th century Wemyss Ware ewer and bowl, the jug $11^1/2$in. high.
(Russell, Baldwin & Bright)
                              $2,200

An attractive Wemyss model of a pig in the usual squatting pose, with ears pricked, painted all over the back and ears with sprays of flowering clover, the ears, snout, feet and curled tail washed in pink, 46cm., mark in green *Wemyss Made in England of Joe Nekola.*
(Phillips)   **$3,785**

Thomas Whieldon (1719-95) was an English potter working out of Fenton Low, or Little Fenton, in Staffordshire. He gave his name to the distinctive earthenware which he produced and which is notable for its range of colors. He was in partnership with Josiah Wedgwood from 1754-79.

No marks were used.

A pair of creamware Arbor figures of Whieldon type, modeled as a musician playing the fiddle in streaked gray topcoat and yellow waistcoat, his companion in a green splashed crinoline and holding a pug dog on her lap, circa 1750, 15cm. high.
(Christie's) **$61,000**

An important Whieldon figure of a bagpiper, the gentleman dressed in short coat, buttoned waistcoat and striped breeches, 19cm.
(Christie's) **$17,600**

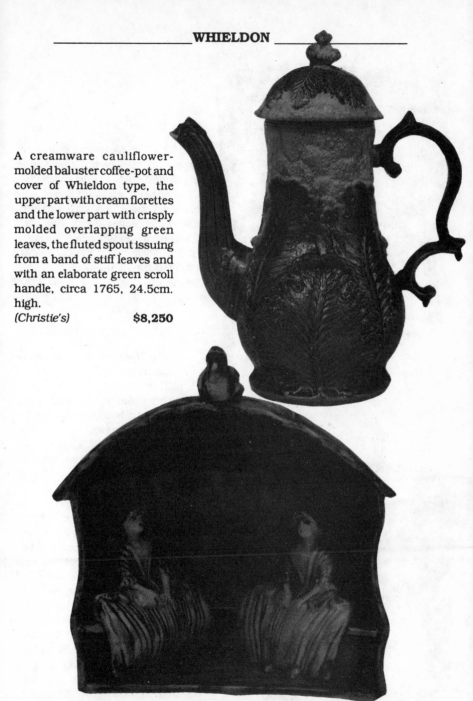

A creamware cauliflower-molded baluster coffee-pot and cover of Whieldon type, the upper part with cream florettes and the lower part with crisply molded overlapping green leaves, the fluted spout issuing from a band of stiff leaves and with an elaborate green scroll handle, circa 1765, 24.5cm. high.
(Christie's) **$8,250**

A creamware arbor group of Whieldon type, modeled as a garden shelter of semi-circular form, a woman in a crinoline sitting on either side of the curved seat, 14.5cm. high. *(Bearne's)* **$65,000**

A George III brass-bound mahogany cellaret of canted rectangular shape, the hinged top inlaid with two satinwood octagonal panels each with a compass medallion with radiating lines of checkered inlay, the plain sides with carrying-handles, the stand with fluted frieze and molded square chamfered legs, 26in. wide.
(Christie's)   **$23,000**

A George II mahogany wine-cooler, the oval top edged with gilt-lacquered brass chain-and-rosette border, the tapering body mounted with pierced carrying-handles cast with foliage, shells and flowerheads and banded with cabochon border, 27³/₄in. wide.

This cistern wine-cooler is likely to have been commissioned by James Herbert, who succeeded to the Tythrop estate in 1720 and was elected Member of Parliament for Oxford in 1739. During the 1730s he created a great banqueting room at Tythrop in the Palladian manner by the insertion of an Inigo Jones style balcony and a stuccoed ceiling in the manner of the Francini brothers (fl. 1730–1760).
(Christie's)

$292,000

A George III brass-bound mahogany wine-cooler of bucket form, the domed circular lid with turned knob and hinged top enclosing a lead-lined interior with detachable brass liner, the sides with Etruscan looped brass handles, 11in. wide.
(Christie's) **$6,750**

A George III brass-bound mahogany cellaret-on-stand, the hinged hexagonal top enclosing a lead-lined interior with compartments, 18^1/$_2$in. wide. *(Christie's)* **$9,600**

One of a pair of William IV wine coolers, each with molded rectangular top around a leadlined well, with gadrooned sides and feet, 35in. wide.
(Christie's) **$16,850**

A German green-tinted puzzle goblet, the waisted funnel bowl with a central column supporting a detachable figure of a stag, the stem formed as a hollow knop with four apertures above two further knops, on a high domed and folded foot, 17th century, 35.5cm. high.
(Christie's)   **$11,677**

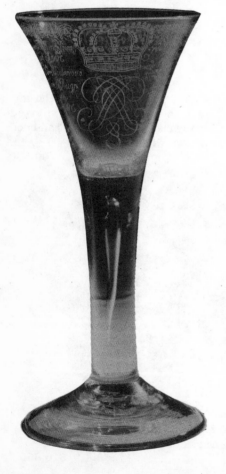

The 'Breadalbane II' Amen glass, of drawn-trumpet shape, the stem enclosing an elongated tear and supported on a conical foot, the bowl engraved in diamond-point with a crown above the Royal cipher of King James VIII, the letter JR direct and reverse and with the figure '8' worked into the monogram at the base, below the word Amen, flanked by two verses of the Jacobite anthem, 1745–50, 17cm. high.
(Christie's)   **$50,000**

A North Bohemian 'Schwarzlot' wine-glass painted by Ignatz Preissler, the flared funnel bowl with three horses in various stances on a continuous grassy band with a tree partially covered in foliage, supported on a merese above an inverted baluster stem with spreading basal knop, on a conical foot, circa 1715, 12cm. high.
(Christie's) **$11,650**

A polychrome enameled armorial opaque-twist wine-glass attributed to William Beilby, the funnel bowl enameled in yellow heightened in iron-red, black and white and gilt with a coat-of-arms and with trailing foliage, circa 1765, 15.5cm. high.
(Christie's) **$18,000**

A very fine pavise shield, of wood, rectangular form with central gutter of rectangular section, of wood, the front covered with gesso painted with a standing figure of St. George in gothic armour, German (perhaps Vienna) or Bohemian, circa 1485–90, 46in.

(Christie's) **$34,000**

Polychromed wood anthropoid mummy case, Ptolemaic Period, circa 300 B.C., wearing a wide striped tripartite wig, traces of original polychroming on the cover, 6ft. high.
(Butterfield & Butterfield)

$9,350

South German baroque carved and polychromed figure of the Archangel Michael, circa 1600, the figure depicted with displayed wings, wearing a plumed helmet, cape and half armor, the figure of the Devil prostrate beneath his feet, 32in. high.
(Butterfield & Butterfield)

$6,600

A James I pearwood armorial standing cup with circular slightly-tapering body with four panels divided by twin-pilasters with heart-filled spandrels, the panels incised with the royal coat-of-arms and supporters above the motto *BEATIPACIFICI*, an ostrich with a horseshoe in its beak, a hart statant with a crown and a rope dated *1621*, 9^1/$_2$in. high.

Despite considerable interest in these cups since the late 19th century little evidence for their use has come forward. With few exceptions the cups bear the arms of James I flanked by the crests of two or more English families.
(Christie's)

$15,074

Painted wood canoe, Old Town. Maine, early 20th century, the painted and stencil decorated wooden canoe with two caned seats, the body with stenciled line decoration, inscribed *Old Town Canoe*, 47^1/$_2$in. long.
(Butterfield & Butterfield)

$12,100

Carved bellows, America, early 19th century, 20¹/₂in. long.
(Skinner) **$3,300**

A late Elizabeth I pearwood cup and cover with circular slightly-domed cover surmounted by a stepped turned finial carved with ogee-leaves and surrounded by a band carved with a lion, a unicorn, a dove and an antelope, with outer arcaded band and conforming concave frieze, the slightly-tapering cylindrical body carved with repeated geometric strapwork divided by flowerheads, 10³/₄in. high.
(Christie's) **$16,959**

A Tyrolean carved pine hallstand in the form of a standing bear holding a tree trunk with young bear on the uppermost branch, the stick-stand base naturalistically carved foliage, 79in. high.
(Phillips) **$2,600**

An important large polychromed wood figure of Guanyin, seated in rajalilasana, the right arm relaxed on the raised right knee, the left arm supportive and left leg lowered, wearing a simple shawl exposing the chest and loose robes knotted at the front, a beaded necklace and bracelets, the face with a calm expression beneath the hair tied up in an elaborate chiffon, $61^1/_2$in. high.

Such life-sized wooden figures were popular from about the 10th to 14th centuries and are associated with Shanxi province.

(Christie's) **$310,000**

An early 19th century carved giltwood relief of a winged lion, gardant, his front paw resting on an open book, 81cm. wide.
(Phillips) **$2,150**

A wood carving of a champion, 17th century, his tunic with old polychrome decoration and carved sun mask, carrying a hand sword, 24¹/₂in. (possibly an old tobacco sign).
(Woolley & Wallis) **$1,153**

Carved and painted figure of Ceres, unsigned, attributed to the workshop of John and Simeon Skillin (1746–1800) and (1756/57–1806).
(Skinner) **$23,100**

A Swiss carved softwood model of a begging dog, on a molded naturalistic base stamped *BERGEN & CO INTERLAKEN*, late 19th/early 20th century, 31^1/$_2$in. high. *(Christie's)* **$14,000**

A Victorian treen tobacco jar, carved in the form of a boxer dog's head, with inset eyes and leather collar, 6in. high. *(Christie's)* **$895**

Scandinavian carved and painted wood beer bowl, 19th century, with two handles carved in the shape of horse's heads painted green, cream, and black, 16^1/$_4$in. high. *(Butterfield & Butterfield)* **$825**

A 19th century Bavarian carved 'Warwick Bear' in standing position with arm outstretched with tray, the other arm holding a twig as support for sticks, insert glass eyes, 48in.
(Locke & England)   **$2,600**

Continental baroque carved pine group of three putti, Italian or German, circa 1700, the scantily draped infants frolicking together, one supported by the other two with his arms aloft, all with smiling expressions and curly hair, 41¹/₂in. high.
(Butterfield & Butterfield)
                              $12,100

Carved and painted figure of Uncle Sam on horseback, America, late 19th/early 20th century, Uncle Sam painted red, white and blue, his horse painted black and white with brown saddle and leather tack, 19in. high.
(Skinner)   **$4,400**

494

Carved and painted American eagle, circa 1900, attributed to John Hales Bellamy (1836–1914), Kittery Point, Maine, wings heightened with gilt, the shield painted red, white and blue, the bannerole painted blue with gilt lettering, 73in. long.
(Skinner)   **$8,250**

A carved and polychrome-painted wood panel carved with the Royal arms of King William III supported by a lion and a unicorn, each with a putto at their feet and surmounted by acanthus scrolls, 19th century, 28in. x 36in.
(Christie's)   **$7,700**

New Mexican Santo figural group by Jose Benito Ortega, 1875–1890, depicting San Ysidro Labrador, of 'flat-figure style', standing with one arm raised, the other held forward, wearing a wide-brimmed hat with sheet metal plume, painted garments and attached pin of the Virgin and Child on his chest, an angel stands at his side steering a plow pulled by a pair of oxen wrapped in animal hide, all mounted on a rectangular wood base, length of base 20³/₄ inches.
(Butterfield & Butterfield)

$15,400

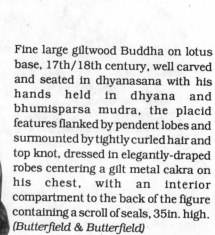

Fine large giltwood Buddha on lotus base, 17th/18th century, well carved and seated in dhyanasana with his hands held in dhyana and bhumisparsa mudra, the placid features flanked by pendent lobes and surmounted by tightly curled hair and top knot, dressed in elegantly-draped robes centering a gilt metal cakra on his chest, with an interior compartment to the back of the figure containing a scroll of seals, 35in. high.
(Butterfield & Butterfield)

$20,000

Franconian School, circa 1500, Christ on a Donkey, polychrome wood, 58 x 49¹/₄in.

Palmesels, representing Christ's Entry into Jerusalem, were drawn in procession on Palm Sunday. These were very popular in South Western Germany, Austria, Tyrol, Switzerland and Alsace from the 14th century until the Reformation. Relatively few have been preserved, this example is remarkable for the survival of its original platform and wheels.

(Christie's) **$94,248**

A pair of polychrome-painted Venetian blackamoor torchères, each with a boy holding a torchère with a glass shade, 19th century, 69in. high. *(Christie's)* **$35,000**

Pair of Venetian parcel-gilt and polychromed blackamoor monkeys on pedestals, late 18th/early 19th century, each figure depicted wearing a perruque, red and black foliate-patterned coat, vest, shirt, breeches and slippers, holding a blue and white-painted 'Delft' wooden dish in outstretched hands suspending wood link chains, 4ft. 6in. high.
(Butterfield & Butterfield)

$33,000

A good late 17th century Norwegian birchwood tankard, the lid carved GT.KL, two coats of arms surmounted by doves and 1693, the thumbpiece with a bear, the body with three circular panels representing Diana and Endymion, Apollo flaying Marsyas and Fortune, two smaller circles with a bird and a mythical beast, between are trees, animals, fences and buildings, the scroll handle carved with foliage, 7¹/₄in. high, circa 1830.
(Woolley & Wallis)

$87,500

The history of porcelain making in Worcester is a complex one, involving a number of principal factories. The process began around 1751, when the Worcester Tonquin Manufactory was set up by a consortium of 15 local businessmen. The leading figures in the group were a local surgeon, John Wall, and an apothecary, William Davis. During this earliest, or 'Dr Wall' period, a soaprock body was perfected from experiments at Bristol. The wares were decorated both in blue and white and a colorful polychrome, in a manner which amalgamated both oriental and European influences to form a highly distinctive style of their own.

'The Aesthetic Teapot': a fine and rare satirical teapot and cover probably designed by R.W. Binns and modeled by James Hadley, one side as a soulfully intense young man wearing a sunflower, the reverse as a lovesick maiden sporting a lily, their costume shaded in bright 'greenery-yallery' enamel, the base inscribed *Fearful consequences through the laws of Natural Selection and Evolution of living up to one's Teapot*, date code for 1882.

Gilbert and Sullivan's comic opera 'Patience' opened in London in 1881 as a satire on Oscar Wilde and the whole Aesthetic movement. The Worcester teapot is based on Gilbert's costume designs for the play. The inscription pokes fun at an exhibition held by the Grosvenor Gallery where a single Japanese teapot was put on display and visitors were invited to go home and 'live up to it'. *(Phillips)* **$1,870**

A rare Worcester eye bath of boat shape on a slender stem with a spreading foot, painted in blue with trefoil leaves and cell borders, 4.5cm. high.

(Christie's) **$3,200**

A Worcester marbled-ground vase of urn shape, the richly gilt angular handles with Bacchus-mask terminals, painted in the manner of Thomas Baxter with shells and seaweed on a marble edge within a gilt band shaped rectangular cartouche, the interior to the everted rim enriched with gilt trellis, circa 1810, 36.5cm. high.

(Christie's) **$14,000**

A rare first period Worcester bell-shaped mug, printed in puce with a profile portrait of George III taken from plates engraved by Robert Hancock after the original by Jeremiah Meyer, the reverse with a similar portrait of Queen Charlotte.

It is exceptionally rare on Worcester porcelain to find the portraits of both the King and Queen reproduced on the one ceramic item.

(Bonhams) **$5,250**

A Worcester partridge-tureen and cover, its plumage enriched in shades of brown, the edge of the cover with stylized entwined straw in green and yellow and applied with colored feathers, the white basket-weave base with colored feathers and corn, the interior to the base with iron-red painter's mark, circa 1765, 17.5cm. long. *(Christie's)* **$15,000**

A pair of Worcester shagreen-ground Imari pattern tapering hexagonal vases and domed covers, painted with fabulous winged beasts sinuously entwined about flowering shrubs, circa 1770, 30.5cm. high. *(Christie's)* **$46,000**

A Worcester plate from The Duke of Gloucester Service, gold crescent mark, circa 1775, 22.5cm. diameter. *(Christie's)* **$25,000**

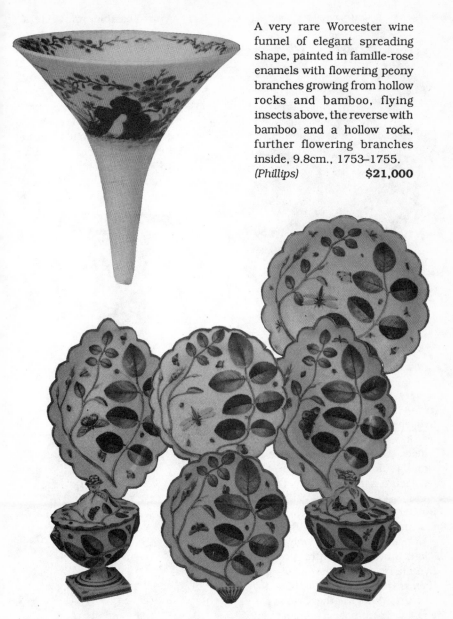

A very rare Worcester wine funnel of elegant spreading shape, painted in famille-rose enamels with flowering peony branches growing from hollow rocks and bamboo, flying insects above, the reverse with bamboo and a hollow rock, further flowering branches inside, 9.8cm., 1753–1755.
(Phillips)   **$21,000**

A remarkable Worcester 'Blind Earl' dessert service, Chamberlain and Flight, Barr and Barr, circa 1840, the popular embossed design of rose leaves picked out in colors, the ground finely painted with ombrierte butterflies and a variety of other insects.
(Phillips)   **$29,000**

A rare Yuan blue and white jar, guan, the globular body painted in vivid blue tones with an arching peony scroll comprising six flower-heads alternately shown full faced and upright below twenty three pendent lotus panels enclosing mixed emblems alternating with flaming pearls, 1350–1360, 46.5cm. high.
(Christie's)

$213,000

A very rare blue and white vase, Yuhuchun, freely painted to the body in deep purplish tone with two figures within a rocky landscape divided by a willow tree and a cliff opposing a waterfall flowing from behind rocks, between a band of classic scroll and another of cash motif, all above a further band of lotus panels above the foot repeated on the neck, 9³/₈in. high.

Human subjects are rarely found on Yuan blue and white porcelain. Symmetry and the novelty of secular themes may have something to do with this, though earlier Cizhou pieces employed a number of human themes. The Romance of the Three Kingdoms became highly popular at this time, and was adapted for blue and white decoration.
(Christie's)   **$133,250**

INDEX